14073

ON BELAY!

- THE LIFE
- OF LEGENDARY
- MOUNTAINEER
- PAUL PETZOLDT
-

RAYE C. RINGHOLZ

THE
MOUNTAINEERS

Published by
The Mountaineers
1001 SW Klickitat Way, Suite 201
Seattle, WA 98134

Published simultaneously in Great Britain by Cordee, 3a DeMontfort Street, Leicester, England, LE1 7HD

Manufactured in the United States of America

Edited by Cynthia Newman Bohn
Cover and book design by Alice C. Merrill
Cover photograph: *Grand Teton Peak* ©Galen Rowell/Corbis.
Cover inset photograph: *Paul Petzoldt climbing a chimney on Mount Owen, 1940.*
    Courtesy the American Heritage Center, University of Wyoming
Back cover photograph: *Paul Petzoldt on Mount Owen, 1940.* Courtesy the American Heritage Center, University of Wyoming

Library of Congress Cataloging-in-Publication Data
Ringholz, Raye Carleson.
    On belay!: the life of legendary mountaineer Paul Petzoldt/Raye
C. Ringholz.
        p.   cm.
    Includes bibliographical references (p.   ).
    ISBN 0-89886-558-1
    1. Petzoldt, Paul. 2. Mountaineers—United States—biography.
I. Title.
CV199.92.P48A56 1998
796.5'22'092—dc21
[B]   97-41247
                                                                 CIP

♻ Printed on 100% totally chlorine free/acid free paper

contents

To my family

introduction

Mention the Grand Teton and the name Paul Petzoldt comes to mind. Ever since he and a friend successfully scaled the peak at the age of sixteen to become the fourth party to do so, Petzoldt and the Tetons have been almost synonymous.

Petzoldt's name marks numerous routes, ridges, and caves in the Wyoming range. He has been credited with many first ascents and, not content with regular seasonal climbing, he introduced winter expeditioning in the Tetons and later became known for his legendary annual New Year's climbs. At the age of twenty-one, when he was awarded the original climbing concession in Grand Teton National Park, he took his place as a pioneer in professional mountain guiding in the United States.

Paul Kiesow Petzoldt was a maverick in the mountaineering world of the early twentieth century. By the late 1800s, explorers seeking migration routes across the country or government surveyors charting remote geological features had traversed most of America's mountainous regions. Then, once the topographical profiles were established, men, and a few women, began to climb for fun and the pure challenge of the experience. Many of these climbers were well-to-do doctors, clergymen, industrialists, and Ivy Leaguers who possessed the means and time to embark on extended expeditions. But Petzoldt, born January 16, 1908, on an Iowa farm, did not come from the roots of wealth and position enjoyed by most mountaineers of those days.

His father, Charles, born in Castorland, New York, was the son of William Petzoldt, one of scores of German liberals who migrated to America prior to the Civil War. His mother, Emma Kiesow, a small woman of Slavic descent, came to the United States from Germany when she was twelve. She was still living with her parents in New York and working at the Hickey-Freeman Company stitching velvet collars on men's topcoats when she met and married Charles. They soon left New York to homestead a barren plot of ground in mid-America, and Emma produced nine children (and lost a tenth) in less than twenty years.

Petzoldt developed the traits of a survivor early in life. The youngest of nine siblings, and having little in common with his four brothers and four sisters, he learned independence. When he was three years old, his father died and he compensated for the lack of bonding with a male model by imagining himself emulating the exploits of adventurers pictured in storybooks. Schooling whet his curiosity and desire for knowledge and revealed a talent for friendship.

By the time he was a teen, and his struggling family finally disbanded under financial pressures, he was on his own, making his way with odd jobs, an engaging smile, and the knack of telling a good story. He supported himself and gained an education by seizing opportunity whenever and wherever it arose, and by being willing to stumble through unfamiliar territory to achieve his goals.

Petzoldt's career as a mountaineer evolved from several such propitious twists of fate. After his near tragic, but ultimately successful, adventure on the Grand Teton at the age of sixteen, Jackson Holers and visiting dudes from the big city hounded him to take them to the top of the mountain. Suddenly, he was in the guiding business. The need to increase safety measures for growing numbers of inexperienced clients triggered his invention of an innovative voice signal system and several technical maneuvers—procedures which solidified his reputation among the climbing fraternity.

A fortuitous meeting with the Dean of St. George's Chapel at Windsor Castle, who was visiting in Jackson, resulted in his being invited to England, touring Europe and climbing in the Alps. And in 1938, a last-minute cancellation by a member of the First American Expedition to K2 in the Himalayas occasioned his invitation to join the climb, where he distinguished himself by reaching a record elevation without auxiliary oxygen and obtaining a view of the summit to verify that K2 was climbable.

Wanderlust, restlessness, and a relentless drive for adventure mark the mountaineer. Petzoldt combines these qualities with the passion of mission. At midlife, when most careers peak, he set aside his achievements as a climber and reached his true zenith as an educator. After working for the Lend-Lease program and serving in the Tenth Mountain Division ski troops during World War II, he recognized the need for educating qualified leaders for the ever-increasing outdoor programs being geared to American youth. In becoming chief instructor at Colorado Outward Bound, and later founding the National Outdoor Leadership School, he not only put his mountaineering, camping, and organizing skills to good use but became a forerunner in developing a code of wilderness ethics and conservation practices. In later years, he expanded his horizons to reach professional outdoorsmen through the Wilderness Education Association.

Not content with his successes in teaching youngsters how to find safe, socially acceptable adventure in the out-of-doors and educating those aiming at careers in outdoor recreation and conservation, he is now proselytizing for new standards and ethics to be practiced by every sportsman and recreationist who ventures into the backcountry. Through his lectures and in his writings, he hammers away at the same theme—the urgency of educating all users of America's wild country so that people can travel safely beyond the roadhead without harming it. And, if he had his way, without being restricted to designated paths and improved areas.

Petzoldt is at his best on top of a mountain or in front of an audience. In either case, he is intelligent, entertaining, and has command of the situation. He has packed a lot into his ninety years. Stories about his exploits abound. Some are true, some not so true. Winnowing the truth from rumors and common gossip is a daunting task. Especially when so much time has elapsed, memories have dimmed, the people involved are deceased, or the records have been lost.

But Petzoldt is a man who faces reality as he sees it and acts and speaks accordingly. His free-spirited nature generates both friends and foes. A natural charisma attracts near adulation from the thousands of young people who attend his courses in the mountains or hear his litany of oft-repeated stories at conferences. Environmental and educational organizations award him their highest honors. Still there are detractors who question his integrity, claim he lacks business skills, berate his single-mindedness, or perpetuate unflattering, often un-founded, rumors about his past. Some of the more persistent rumors that have dogged Petzoldt over the years are put to rest in these pages.

In reflecting on his long life, Petzoldt admits he bucked the sys-tem, but it was a great ride. "I didn't take on the reponsibilities that most people desire to have of a steady job and raising children," he says. "I wouldn't get into that trap. I wouldn't take a job where I had to go and work every day for the rest of my life for Sears and Roebuck. I'd rather die than do that. But I'm living the kind of life I want to live."

Petzoldt has always taught that the primary reason for climbing a mountain, venturing into the wild outdoors, or merely existing is for enjoyment of the environment, the companionship, and just plain fun. Reaching the summit, gaining fame, or making a lot of money is a bonus, not a measure of success.

Now that he suffers from advanced glaucoma, Petzoldt's own climbing days are behind him. His fortitude in getting to 11,000 feet on his seventieth anniversary ascent of the Grand Teton in 1994 was inspirational. His good judgment in deciding not to try for the top on this commemorative occasion was typical. Renowned for his one-liners, he says, "There are old climbers and there are bold climbers, but there are no old, bold climbers."

On October 10, 1995, his courage faced a severe test. A field and vision examination showed that his glaucoma was so progressed that he retained only a little peripheral vision in the left eye and tunnel vision in the right eye. Alan S. Crandall, a specialist at the University of Utah Moran Eye Center, told him that he would probably be blind within a couple of months unless he underwent an operation as soon as possible. Dr. Crandall warned that there would be some risk. Petzoldt agreed to the surgery without hesitation.

"I'm facing reality. I'm ready now to live blind," he said. "As long as I can talk, write and go around and meet a few people it will be okay. In many ways, I'm a dreamer and do silly things. But in many ways I'm a realist."

The operation was relatively successful. Although Petzoldt's vi-sion is still greatly impaired, there is a good possibility that it will not worsen. At the age of ninety, he still maintains a hectic schedule that keeps him "spreading the word" back and forth across the country.

"After all, eight and nine add up to seventeen," he quipped on his eighty-ninth birthday. "I'm just getting started."

Energy and optimism typify Petzoldt's life. Ever a survivor, he continues to challenge the facts, disturb the norm, and write his own story.

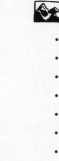

CHAPTER 1

Discovery Years

PAUL PETZOLDT LAY ON HIS STOMACH STARING INTO THE THOUSAND-foot-deep gorge of Snake River Canyon. It was hot and dusty and the bored eleven-year-old did not know what to do with himself.

Daydreaming on the lip of the cliff, he was soon mesmerized by the rugged gorge opening beneath him. The canyon wall revealed little shelves and projections he had not seen before. It looked like a natural stairway. He imagined himself wedging his hands into cracks and balancing his feet on the ridges to lower himself to the river. It would be much more fun than hiking on the path. He gingerly slid his legs over the edge.

Clinging to the rim of lava rock, he panicked. He could not follow the line he had seen from above. He hung on the precipice, fumbling for an anchor with one foot as he reached for a lower handhold. Then the other foot scratched around for a contact point and his fingers grappled for another projectile to hang onto. Not daring to look down, he tried to convince himself that he had seen a climbable route in the rocky face.

His arms and legs moved mechanically as he scraped his way downward, too intent on his movements to heed the tightness in his belly. Finally, the welcome gurgle of the river broke his concentration, and

11

he felt solid ground beneath his feet. Standing on the riverbank he looked up at the towering bluff and marveled at his accomplishment.

He rested awhile and then began to study the upward route. It looked as though it would be easier going because he could anticipate the cracks and knobs of rock that would lead him to the top. Full of his success, he decided to try it again. Eager to tell his mother about his daring feat, he climbed to the surface quickly and then ran all the way home.

"You must be careful," Emma Petzoldt said, knowing her doughty youngster was bound to repeat his adventure. She had given up trying to keep him from the gorge.

Since moving from the Midwest to Twin Falls, Idaho, he had adopted the canyon as his playground on most summer days. He scrabbled down faint paths to the river bottom, hiked to Pillar Falls, where foaming torrents exploded over two massive boulders, or explored mysterious caves that eons of pounding wind and water had chiseled through cliffs of layered red, yellow, and black lava. He spent hours at the springs bubbling from lost rivers that had disappeared into the porous volcanic bedrock miles away. That is where he and his big brothers pulled in rainbow trout and sturgeon or fired their shotguns at dozens of geese and mallards that filled the sky.

Sometimes, after long hours of rambling, he wandered to a place where the river narrowed and orchards of sweet cherries, apples, peaches, and plums grew along its banks. Spreading his bedroll beneath the trees, he slept there, soothed by the whispering current, smelling the fragrance of ripening fruit, and fancying he saw pictures in the stars.

Emma prayed often for her spirited child but thanked God that he had responded so well to the westward move. Idaho's rugged terrain suited him well.

PAUL WAS BORN ON A FARM NEAR CRESTON, IOWA, WHERE THE CLOSEST things to a mountain were 300-foot mounds of prairie sod rising abruptly from the windswept floodplain of the Missouri River. The family lived in an L-shaped frame house on an isolated plot of ground in the unbroken grassland. It was a home of kerosene lamps and wood-burning stoves, with a root cellar on the side, a hand water pump in the front yard, and a privy out back.

In his constant struggle to improve the land and support his wife and nine children, Charles Petzoldt combated sleet, wind, frost, and drought from the time he left the breakfast table before daylight until the skies turned dark. He plowed and planted the fields, picked corn, harvested Ben Davis apples in a small orchard, tended to livestock, and delivered cream to the neighbors, then spent the few remaining hours building a bigger house on a new homestead he called the Enterprise. His goal was interrupted when he died of diphtheria before Paul was four.

Paul had few memories of his father. He remembered looking forward to harvest time when Charles drove up with wagonloads of shucked corn to toss into the storage crib by the barn. The bin was built with air slots between the boards so that the corn would dry out and not rot. Every once in awhile, an ear would drop to the ground and the barnyard pigs would fight over it. Paul's job was to dash for the stray ears and throw them back in the pile before the hogs could get them.

He remembered evenings when his father led evening prayers or played hymns on the pump organ in the parlor while the rest of the family sang. And the Sabbath, when everyone crowded into the wagon and bounced down the rutted road to chapel. The little church resounded with shouts of "Hallelujah! Come to Jesus!" rising from the crowd of farm folk dressed in their Sunday best. Paul slumped down in the pew to muffle the noise, and when the mellow chords of "Amazing Grace" and "Little Church in the Wildwood" calmed the fervor, he fell asleep.

Camp meetings on the banks of the Grand River were better. The preacher waded into the stream and dunked believers underwater with the turtles and the catfish. Paul's usually staid parents joined the chorus of "Praise the Lord!" then his mother and the other women brought out huge picnic baskets of fried chicken, potato salad, and fruit pies.

Paul sensed that something was terribly wrong the day his father left the cornfield in the middle of the harvest and took to his bed. With his eldest son, Louie, just back from a job in South Dakota, and Willie, the next in line, attending college in Oskaloosa, Charles had been working exceptionally hard, trying to get in all of the crop so that he could finish the new house he was building on the Enterprise before winter set in. It was not like him to quit in broad daylight.

When the doctor came the next day, he swabbed thick yellow mucous from the sick man's throat and uncovered a telltale layer of grayish membrane. Charles shook with fever and coughed uncontrollably. The physician posted a quarantine notice on the front door and told Emma that no one could enter the house. Willie could not come home and her daughters, Lily and Rosie, would have to remain in Creston, where they were finishing high school and working as mother's helpers in return for room and board. The rest of the family, Emma, Paul, his brothers Louie, Herman ("Dutch"), Eldon ("Curly"), and sisters Gladys and Violet, had to be inoculated and isolated until the crisis passed.

Paul was sorry that his favorite sister Lily could not come home. She often read him stories about Daniel Boone, recited poetry, and showed him picture books of faraway places. She told him about adventurers who sailed the seas and climbed high mountains such as he had never seen. He sat alone thumbing through the tantalizing pages as his mother nursed her husband and the other children waited glumly in the parlor.

For two days the family kept vigil while Charles's coughing worsened. By the time the doctor returned, the dying man's breathing was faint and raspy. Then it ceased. Emma knelt and placed her head on a chair. When she beckoned the older children to kneel beside her and pray, Paul saw that she was crying.

Paul felt cold. He did not know the words of the prayer his family was chanting, and no one had noticed him. He crept into the kitchen and climbed up on the open door of the Majestic oven. As heat from the wooden embers toasted his back, he swung his legs in contentment, listening to the soothing sounds in the other room. The doctor came in and patted him on the head. "Poor little fellow," he said, and then walked out to his waiting buggy.

There was no funeral. Emma bathed and dressed her husband and the next day the undertaker came with a casket. The quarantined family stood by helplessly as the body was removed from their home and taken to the churchyard for burial. They watched from the windows as a few neighbors gathered in the field a safe distance from the infected house to bow their heads in memory of their friend.

The Petzoldts moved into the square frame house on the Enterprise soon after. Besides providing more space, Charles had worked out a unique system for gas lighting in which water dripped onto a carbide tank, causing gas to travel though pipes into upstairs rooms. It was the first such system in the county.

After Charles's death, Willie and Louie assumed responsibility for the farm and established a chain of command. Willie would tell Louie to do a job and if he didn't want to do it, he would pass it on down the line to Dutch or Curly. If Dutch and Curly thought their little brother could handle the chore, Paul got stuck with it. He was the one who had to run out and bring in the cows, carry messages to the field, slop the pigs, and feed the chickens and horses. Worse yet, Curly teased him unmercifully, scared him with stories about ghosts and goblins hiding in dark places, and even poured a handful of dried hot peppers into Paul's mouth while he was sleeping.

Paul was close to his mother, however, and did not mind doing chores for her, braving the scary root cellar to fetch home-canned fruit or some potatoes. Whenever she wanted a rooster for dinner, he ran out and cornered a bird against the fence, tackled it, then carried the flapping critter over to the chopping block to lop off its head with a hatchet. He always tossed the carcass away very fast so the blood would not squirt all over him while the chicken gyrated in its death dance.

Paul enrolled in school before he was five. By then, the Petzoldt mark was already on the little one-room Prairie Lawn schoolhouse. Lily had excelled as a serious scholar. Curly immortalized himself by tossing 12-gauge shotgun shells into the woodstove and blowing up the chimney. Paul got attention by devising a game to play at recess.

The Petzoldts had a stud horse that was in great demand with the neighbors for breeding their mares. Paul often watched as a horse was unloaded, tied under a tree, and protected from the stallion's flailing hooves by a "snorting pole" placed beside her. Paul had seen the process so many times that it seemed like a natural occurrence to him.

One day when his classmates were chasing each other, playing cowboys and Indians, he thought it would be much more fun for them to play something different. So he organized the game of stud horse. The children caught on fast and went through the antics with great enthusiasm until somebody ran into the school and told the teacher. When she rushed out, Paul was directing the action like a miniature Cecil B. DeMille. The teacher grabbed him by the shoulders and sent him rolling in the grass.

"What did you do that for?" he asked, fighting back tears. The teacher simply threw up her hands and announced that recess was over.

When Paul got home that afternoon, his mother did not greet him at the door with the customary glass of milk and piece of home-made pie. She just stood in the doorway looking at him. Pretty soon she started to laugh and went to get the milk and pie. She waited until the next morning to admit that she knew about the episode and to explain to him the difference between animals and people.

Not long after his stud horse fiasco Paul transferred to a school several miles away where Lily was teaching. His older sister fired his interest in reading and taught him to appreciate the classics and memorize poems. She introduced him to stories about George Washington and Jim Bridger and the western yarns of Zane Grey. He read about the Swiss Alps and longed to see them. He devoured tales about Jack London and dreamed of a life like his, following random roads, not knowing where they led or what unexpected happenstance would occur.

While Paul fantasized about fictional adventures, real life became more difficult. Willie and Violet both married and moved to homes of their own. Louie took charge of the family farm, with Dutch and Curly working in the fields after school, and the other two girls helped their mother with household chores. Six-year-old Paul took over the trap lines along the banks of Grand River, running from one location to the next collecting muskrat, mink, possum, coon, civet cats, and the prized skunks that brought one to two dollars per pelt, depending on the width of their stripes.

But at 160 acres the Enterprise was twice as big as the original homestead. When Willie and Louie sold the old farm, their mother was forced to move into the new house even though her husband had not finished paying for the land. She had not been able to get out of debt, and it was getting harder and harder to make ends meet.

The advent of World War I was the final blow. On June 28, 1914, the Austrian Archduke Francis Ferdinand was assassinated in Sarajevo. One month later, Austria-Hungary declared war against Serbia. Germany followed by declaring war against Russia and invading France and Belgium. Soon England was involved, and America jumped into the fracas on April 6, 1917. Despite his exemption from the draft because he was operating his mother's farm, Louie enlisted in the army and shipped overseas to join the fight. Seventeen-year-old Dutch was left in charge of the struggling family homestead.

Despite having a son on the battlefront, Emma and her remaining children were suddenly persona non grata in the neighborhood because their name was "Petzoldt." Propaganda against the infamous Kaiser was so pronounced that American citizens of German descent were looked upon with suspicion. With high, pronounced cheekbones and dark hair, Emma not only appeared foreign, she also spoke with a guttural Slavic accent that was considered suspect.

When Louie came home from war, the family, having been unable to keep up the payments on the Enterprise, was living in a rented home and struggling for subsistence on a small plot of ground. Willie had joined his brother-in-law working on an irrigation project near Twin Falls, Idaho, and finally bought a little potato farm. He urged Louie to follow him. "Come west," he wrote. "The crops are thriving. Business is great."

Louie knew things were certainly not going well in Iowa so he and Violet's husband, Dick, jumped into their old jalopy to give Idaho a look. They liked what they saw and returned to convince Emma that she and the whole family should head west.

PAUL COULD SEE THEIR DIM SILHOUETTES IN THE DISTANCE—MOUNTAIN peaks over 11,000 feet high. The ragged Sawtooth Range loomed to the north of the new farm, breaking out of the broad Magic Valley tableland where fields of potatoes and alfalfa grew among the moonscape lava beds that surrounded Twin Falls. He was disappointed that the mountains were not closer so that he could explore them, carrying an alpenstock and yodeling like the Swiss mountaineers he had read about in Lily's books. He promised himself that one day he would do so.

He thrived in Idaho. He grew tall, until he towered over Curly and was able to subdue his former tormentor. But he had little in common with his siblings and spent much of his time alone. He soon developed a strong sense of independence, a trait his mother recognized and nurtured.

For the first year he satisfied his adventurous spirit by exploring the Snake River Canyon. The fabled gorge became as familiar as his own backyard. But when he was about thirteen, the allure of the Sawtooths became irresistible. He imagined himself scaling the needle-sharp spires and deep saddles like an Alpine climber, and he was determined to see the peaks at close range. But he knew that getting his mother's approval would be difficult. He hoped that if he made detailed plans for the trip ahead of time and invited his buddy Chico Martinez to join him on the lengthy trek she would agree to let him go.

Paul took his time studying maps and making lists. When he was satisfied that nothing had been forgotten, he told his mother how many jars of home-canned peaches, vegetables, and jam, cans of pork and beans, loaves of bread, sacks of eggs, slabs of bacon, cooking utensils, and blankets he planned to take. He promised to carry an extra-long tether rope, hobbles, and a couple of bags of oats if she would let them take Old Shorty and the one-horse buggy. Ranger, the sheepdog, would tag along for protection. There was nothing to worry about, he assured her. His mother sighed deeply, then promised to bake some cookies and apple pie to add to his supplies.

In a few days, the two youngsters piled their gear in the buggy, climbed atop it, and headed south along the canyon rim toward Shoshone Falls. When they could hear the steady roar of water, they knew they had only a short distance to go to reach the crossing point above the cascade where the river was quiet. There was no bridge in those days, so they had to drive the buggy onto an old wooden ferry that was pulled to the opposite side by cable. Then they struck out across the surreal landscape of lava beds and bumped along a dirt road to the outskirts of Shoshone, twenty miles from home.

The boys made camp before nightfall. They found a sheltered spot, cut a bed of cottonwood boughs for their blankets, and lit a small bonfire to warm the summer night. They fried bacon for sandwiches and ate a quart of Emma's peaches, pleased with themselves that they had come so far without incident. But when the sky grew black and they crawled into their bedrolls, neither admitted to little pangs of fear as strange, unidentified noises moaned and creaked around them.

The next morning they steered Shorty onto Shoshone's Main Street. The sheriff stopped them on the edge of town. Certain that two underage boys traveling alone could be up to nothing but mischief, he tried to send them home. Paul looked the officer in the eye and, attempting to be very polite and grown up, succeeded in convincing him that their mothers had given permission for the excursion.

The mountains became more visible and their excitement increased as they neared the Wood River, where they made a second camp on the fringe of the forest. The next morning they entered the Hailey valley, where herds of jerseys lazed behind barbed wire fences.

As the foothills steepened into mountains, Paul urged Shorty over rocky tracks and across shallow fords in the river until the buggy could go no farther. The boys unloaded their supplies by a stream, tethered the horse where he could reach water and graze, and then anticipated the morning's climb.

They started early. Nothing was as they had imagined. Game trails wound through dense thickets, house-sized boulders and fallen trees blocked the trail, and sheer pitches left them short of breath. Even the summit wasn't the steeplelike cone of the "towering giants" they had seen in picture books of the Alps. It was a broad meadow surrounded by tall pines and spruce that obliterated any view of the valley below. They might just as well have stayed in Hailey, Paul thought.

They spent a few more days fishing and unsuccessfully seeking better peaks to climb. Disappointed, they hitched up Shorty and started home.

All went well until the rough mountain trail fed into a deep ravine and the buggy began to pick up speed. Paul pulled on the reins with all of his strength, but the wheels spun faster and faster. Shorty broke into a run, trying to control the buggy, but wasn't able to hold it back. It was too much for him. He had spent his long life as a saddle horse and wasn't used to towing a vehicle behind him.

Suddenly the buggy careened off the path and sailed into a ditch at the bottom. The reach, a brace connecting the front and back wheels, snapped with a bang. Shorty shied and lurched forward, the reach stabbed into the ground and pitched the hind wheels and buggy high into the air before they landed with a thud and shattered. Shorty, still attached to the front wheels, trotted a few feet down the track and stopped. Paul and Chico had crashed into the culvert—they were dazed but unhurt.

"What am I going to tell Mother?" Paul moaned. "What are we going to do?" Chico said, more worried about being stranded over one hundred miles from home than facing punishment.

The boys stood up and dusted themselves off, then started to assess the damage. The buggy and back wheels were demolished. But the front wheels were still connected to the shafts. They figured they could weave the tethering rope from the front axle to the shafts that were still attached to Shorty's harness. Then they could pile the bedding and remaining food and equipment on top of the rope. It would be impossible for them to balance the load and ride on it, too, so they sat on the wooden axle part of the time and walked much of the way home.

The two adventurers were covered with lava dust when they limped into Twin Falls. Even Shorty and Ranger showed the effects of the long trek down steep mountain trails and through the dry, hot desert. Emma was so relieved to see them home safely that she made little comment on the missing buggy. Paul assured her that his wanderlust was sated.

But when he was fourteen and starting junior high, his horizons expanded, and he longed for a bicycle so he could ride farther afield with his friends.

"It's an awful long walk to school," he told his mother one day. "Most of the kids have bikes." Emma shook her head. "Too many bills," she said. "We can't afford it."

Then a few days later she told him to follow her out into the field. She marked off an acre of ground and said the plot was his to plant a crop of onions. He would have to do all of the work himself and he could keep any money he earned to buy the bicycle he had been wanting.

Paul set to work immediately. He tilled long depressions in the soil and then crawled alongside the narrow channels and carefully placed tiny seeds on the bottom. Then he covered the seeds with dirt and dug small irrigation ditches between the rows to allow water to soak the plants.

When the seedlings sprouted, he got down on his hands and knees again and thinned the crop. Then, all summer he watered and weeded and watched the stems and leaves grow green and strong.

Near harvest time he broke off the tops of each plant to allow the onions to ripen. He began counting the days until it would be time to dig them up, collect them in wire baskets, dump them into gunny sacks, and cart them to the railhead for shipment to Chicago. Then, with cash in hand, he would buy that bicycle.

But when fall arrived, his mother told him he must leave his onions to rot in the ground. She tried to explain to him that economic conditions had deteriorated in the nation. The postwar boom had been short-lived. It was said that over 450,000 farmers had lost their homesteads and land. While their farm had produced hundreds of acres of potatoes and onions since they had come from Iowa a few years before, and they had always been successful in selling their produce for shipment to the East, now the market had slumped, and the bumper crops they raised were unsalable. It would cost the family more to harvest the summer's yield, haul the loads into town, and ship them by rail than they could realize by selling them.

Paul could see that his mother was as heartsick as he was, but he couldn't really grasp the situation. He was confused and angry. It didn't seem fair. He couldn't understand why the family was unable to sell its crops, why he couldn't have a bicycle after working so hard when all of his friends had spent the summer fishing.

In the months that followed, he realized that there was more to worry about than a crop of onions and a bicycle. He could tell by the fatigue showing in his mother's face and the long hours she spent in prayer. A stack of bills sat on the table untouched while acres of produce decayed in the fields. "It isn't because we're lazy or don't get up at four in the morning to milk the cows," he thought bitterly.

Finally, debts piled up so high that his mother lost the farm, and the family split in all directions. Curly headed for the West Coast to become a jockey. Dutch went along with him to build a career as a horse trainer. Willie and Rosie stayed in Iowa, and Gladys moved to

Long Beach, California, to live with Louie, his wife, and their new baby. Paul and his mother were left alone until creditors finally took over the house.

One day in 1923, just before Paul turned fifteen, his mother told him she wanted to discuss something with him. An elderly cousin in New York State had asked her to move back there and care for him in return for room and board. Paul could go east with her if he wanted or he could finish the school year in Long Beach with Louie's family and Gladys. The decision was his.

He had never been separated from his mother, and he couldn't imagine living so far away from her. But Paul did not have the emotional connection with the East that she did. He had learned to love the West. So he opted to go to California.

Still only a teenager, he was on his own. He had never known his father and there was no one else to take his place. Louie, a driller in the Signal Hill oil fields, was kind, but there were too many years between the brothers for them to be very close. Paul felt like an outsider in the small, crowded home on Daisy Avenue, and he spent as much time away from the house as possible. When he wasn't attending classes at Polytechnic High School or competing at water polo and gymnastics, he hung out at the beach or in the park.

He lingered for hours in the library looking for guidance. He studied the works of Plato who held that "all virtue is knowledge" and true statesmanship promotes a national moral character. He also read about the Fascist dictator in Italy who proclaimed himself *Il Duce* ("the leader") and condoned violence as the fundamental element of social transformation. He joined the crowds at the city park, where Communists, Socialists, Wobblies, and other rabble-rousers spouted radical ideas from soapbox platforms. The maelstrom of philosophical rhetoric fascinated him but offered no solutions and confused him all the more.

Late in 1923, he decided to try the next school year in Twin Falls with Willie's family. But his brother's farmhouse was several miles from the high school and the living quarters were so crowded with noisy kids and Willie's elderly father-in-law that Paul was miserable.

His football coach finally made arrangements for him to move into town and work as a caretaker at the mortuary, where he could live in an upstairs room. The idea of dead bodies in the house soon made him uneasy, so he got himself a better position, including board, as a dishwasher at the cafe in the Prine Hotel. He quickly worked his way up to waiting tables and was even allowed to cook on occasion.

By then, it was almost a year since he had seen his mother and he missed her. He decided to visit her in New York. He couldn't afford a train ticket, so he decided to hop a freight as the migrant workers were doing.

A few days before he planned to leave, he hung around the railroad yards to observe the hoboes in action. Company detectives were on the lookout for illegal riders. Vagrants waited in the shadows until a train started to pull out and then jumped aboard before "the dick" discovered them. Riders always caught the car's forward ladder rather than the back one to avoid being swung under the rear wheels if they fell.

It took a few days to muster the courage, then one summer night, trembling with excitement, he packed a small suitcase and hiked to a railroad siding a few miles out of Twin Falls. Pretty soon he heard the wail of a whistle, and a huge engine pulling a string of boxcars thundered down the track. As the train slowed, Paul ran as fast as he could and gave a flying leap onto the front ladder of a car. He waited a few minutes, gasping for breath, and then climbed up onto the roof, and started to gingerly walk along the moving train looking for an empty car. When he finally found a spot to hide, he flipped himself inside and collapsed in a shivering heap.

He enjoyed his visit with his mother. And, now that his initiation was accomplished, he perfected his bumming skills and rode the freights wherever his wanderlust led him. He learned that there was an art to the system.

It was easier to catch a ride on westbound trains than on those traveling east, since the former were usually empty of cargo. The most comfortable quarters on a lengthy trip were in a refrigerator car called a reefer, which had insulated ice bays on each end. After the meat and produce had been delivered, the vacant compartments afforded shelter from wind and weather. But Paul always wedged a stick under the roof lid in case a railroad employee patrolling the top of the train happened to reach down and lock the hatch.

In the summer of 1924, flushed with his independence and proud that he had supported himself and finished another school year, Paul agreed to hitchhike to Jackson Hole, Wyoming, with his friend Ralph Herron to visit Ralph's relatives.

It took them two long days of thumbing rides to get as far as Rexburg, Idaho, but when they reached a bend in the road on the outskirts of town, Paul knew why they had come. There in the distance against a backdrop of brilliant blue were the three Teton peaks. The jagged points of the snowcapped summits loomed above graceful saddles that swept between adjoining ridges. These were certainly like the Alps of Switzerland he had always dreamed of seeing.

The boys were excited as they hiked to the town of Victor on the Idaho border at the mountain's base. As they walked along the dusty road, Paul told Ralph about his disappointing trek in the Sawtooths and wondered what it would be like to climb the Tetons.

There weren't many cars taking the precipitous, winding road from Victor over the pass into Jackson, but finally a man in a Model T Ford stopped for them. The old car huffed and puffed up the steep road until it looked as if it could go no farther, and the youngsters suspected they would be completing the trip on foot. Then the driver surprised them. He made a quick U-turn and started to back up the sharp grade.

When they finally reached the summit, the farmer reversed the vehicle again, hopped out of the front seat, and started poking around in the forest by the roadside. The boys watched in amazement as he cut down a pine tree and tied it to the rear bumper of the car. "Brake," he said, lurching into the treacherous downhill run to Jackson.

Steering his jalopy down the hairpin turns as though nothing unusual was occurring, the farmer kept up a steady line of chatter during the trip. He told the hitchhikers many stories about the mountains that had been passed down through the ages.

The first people to see the Tetons were Indians who came to the Snake River valley to fish, hunt deer, elk, and buffalo, and collect edible plants, he said. The Shoshoni tribe called the distinctive peaks *Teewinot*, meaning "pinnacles." They avoided going up to the cathedral spires because they thought that was where the sacred spirits lived.

Next came the trappers and mountain men like John Colter, Jedediah Smith, and Jim Bridger, who considered "the hole" a storehouse for beaver skins and buffalo hides. They held yearly rendezvous there to trade goods with the Native Americans and engage in raucous celebrations before holing in for the long winters.

"Some French trappers named the Tetons," the farmer said. "Thought they looked like three tits."

The more staid Astorians of John Jacob Astor's Pacific Fur Company called the peaks the Pilot Knobs, and geologist-surveyor F. V. Hayden thought they looked like shark's teeth.

"Have you ever climbed the big one?" Paul asked.

"Hell no," he said.

"We're going to," Paul said, surprising himself.

Ralph agreed. The old-timer laughed.

As they coasted down into the valley the farmer stopped his car to remove the tree. They continued on, past ranches with fenced pastures, golden haystacks, and skeletal wooden beaver-slide racks.

Soon the Model T chugged into the village of Jackson. The boys thanked their friend and hopped out at the town square, where a few young trees had been planted. The Jackson State Bank, Mercill's general mercantile, DeLoney's grocery store, Porter Drug, the Crabtree Hotel, and some saloons were linked by boardwalks along the dusty streets.

There weren't many people around, but the young hitchhikers attracted the attention of a few locals. When they started asking if anyone knew about climbing the mountains, a crowd of bemused onlookers gathered. Some had hunted deer and mountain sheep in the highlands, but most Jackson Holers looked at the towering range as a damned inconvenient blockade to getting over to Idaho. The idea of two green kids trying to scale the 13,766-foot peak brought nothing but laughter. Then Billy Owen got word of their plan and came to find them.

Owen, who happened to be visiting in town, had successfully led a party to the top of the Grand Teton twenty-five years before. The diminutive sixty-four-year-old didn't look much like the mountaineers Paul had seen pictured in books about Switzerland, but when he finished telling the boys about his 1898 ascent, they were impressed.

Better yet, he didn't ridicule the youngsters for their determination to climb the peak. He had advised three Montana climbers who made a successful attempt the previous August. He would give Paul and Ralph detailed instructions about the route he had pioneered, as well.

A few days later, armed with Owen's rough map, some canned goods, a rope, a pocketknife, and a few skimpy supplies wrapped in a bedroll, the boys started their adventure. They enjoyed the taste of celebrity and attention from the locals and affected nonchalance as one of Owen's friends drove them to the trailhead.

The Tetons were an impressive sight close up. The massive glacial fault-block had been created by a series of gigantic upthrusts which formed peaks that shot straight up from the valley floor. Deep canyons had been cut by streams born of the melting ice and snow, and huge quantities of rock and debris had been scraped away from the granite mountains and deposited in moraines at the bottom.

The adventurers thanked their driver and scrambled into the forest. There were no foothills to ease them into the climb. Right off, they were tramping uphill, following game trails through jungles of fallen timber and thick brush.

Worming their way through the undergrowth as fast as they could, they soon found themselves in a forest of Engelmann spruce and lodgepole pine, with crusty patches of snow in shady spots. As they climbed higher, the trees gave way to broad, open slopes of grass studded with wildflowers.

It was almost noon when they reached a small lake (later named Delta Lake) that was surrounded by tall granite walls. They stopped to eat a can of cold pork and beans and surveyed the succession of cliffs rising beyond them. A giant flight of climbing pitches, later known as the East Ridge, appeared to be much easier than the longer circuitous route that Owen had described.

The day was warm and sunny. The boys were pumped with adrenaline and couldn't wait to stand on top of that magnificent peak. They decided to leave their bedrolls and heavy jackets at the lake, climb the Grand, and then return to their camp for the night.

Their first challenge was a boulder field with rocks as big as boxcars. The leather soles of their cowboy boots didn't have much purchase on the slick surface, and they were pretty exhausted by the time they maneuvered over the giant obstacle.

Next, they tackled a series of cliffs. Handholds and footholds were harder to find and further apart than they had estimated. The climb was difficult, but they were committed to the task and continued to scramble doggedly up the pitch.

About three o'clock, clouds started to gather. Snowfields appeared more frequently and there were icy ledges on the cliff. Worse yet, the route that had appeared so easy from the foreshortened view below fractured into a jumble of pinnacles and canyons. They gingerly made their way to a summit.

Once they were on the ridge, a sheer wall rose behind them and a massive gendarme blocked their way to the north. Paul offered to check out the rocky tower to see if there was a way around it. But when he crept along an out-sloping ledge to pass the gendarme, he was rim-rocked, staring into thousands of feet of nothing. Terrified, he edged back to tell Ralph the bad news.

They decided to explore the south side of the ridge. They dropped down onto a shelf, worked their way up a couple of cracks and found themselves on another ledge. Afternoon shadows lengthened and cold winds screamed. They negotiated sheer slabs of rock, trudged through snow-filled chasms, and felt their way around huge chockstones barricading the path until they ran out of light. They would have to bivouac for the night.

Huddling together for warmth, they thought of their bedrolls at the lake and wished they had their warm jackets to cover their sweat-soaked cotton shirts and overalls. Thunder rolled and lightning streaked the sky. Then it began to snow. As a wind-whipped blizzard raged through the night, they felt more like scared little boys than brave mountaineers.

The storm stopped before morning. They were numb and aching but thankful to be alive. All thoughts of standing on top of the Grand had vanished, and they were ashamed that they had ignored Owen's instructions.

Looking for an easier route down, they slid on their stomachs from a slanting ice slab to another shelf. They were rim-rocked again! Trying not to cry, Paul took the pocketknife from his pants pocket and started to chop small hand- and footholds into the icy wall. It took him an hour to chisel steps back up to the ridge where they had spent the night.

Luckily, the sun finally broke through the clouds, and they shivered as their bodies warmed. When the new snow and ice started to melt into small rivulets, they carefully made their way back down to their camp at the lake.

They rested the next day and wrestled with the decision of whether to return to Jackson as failures or attempt the ascent again. They had enjoyed all of the notoriety on their departure. They couldn't face the ridicule they would surely receive from the cowboys on their unsuccessful return. They decided to give the mountain another try. But this time, they would take the less direct southwest route that Owen had advised.

At dawn the following morning, they traversed the boulder field and then turned south. The trail was just as Owen had described it. They tramped across the snowfield, kicked steps up the glacier, and scrambled onto the Lower Saddle, a broad sweep between the peaks, where they could look down into Idaho and even see the distant outline of the Sawtooth Range.

They then climbed up a talus slope leading to the Upper Saddle which was wedged between the West Face of the Grand and another peak. Below them a deep chasm of ice and snow plunged thousands of feet to a mass of rocks. Ahead, a massive cliff blocked the route.

For a minute they thought they were stymied again, but another look at Owen's map reassured them. They continued on to a huge bulge in the mountain that seemed to obstruct the way. Following Owen's instructions, they walked their hands over a rough edge in the boulder and stretched their legs to reach small footholds so they could work their way around what was later dubbed the Belly Roll.

Soon they reached a narrow platform where the next challenge awaited—a slim shelf under an overhang where they had to inch along on their hands and knees across an eighteen-foot-long ledge called the Crawl. They didn't dare look down at the open space that gaped beneath them.

Once across the Crawl, Ralph boosted Paul up into a steep-walled chimney, where he laboriously climbed to the top and then helped his partner up. From there, they clambered over rocky slabs onto the final pitch.

At two o'clock in the afternoon of July 25, they stood on the summit of the Grand Teton. Far below stretched miles of sage meadows fringed with evergreens and dotted with glistening lakes. Ragged mountain peaks capped with glaciers rose in the distance.

After a few minutes of hilarious laughing, crying, and back-patting, the fledgling mountaineers shook hands. They found Owen's lightning-scarred plaque engraved "Rocky Mountain Club," his autograph chiseled in the granite, and the bottle that held the names and addresses of the 1898 Owens party and the two groups that had summited in 1923. They wrote their own names on a paper and placed it in the container. Paul did not realize it then, but his life had taken a new direction.

CHAPTER 2

The Teton Guide

WHEN THE TEENAGERS HITCHHIKED INTO JACKSON, WORD SPREAD FAST that the two bedraggled hikers were back. People swarmed out of the clapboard stores and saloons and crowded around the boys in the town square.

"Did you get to the top?" they asked.

"Sure did."

The cowboys were skeptical. "All the way?"

The kids looked as though they had been through an ordeal, and their boot soles were nothing but ragged scraps of leather. Certainly they had done a lot of rough hiking, but could they prove they had gone to the summit?

Billy Owen arrived just in time. "What did you see?" he asked the boys.

Petzoldt and Herron described the jumble of broken boulders on the topmost pinnacle and told of seeing lightning burns on the metal commemorative plaque and Owen's name chiseled in a rock.

Owen nodded solemnly. "These youngsters have been to the top of the Grand Teton!" he proclaimed.

Everyone cheered.

Being "the kids that climbed the Grand" was fun. Strangers waved or stopped them on the street to ask about their adventure. Petzoldt became good at embellishing the story, especially the parts about bivouacking overnight in a blizzard and cutting steps in an ice wall with a pocketknife. Herron went back home, but when rancher Bill Lucas befriended Petzoldt and offered him a summer job haying, he decided to stay awhile. Lucas even bought him a new pair of boots.

Petzoldt and Billy Owen became friends, too. Soon the old man was talking about making another attempt on the mountain together. He wanted to settle a long-standing dispute about the first ascent.

IN 1872 NATHANIEL LANGFORD, THE FIRST SUPERINTENDENT OF Yellowstone National Park, and James Stevenson, Chief of the Field Division of the U.S. Geological Survey, claimed to have reached the summit while they were conducting the Hayden Surveys, a federally sponsored expedition to map the Yellowstone area. Langford later chronicled the event in a story for *Scribner's Monthly*.

Owen, then an adventurous young surveyor from Laramie, Wyoming, who had run geodetic surveys on foot in the Wind River Range, had reason to doubt Langford's claim. He had made several abortive efforts to follow the Langford/Stevenson route on the Grand Teton. He got as far as the Upper Saddle, but further progress was blocked by the West Face, an immense cliff that neither he nor the Langford party had the necessary hardware to maneuver.

A high, rounded pinnacle on the ridge west of the Upper Saddle contained a large circle of rock slabs that had probably been placed by Indians or early trappers as protection against the elements. Owen named the man-made formation the Enclosure and concluded that was as high as Langford's party had gone. His suspicions were heightened by common gossip in Jackson that "Beaver Dick" Leigh, guide for the Hayden Surveys, had said that the party got close enough to the top that they figured it didn't matter whether or not they actually reached the summit.

When Owen, along with F. Spalding, J. Shive, and F. L. Petersen, made the ascent in 1898, he was convinced that his party was the first to reach the top. Langford and Stevenson had not even mentioned the terrifying Belly Roll and Crawl that Owen found to be the keys to avoiding the steep cliff of the West Face and getting to the top.

Langford and Stevenson's description of the summit as "a bald, denuded knob worn smooth by elemental warfare" was more consistent with a large, solid slab above and east of the Upper Saddle than it was with the mass of broken rock at the actual mountaintop. Furthermore, when Owen and his companions reached the summit, there was no traditional cairn, no container holding names of the climbers, no sign that any human had ever been there. Owen was certain that he had made the initial ascent.*

NO ONE ELSE MADE IT TO THE TOP UNTIL AUGUST 1923, WHEN TWO different parties succeeded: A. R. Ellingwood from Lake Forest, Illinois, and Eleanor Davis from Colorado Springs, Colorado—the first woman to scale the Grand; and Andy DePirro, Quin A. Blackburn, and Dave F. DeLap, the group from Missoula, Montana, that Owen had advised. Petzoldt and Herron could be credited with the fourth successful trip.

Petzoldt agreed to guide his friend up the mountain in August to celebrate Owen's sixty-fifth birthday. When word of the planned trip reached the Jackson grapevine, locals who had rarely given the Tetons a second thought, clamored to make the ascent.

Bill Lucas's sister Geraldine, signed up. When Mrs. Eugene Amoretti, who operated a dude ranch, heard that Geraldine was going, she insisted on joining the party with horse-packer Gibb Scott to help her. Frank Petersen, a member of Owen's 1898 party wanted to try it again, and Jesse Dewey, Fred Koerner, Jack Crawford, and Charles Purdy completed the roster. Young Yvonne Deloney got permission from her mother to accompany them as far as base camp.

They started out on August 12. Eleven impatient hikers milled around the trailhead while horse-packers tried to organize an unwieldy assortment of food and equipment. Finally, a few of the younger members took off on their own, while the remainder of the party made last-minute adjustments to their gear before stringing along behind the leaders. Petzoldt scuttled back and forth between the pack outfits, horsemen, and hikers to lead them over the rougher

---

*The debate about who made the first ascent of the Grand Teton still rages. Petzoldt is convinced Owen deserves credit for the feat.

terrain and on up to timberline, where they camped for the night.

Before dawn the next morning, the younger climbers resumed their fast pace. Petzoldt stayed in the rear with Owen, who despite a bad heart, tried to keep up with the stronger climbers. He took his pulse periodically and complained that his heart was racing. But he refused to slow down.

After several hours of hiking, Geraldine Lucas said she was too exhausted to continue. Mrs. Amoretti, feeling dizzy and short of breath, decided to turn back, too.

Owen did not even reach the Lower Saddle before he gave up the climb. He told Petzoldt to hurry ahead to catch the others "and keep them from getting killed up there." Petersen and Purdy went back to the valley with Owen.

Unencumbered by his worn-out companions, Petzoldt worked his way up the rugged boulder fields and glaciers to meet the remaining climbers at the Upper Saddle. He realized that, having seen the treacherous North Face of the Grand Teton and the frightening exposure to the icy chasm below, they had lost some of their confidence. Taking charge, he told them to take turns tying into the rope while he belayed them over the Belly Roll and the Crawl, which lay ahead.

"It will be hard to hear each other up here," he said. "We might not be able to see one another around a corner or in a chimney when I am holding you on the rope. Speak slowly and loudly and use as few words as possible to say what you mean so your voice won't get all garbled in the wind."

With the climbers gingerly following his orders, somehow Petzoldt guided them safely to the summit and back to Jackson. But he didn't deem the excursion a success. Billy Owen had not made it.

The next day Geraldine Lucas drove out to the ranch and asked Petzoldt for another chance to go up the Teton. Eleanor Davis, who had climbed with A. R. Ellingwood in 1923, had reached the top. Lucas wanted to be the first local woman to stand on the Grand.

Lucas was a stocky fifty-nine-year-old with a reputation as a crusty westerner who knew what she wanted and generally got her way. Petzoldt liked her and was grateful for the hospitality she had shown him at her ranch. He agreed to guide her once more and resolved to do everything possible to help her reach the summit.

But by now he had experienced two poorly organized climbs. Lucas had tired early on the previous attempt and had to turn back. He was determined not to make the same mistakes again. This time, he would analyze what had gone wrong on the other trips and make his plans carefully.

When he arrived at the Lucas ranch, despite his adolescent appearance, Petzoldt had the bearings of a seasoned mountaineer. Tall and trim, he wore a sturdy shirt and trousers with the five-dollar high-laced boots that Bill Lucas had bought him after his first climb. An unruly thatch of thick brown hair defied its middle part and bushy eyebrows shaded his pale blue eyes. A properly coiled climbing rope was slung around his neck and under one arm he carried an ice ax.

Lucas had invited her friend Jack Crawford to join them again and had asked packer Ike Powell to furnish each of them a saddle horse so that everyone could ride to timberline. They took extra pack horses for carrying gear.

Petzoldt told the group that he had learned the hard way what disorganization and forced marches would do. This time there would be no racing uphill; when they started out on foot, they would keep a steady pace dictated by the slowest walker.

He planned to take one more day and make a second camp under an overhanging rock above a waterfall that flowed into a high meadow east of the Middle Teton. Lucas could rest there before the difficult technical climbing began.

He told the party to make light packs but to bring warm clothing in case of a storm like the one he and Herron had endured. He warned them to drink plenty of fluids and nibble candy and other energy-building snacks on the trail. When everything was arranged, the foursome, and a wrangler to stay with the horses at timberline, started up the mountain. Geraldine Lucas reached the first camp in fine shape.

The next day they climbed slowly as far as the "Petzoldt Caves" above the waterfall. Refreshed, they started early on the third morning. Petzoldt cut Lucas an alpenstock to help her balance on the uneven trail and told her to follow his lead and imitate his moves over snowfields and on the rock. When the grade steepened, he tied her into a rope and belayed her over difficult pitches.

As they approached the Upper Saddle, they spotted four men

coming up behind them. Lucas recognized them as ranchers from Kelly, Wyoming. The group appeared to be ill-prepared for an overnight camp and wasn't even carrying a rope.

The climbers soon caught up with Petzoldt's party and explained that they wanted to plant an American flag on top of the Grand. Petzoldt thought that was a great idea and offered to help them. But when they reached the Belly Roll and Crawl, where thousands of feet gaped below them, two of the cowboys backed out of the trip.

With a great deal of coaxing, pushing from below and tugging from above, Petzoldt succeeded in getting all five climbers to the summit. The two remaining Kelly men attached their flag to a tepee pole and wedged it into the boulder stack. Geraldine Lucas climbed to the topmost pile of rocks and posed, with arms dramatically outstretched, for a picture in front of Old Glory.

Within a week of their return, Billy Owen insisted that if Lucas could make it, he could, too. Petzoldt had no doubt that the wiry little man was an accomplished athlete. He had ridden a high-wheeled bicycle all around Wyoming and even through the untamed backcountry of Yellowstone Park. And he had certainly done his share of mountain climbing in the Wind Rivers and Tetons. The only problem would be curbing the old fellow's boundless energy so as to keep his heart rate under control.

He agreed to guide him again if they took no one but the packer Ike Powell. This time they would start up the Idaho side and ride horses all the way to a basin at the bottom of the Middle Teton. From there they would make the climb slowly, and Owen could study the terrain carefully to further verify his theory that the Langford party had not reached the top.

The trio made three camps along the way and then on the fourth morning left the hobbled horses to start the ascent. The leisurely pace kept Owen's pulse in the normal range and did not tire him.

When they reached the Enclosure, Owen scrambled up the rounded pinnacle to see if he could get a better view of the summit. He couldn't see it. He also verified his suspicion that the Belly Roll and Crawl were hidden from that vantage point. In all probability, Langford had figured that the large granite slab southeast of the Enclosure was the highest point on the mountain, and thought it was impossible to go further. No one would ever know for certain, but Owen was more convinced than ever that Langford's party had gone no further than the Enclosure.

At noon, the old man and his young admirer reached the top of the Grand Teton (Powell had remained at the Upper Saddle). Petzoldt let his companion climb the last few yards alone to savor the moment. Then they stood together looking at the panorama of Jackson Hole and Jackson Lake stretching on into Yellowstone to the north of them. Owen scanned the horizon that twenty-five years earlier he had estimated as a circular field of vision embracing some 50,000 square miles. There were the mountains he had surveyed on foot; the primitive roads he had ridden on his bicycle as a boy. The two men didn't speak for a long time. "I never thought I'd get up here again," Owen finally said.

They silently signed the register and sat to rest awhile before starting the descent. It was hard for Petzoldt to believe that he had been there four times within a month. And now with Billy Owen.

It was almost the end of August when he returned to the valley. He would have to leave for home soon to get settled before school started. After Bill Lucas assured him he could have a job on the ranch the following summer, he hitchhiked back to Twin Falls.

AS SOON AS SCHOOL CLOSED FOR THE SUMMER, PETZOLDT RETURNED TO his job at the Lucas Ranch. He invited his friends Ralph Herron and Melvin Whitehead, one of his Snake River Canyon buddies from Twin Falls, to come that July and do some more climbing in the Tetons. He wanted to make another attempt on the East Ridge of the Grand, where he and Herron had been blockaded by a gendarme (the Molar Tooth) the year before. Petzoldt had observed the pinnacle on his other climbs and thought there might be a way around it or the possibility of making a north traverse.

By then he had learned the importance of good equipment. He made certain that each of them was outfitted with sturdy layered clothing, hobnail climbing boots, extra jackets, gloves and rope, and plenty of food.

The threesome was camped at Jenny Lake when they met Harold Criger, who had climbed in Alaska, and invited him to join them. They got an early start the next morning, hiked to Delta Lake, and were at the Molar Tooth in record time the following day. The sheer drop down the North Face to the glacier thousands of feet below was disconcerting, and they debated whether to try to scale the huge granite slab or take the traverse. Herron opted to climb the pinnacle and asked if he could be lead man. Petzoldt agreed and said he would belay him from below.

Herron started up cautiously, but being inexperienced at leading he got himself into an impasse midway up the cliff. He couldn't move up or down. The muscles in his legs began to shake as he clung to the rock. As there was no one belaying from above Petzoldt quickly gave the rope to Whitehead and scrambled up the pinnacle in an attempt to guide his friend's feet on the descent. But Herron slowly started slipping from his position. Petzoldt knew if Herron fell and he stayed where he was, unprotected by rope, they would both be swept off the cliff. Keeping his eyes on his friend, he carefully retreated, took the rope from Whitehead, and coiled it around a rock, bracing himself to hold the belay just as his companion fell.

Herron came down almost in slow motion, bumping over rocks as Petzoldt took in the rope, and finally bouncing over the edge of the precipice where he dangled unconscious. Petzoldt desperately tied the rope to another rock and the three other climbers gradually hauled their injured teammate back to the ledge.

Herron slowly regained consciousness. His body was cut and bruised, he had probably broken some ribs, and he was unable to use one leg, but there appeared to be no serious damage to his head or back. The others took turns carrying him piggyback over ledges and boulder fields, carefully belayed him down snowfields to the campsite at timberline, and had him under doctor's care by the next afternoon.

With Herron recuperating and the others gone, Petzoldt returned to Bill Lucas's ranch for his summer job pitching hay. He was working in the field one day when a couple of eastern dudes approached him and asked if he would show them the way up the Grand. Then they asked him what he would charge for the trip.

Without thinking, he said, "$100."

"Fine," said the dudes.

That was a whole season's wages for two days of "work!" As the summer progressed other tourists hired him to take them up the mountain.

Gibb Scott, the packer who had been on Petzoldt's first climb with Owen, started guiding, too. That August, he successfully led Theodore Teepe and W. D. Young to the top of the Grand. But on the descent, Teepe slipped on a massive snowfield and plummeted downhill into a pile of sharp boulders. His skull was crushed and he died instantly.

Late the night of August 4, Bill Lucas awakened Petzoldt and told him the sheriff had sent for him and was asking him to lead an expedition to evacuate the body. He gathered his climbing gear quickly and met the sheriff at Jenny Lake. Bill Scott and Jimmy Mangus volunteered to help with the rescue and the trio strapped on wooden "Trapper Nelson" packs and started their all-night hike.

A little past noon the party crossed a moraine into the snowfield where Gibb and Young waited with the body. The two men appeared to be exhausted and shaken by the episode as they pointed out the rutted track where Teepe had cartwheeled down the steep slope.

Petzoldt saw that Gibb had brought some sturdy tarps with him on his return from notifying the authorities. They planned to wrap the body and secure both ends with long rope so that a person could be on each end to carry the body or slide it over smooth terrain.

But then Petzoldt remembered a long snow chute that he and Herron had climbed on their first ascent. He convinced Gibb that it would be easier to steer and belay the body down the slide. So they tied a rope around Teepe's ankles and lowered him in relays as far as the rope would reach. Once down, they were able to carry him to Amphitheater Lake, where pack horses waited. Petzoldt later suggested they name the snowfield Teepe's Glacier to commemorate the tragedy.

That fall, Petzoldt returned to work at the Prine Cafe in Twin Falls. His former boss had moved to his hometown of Toledo, Ohio, and sold the hotel to "Pop" Weiner. "Pop" liked his young dishwasher and soon made him the night cook's helper.

The cook, a volatile ex-prizefighter with a reputation for chasing people with cleavers, was an avid fan of Gene Tunney and had once been his sparring partner. He befriended Petzoldt and when the Tunney–Jack Dempsey fight was announced, he told the boy to bet everything he had on Tunney. Petzoldt took his friend's advice and won $400. It was the most money he had ever had.

Gambling appeared to be a fast, easy way to earn money. He had watched card players in the Jackson saloons sweep up armloads of chips and turn them into cash. He tried the game for small stakes and was generally lucky, so one night he asked some poker players at the Prine if he could sit in on a game. He lost his entire week's salary.

"Pop" took him aside.

"Look, if you're determined to become a card player you'll be broke unless you know what you're doing," he said. "I'm going to teach you.

"If there's $2.00 in the pot and you think you have a 50–50 chance of bluffing, bluff. If the guy doesn't call you, you show him and let him see you're bluffing. You go along like that and get him set up. You have to act it out. When you really know you've got a cinch hand, then you throw in the chips like you do when you're bluffing and he thinks you're doing it again. Nothing to it."

When he wasn't in school or at the restaurant, Petzoldt rode the reefers to see his mother in New York or visit places like Pittsburgh, Omaha, Los Angeles, and Chicago. He became so adept at bumming rides that he graduated from freight cars to passenger and mail trains. He bought tickets to nearby towns, got off, and then sneaked up behind the engine and hopped into the steel blinds, a protected section behind the water tank. On long layovers, he took shelter in local libraries, where he avoided being picked up for vagrancy by the railroad "dicks."

In 1926, after a summer of guiding in the Tetons, he looked up his old Prine Hotel boss in Toledo, got a job in his new restaurant, and enrolled in Scott High School. He earned extra money caddying at the local golf course, taught himself how to play the game, and soon supplemented his income with a few well-placed bets.

He returned to Jackson every summer to operate his guiding concession. Teepe's accident and Herron's fall had had a sobering effect on him. He decided if he was going to take people into the mountains, he would operate by his own rules. He would not only do all of the outfitting, he would take charge of making decisions about time and weather factors as well as deciding when to rope up and perform other technical functions.

The difficulty in communication between climbers was another problem he tackled. Many European climbers got messages to one another by jerking on the rope one, two, or three times, with each jerk signifying a special movement. More often, climbers just yelled, but Petzoldt had already realized that using too many words often resulted in sentences being lost in the wind or muffled around corners.

Instead of yelling to a client that he was belaying up a cliff, "Okay, Jim, I've got a pretty good belay over here and think I can hold you all right," he devised the Teton system of voice signals based on the number of syllables in each message.

The belayer would call only, "On belay." Three syllables.

The climber would call, "Climbing." Two syllables. Then, as a failsafe signal, the belayer would say, "Climb."

Petzoldt constructed similar phrases for rappelling, handling rope, and other technical moves.

His unique approach of teaching his clients a few climbing skills rather than hauling them up the mountain in the European tradition, and his strict attention to safety paid off. When Grand Teton National Park was established in 1929, he was, at the age of twenty-one, awarded the mountain-climbing concession. Under the name of the American School of Mountaineering he operated out of a small wall tent pitched near Jenny Lake.

With a new road connecting Yellowstone and Teton National Parks, the tourists started to arrive. Many of them spent a couple of days at the Jenny Lake campground, where Petzoldt hooked up with local artists Archie Teater and Olaf Moller.

The two painters spent the days hiking with canvas and brushes in hand to reproduce the exquisite scenery. In the evening, they returned to the campground and leaned their finished works against the trees for the other campers to see.

By then, Petzoldt had struck up a conversation with strangers and invited them to look at the paintings. If a tourist wasn't interested in a landscape, he gave a convincing little spiel on the romance of walking on a glacier or standing on a mountaintop. With a guide! The trio made a modest living selling art and two-day treks up the Grand for $25.

The following season, Petzoldt and Teater were able to sleep under a roof. Pioneer photographer Harrison R. Crandall had sold his homestead to the park and moved two of the larger log buildings to Jenny Lake. He used one cabin for his studio and offered the other as a museum. While the Park Service was making plans for the museum, they allowed Phil Smith, a ranger who also worked as Petzoldt's climbing assistant, and Glenn Exum, a musician by night and park trail crew member by day, to bunk there with Petzoldt and Teater.

Petzoldt and Exum, who had Idaho roots in common, hit it off immediately. Petzoldt thought Exum played "a wicked sax," and Exum, who was four years younger than Petzoldt, admired his new friend's feats on the mountain. When Petzoldt invited him to climb the Teton with him that August, he accepted without hesitation.

It was Exum's first climbing experience. Pitifully unequipped, he put Petzoldt's size 13 cleated football shoes on his size 9½ feet and tied a couple of rolled army blankets around his back to use as a bed.

But once on the mountain, he maneuvered over the rock and snowfields like a veteran. It took very little coaching for him to learn how to seek out hand- and footholds and he was quick to master the art of belaying and rappelling down cliffs. Petzoldt started taking him along on other climbs with clients. He saw that Exum had a natural knack for putting people at ease. Before the summer ended, he hired him as a guide.

More and more tourists sought adventure in mountaineering, and Petzoldt became an expert at making the experience enjoyable. He viewed his role not only as a mountain-climbing teacher and leader but as an entertainer and psychologist as well.

The big man with the ragged, tumbleweed eyebrows often held court in camp. His clients forgot their fatigue and aching legs as he regaled them with stories of his adventures. He would punctuate the tales with coyote howls and yodels that echoed from one isolated peak to another.

He enjoyed poking fun at himself, as well as Wyoming cowboys who scorned mountaineering because they "ain't lost nothing up there," and "those Harvard types who think they know it all." His voice boomed, whispered, and paused for effect as he recounted episodes of adventure and humor, and his bellow of a laugh came from deep within.

Sometimes he played a trick on clients who reached the summit of the Grand.

"Boy, I'd give ten bucks for a beer about now," he would say.

"Me, too," the client agreed.

Then Petzoldt would stroll over to a secret cache he had hidden in the rocks and pull out a lager.

All kinds of people signed up for a climb. Most of them came for sport and adventure, some to prove themselves, a few to overcome fear or inferiority complexes. Petzoldt became adept at reading character and handling psychological problems.

One time, a hysterical client clung to him in terror as they stood on the East Ridge of the Grand Teton. The man pleaded with him to get him off that mountain. But it was getting dark, and Petzoldt knew it would be life-threatening to attempt retreating, especially with a person in panic. The only safe move was to climb to the top and descend on the regular Owen route.

Petzoldt patiently explained the situation. At last, the man calmed down a bit and released his grip.

"I had to get tough then," Petzoldt said later. "I told him that no matter how he felt about it I was not going to get myself killed. So we inched along the ridge, made the top at last, and spent the night in sleeping bags that I had cached there for the purpose."

As the official park concessionaire, Petzoldt was able to charge regular fees for his services. He started to save part of his profits for a college fund. But one night, he weakened and tossed his savings into a poker pot. Luckily, he remembered "Pop" Weiner's bluffing techniques. He built his winnings to $2,000 then folded his cards. The windfall enabled him to enter the University of Idaho that fall of 1930.

Petzoldt was twenty-two years old. Despite the onset of the Great Depression he had managed to complete high school in Toledo and had spent succeeding years learning tougher lessons by scrambling for existence in cities and hobo jungles. It had been a balancing act between finding honest work and gambling for money to get an education and sharing "billy-can" meals around bonfires with freight-hopping drifters to satisfy his wanderlust.

College brought him into the mainstream. He was popular with former classmates from Twin Falls High School and his reputation as a mountain climber added a special luster to his image. He joined the Kappa Sigma fraternity, was named to both the debate and swim teams, and was even voted president of the freshman class. But his heart was in the Tetons. He much preferred learning his lessons through experience rather than memorizing and spewing out facts in the classroom.

By the summer of 1931, the rugged mountain climber and Exum, the tall musician with the chiseled features of a movie star, were back in Jackson Hole. They were in demand by the girls, especially as escorts for the daughters of wealthy easterners.

One Saturday night Exum asked Dorothy Redman, a popular local girl, for a date with the intention of going to the Jenny Lake Dance Hall, where he was playing in the band. As Dorothy had an out-of-town guest, they asked Petzoldt to join them. It was agreed that he would alternate dancing with the two young ladies until Exum was able to take a break from the bandstand.

The old log building thundered with heel-stomping cowboys when Exum sat out from the band around midnight. By that time, just about everybody had made a few trips outdoors where Ben Goe was dispensing moonshine whisky from his Buick parked in the shadows.

John Emery, a burly rodeoer and wrangler from the Bar-B-C, was pretty well "liquored up" when he stomped onto the dance floor, roughly pushed Exum aside, and demanded to cut in on the dance. Exum politely refused. Emery let out an oath and gave him a shove then grabbed for Redman. Exum lunged, seized the cowboy by the shoulder, and punched him on the jaw.

Emery reeled and started to pounce again. A couple of men jumped in to hold back the two fighters and yelled for Redman to run. But Emery was riled and strong. He wrenched loose and chased the terrified girl through the dance hall. He caught her as she fled towards the midnight buffet counter and punched her between the eyes.

Petzoldt had been outside with his date during the fracas. He ran back in the hall to see what had happened and saw Redman crying. When Exum told him Emery had hit her, he went for the cowboy, and with a single blow, sent him caromming across the porch and down the steps. Emery got back to his feet and Petzoldt knocked him down a second time. He struggled back up, but as Petzoldt lunged for him again, he saw the glint of a knife in Emery's hand. Luckily, some cowhands from the Bar-B-C grabbed their friend, threw him into their pickup, and beat a fast retreat.

The next morning Petzoldt was in the Jenny Lake general store when Gabbey, the owner, approached him.

"Petzoldt, you're in trouble," he said. "John Emery is saying there ain't enough room for you and him in the same country. Unless you get out of Jackson Hole, he's going to kill you on sight."

Petzoldt knew about Emery's temper. Everybody in the Hole was afraid of him, including the sheriff. There was a story that a fellow had pulled a pistol on him in an argument over a poker game. He knocked the guy down, grabbed the pistol, stuck it in the attacker's mouth, and pulled the trigger. When the gun misfired, Emery got so mad he bit off part of the man's ear.

"You'd better protect yourself," Gabbey said. "I'll loan you my revolver."

"I'm not going to be dodging around trees at night and I'm not going to leave the country," Petzoldt said, accepting the gun.

That Saturday night, with the gun in his coat pocket, he went into Jackson with Exum. They found Emery shooting dice in one of the saloons. Petzoldt sauntered up to the table.

"John, I hear this country isn't big enough for us and if I don't get out of here you're going to kill me," he said.

Then, with all of the gamblers watching, he said, "Tell me right now you're going to kill me and make a move because I've got my hand on a pistol and I'm going to blow out your guts!"

Emery straightened up slowly and stared at Petzoldt. Then he grinned.

"You goddam mountain-climbing son of a bitch, let's go have a drink," he said and held out his hand.

Petzoldt hesitated, wary of a trick. Then he released his grip on the gun and headed for the bar.

Later that season, Emery's crush on Redman reached a violent climax. She was dating Fernie Hubbard, another cowboy. One night Hubbard was shaving in his cabin when Emery suddenly burst through the door and shot him twice in the back. Hubbard almost died. Emery ended up in jail. But in the middle of the night, he kicked out the roof of his cell, escaped, and disappeared. Hubbard recovered, and got the girl.

In mid-July 1931, Petzoldt offered Exum an opportunity for an adventure of his own. The guiding business had grown and dude ranchers were recommending the American School of Mountaineering to their guests. The Park Service was even telling tourists about Petzoldt's services in its campfire programs.

He felt the need to develop new climbing routes in order to offer clients a variety of experiences. He had climbed the Middle and South Tetons, Mount Teewinot, and Mount Owen, but the only alternative to the Owen Route on the Grand Teton was the East Ridge Route that had not been climbed since Bob Underhill and Kenneth Henderson summited in 1929.

Petzoldt was curious about a ledge on the south side that he thought might be climbable. He had trained himself to observe the mountains closely and imagine ways to surmount perceived obstacles. He would climb the Middle Teton or Mount Owen and study neighboring peaks with field glasses. Soon he was able to judge actual heights of pillars and cliffs from great distances and, by looking at them under varying light conditions, to identify cracks and shelves not easily seen.

One day he and Exum were leading the Fred Wittenbergers, who had just returned from climbing in Austria, on the Owen Route. Petzoldt decided to send Exum to explore a ledge he had spotted on the south wall of the Grand. It appeared to him that the wide shelf narrowed and might lead to a place where he could get around the corner and proceed to the top.

Exum was eager to give it a try. He left Petzoldt's party, crossed a gap, and started up the ledge. The route appeared to be as Petzoldt had imagined until Exum reached a sheer wall that towered above him and was over one hundred feet tall. It was a dead end. There was no way around the cliff. The shelf ended abruptly and dropped about fifteen hundred feet into the Middle Teton Glacier. A huge boulder sat on the other side of the gap at the base of the southwest ridge. Nothing but air lay between. Exum yelled for Petzoldt to let him know he was blocked. But his voice was lost in the whistling wind. He didn't know what to do. He tried to call again with no success. Pacing the ledge, he mulled over his predicament. He could retreat to the valley, try to catch up with Petzoldt on the Owen Route, or jump across the gaping hole. None of the alternatives was appealing.

He started back down the ledge to where he could see Petzoldt and shouted again. This time Petzoldt tried to tell him to come back and join him on the Owen Route, but the wind-whipped words sounded like he said, "Any old woman can climb that!" Exum was furious. He was damned if he would attempt to join Petzoldt's party after that so he worked his way back to the crevasse.

Studying the rock carefully, he was able to locate a series of hand- and footholds on the rock face that could possibly get him close enough to the gap to leap across. Mustering all of his courage, he inched along the wall, took a deep breath, and threw himself over the eight-foot opening. Once safe, he clung to the granite boulder and shuddered at what he had just done. After a short rest he felt reassured. He made his way along the ridge and through a system of cracks and buttresses and was at the summit a few minutes before Petzoldt's party arrived.

"Exum, do you know what you have done?" Petzoldt said, giving his friend a bear hug. "You've made the new Exum Route on the Grand Teton." Exum grinned.

It was a great day on the Teton. Not only the Exum Ridge was discovered, but Bob Underhill, Phil Smith, and Frank Truslow pioneered another route, now known as the Underhill Ridge, over the easternmost of three prominent south ridges. Counting Petzoldt and his clients, three groups stood together on the summit and celebrated their accomplishment.

Curious to try it himself, Petzoldt retraced Exum's route alone and, after reaching the summit, quickly descended by the normal route, catching Exum and their two clients near timberline. Thus the Exum Ridge, destined to become the most popular rock-climbing route in the park, was climbed twice on the same day, and both were solo ascents.

Prentice Gray, president of the J. Henry Shroeder Banking Corporation in New York, caught the excitement and was one of the first to ask Petzoldt to guide him up the Exum Ridge.

The banker and his estranged wife, who both owned ranches in Jackson, had befriended Petzoldt and Exum. The two young men were often their dinner guests and Petzoldt had started to date their daughter, Barbara, a rather impish-looking brunette who was lively, agile, and intelligent. Petzoldt taught Barbara to climb, and she became the first woman to summit Nez Perce peak.

Prentice Gray had never climbed a mountain but was an able sportsman. Late that summer he hired Petzoldt and Exum to guide him up the Exum Ridge. It was on that trip that Exum named the ledge where he had leaped across the gap Wall Street in Gray's honor.

Petzoldt found Barbara Gray different from most of the city girls he dated. She wasn't snobbish and was a fun-loving companion as well as an interesting conversationalist. The young couple spent an idyllic summer. If Petzoldt was not busy with clients, they would trek in the mountains or sit by the fireplace and solve all of the world's problems. In the evenings, they were popular guests in the Jackson social scene. By the end of the season, they were in love.

That fall Barbara told her father that she was getting serious about the handsome mountain climber. Gray liked the young man who had introduced him to mountaineering and approved of the relationship. He invited Petzoldt to join them in New York for the holidays and sent him a railroad ticket.

Despite the comforts of sleeping in a train berth rather than hunkering down in the reefers, living in a plush Manhattan apartment, riding in a Pierce-Arrow car, and celebrating New Year's Eve at the Roosevelt Hotel, where Duke Ellington played, Petzoldt became leery of the millionaire's overtures about sending him to law school. He envisioned himself as the kept husband of a rich girl whose father was going to tell him what to do. Barbara Gray must have sensed his cooling ardor. The following summer her father sent her to Europe, and the relationship gradually dissolved.

That season of 1931, Petzoldt's guiding business was so successful that he hired Exum as his assistant and changed the name of his concession to the Petzoldt-Exum Climbing School. Still anxious to complete his education, he was able to save enough money to transfer that fall to the University of Wyoming in Laramie.

The university was a small institution with approximately fifteen hundred students, most of whom came from farms and ranches around the state. A few old brick buildings clustered above town on a broad, rolling lawn that was studded with clumps of giant evergreens.

One chilly November evening Petzoldt was tramping across the snowy campus when he decided to stop for a cup of coffee at the Campus Shop. He slammed the door against the sub-zero temperature outside and stomped the snow off his boots as he entered the warm room.

The place was almost deserted. A bored-looking clerk stood behind the counter and a young girl rubbed her hands before a gas stove that sputtered in the corner.

The girl looked about eighteen. She was tall and slender, with curly brown hair and fair skin that was slightly sunburned.

Petzoldt threw his jacket on a chair and went over to the stove. They warmed themselves silently for awhile then he smiled and asked her name. "Bernice McGarrity," she said. "Would you like a bowl of soup?" he asked.

In her book, *On Top of the World*, Bernice* described the rest of their first meeting:

> I would have loved a bowl of soup with lots of crackers in it, because I liked to eat. But suddenly, I cared a great deal about how I looked, and I quickly decided I would look better drinking a lemon coke. So I said that I didn't care for soup but that I would enjoy a lemon coke.
>
> While he broke his crackers in his soup, we discussed many things.
>
> He said his name was Paul Petzoldt and that he climbed mountains in the summertime to make a living. He didn't have the smart nonchalance and easy chatter that college boys of that time affected.
>
> He didn't talk about the fellows at the house or try to entertain me with witticisms. He talked seriously of different things, but mostly of mountain climbing.
>
> In spite of my dazed and smitten condition, I gradually grew more interested in what he was saying.
>
> I said, "You mentioned climbing mountains to make a living. How does one make a living climbing mountains?"

---

*Bernice Patricia was her given name. I assume that she considered the alliteration of Patricia Petzoldt to look better in print as a byline. She answered to both names.

He laughed. "People pay me to take them to the tops of mountains."

"But don't they know the way? It seems to me they could stand at the bottom and decide which way to go up."

Petzoldt described the thick timber and sheer granite walls of the Tetons. He told her about the thousands of feet of exposure beneath perpendicular cliffs, about finding hand- and footholds, and tying into rope.

Finally he said, "Have you ever watched an eagle soar high into the clouds and envied him as he sailed away? Or have you dreamed of flying?

"Do you remember that breathless feeling of wanting to go up and up?"

I sighed. "Yes, of course. When I was young I tried to fly. I jumped from a barn loft with an umbrella tied to my wrist, hoping somehow I'd take off—but I fell and broke my leg instead."

Petzoldt laughed. He liked this girl with the inquiring mind and sense of humor. They talked until closing time and then he walked her back to the dormitory and asked to see her again.

The next few weeks were full of Bernice McGarrity. Moonlight walks. Studying at the library followed by chili in the Campus Shop. A fraternity formal.

They had long conversations about the Depression at home and uneasy conditions abroad. A gifted mimic, she entertained him with hilarious imitations of campus big shots.

But as Christmas approached, Petzoldt grew silent. The little town of Laramie was struggling economically, and his savings were almost gone. It was hard for him to find any kind of work to supplement his income. Just before the holiday break, he told her he was moving to Salt Lake City. Hopefully, he could get a job there and finish the year at the University of Utah. He promised to keep in touch, but she was sure that she would never see him again.

Petzoldt's stay in Utah was brief. His few months there were highlighted by winning a golf championship. He also picked up extra cash by gambling on local courses, but the impact of the Depression made it hard to find work and he resumed his nomadic existence.

Despite his breakup with Barbara Gray, his friendship with her father continued. Late in the summer of 1933, Gray told Petzoldt he was entertaining a very important guest from England who liked to hike every day. He hired Petzoldt to guide his friend and gave him the use of his Model A Ford for showing the Englishman around the Jackson Hole area.

On the appointed day, Petzoldt arrived at Gray's ranch to meet his new client. It was Sir Albert Victor Baillie, Dean of St. George's Chapel at Windsor Castle.

Petzoldt immediately took a liking to the private chaplain of the king and queen of England. He was a portly, fairly tall man around sixty years old, well-coordinated but in need of a walking stick. And he enjoyed lively political discussions as much as Petzoldt.

The Dean was amused at some of Petzoldt's naive ideas but surprised that the young Wyoming cowboy and guide could converse so knowledgeably about world affairs. The hours Petzoldt had spent in libraries when he was on the road as well as listening to the rabble-rousers in Long Beach's city park had served him well.

The pair walked for hours through the glens of pinyon and aspen, decrying the hunger, unemployment, runs on banks, and depletion of national income triggered by the Great Depression. They argued about the ability of America's new president, Franklin Delano Roosevelt, to restore the nation's economy and debated the probability of European leaders maintaining world peace in the face of exploding Fascism and Nazism. Once the Dean became so agitated while emphasizing a point that he broke his favorite cane over a log.

After a day's stroll, the Dean enjoyed sipping a bit of whisky. With Ben Goe's still at Cache Creek, Jackson never really experienced prohibition, so Petzoldt always had a Mason jar full of moonshine for the reverend's cocktail hour. Sometimes he joined the Dean for a drink in the evening and asked him about life in England and at Windsor.

On the morning Baillie's ten-day visit ended, Petzoldt went to Gray's ranch to bid his friend farewell. He brought along a parting gift of two quarts of Ben Goe's best, wrapped in a brown bag. The clergyman chuckled and put the package in his suitcase.

A few weeks later Petzoldt received a letter from England.

"How would you like to be my guest to study for a year at Windsor Castle?" the Dean wrote.

Petzoldt couldn't believe what he was reading.

"If you need help to pay for passage let me know," the note continued. "You can come in the fall when climbing season ends."

His acceptance was in the next mail.

CHAPTER 3

Windsor and Beyond

AFTER THE DEAN'S GENEROUS OFFER TO HOST HIM AT WINDSOR, Petzoldt was too proud to admit that he couldn't afford the passage to England and back home. Sure, he had saved $1,500, but that would barely serve for spending money and incidental expenses on a year-long trip.

And what about clothes? What did you wear at a castle? He had no idea. So he decided just to be himself and take his good suit, a warm overcoat, the trousers and shirts he wore at the university, and, of course, his Stetson hat and cowboy boots.

As for hobnobbing with royalty and the British uppercrust, he couldn't even think about that. He had gotten along with the Dean very well. He would just have to hope his manners were up to the expectations of others.

With Glenn Exum teaching in Idaho during the winter, Petzoldt arranged for Phil Smith to take over the guiding service while he was away. He left Jackson in October 1933 and thumbed a ride on a truck as far as Rock Springs, Wyoming. After shipping his luggage to the American Express office in New York, he filled up on chili and coffee at an all-night cafe and waited until it was time to hop a late freight train to Chicago. From there, he was lucky to catch a fast mail carrier that sped him the rest of the way to the East Coast.

As he lay in his hiding place listening to the *rick-a-tick-a, rick-a-tick-a, rick-a-tick-a* of the wheels he grew more excited about his trip. And more worried about how he was going to get across the Atlantic Ocean. Stowing away on a ship wasn't as easy as bumming rides on the railroad. There would not be enough time to earn his fare in New York before setting sail. He decided his only alternative was to try to work his passage overseas on a freight ship.

When he reached Manhattan he collected his luggage, checked into a cheap hotel, and started to make plans. The first priority was to clean up and get a decent meal. Then he would take a cab to the port and see if he could talk with someone at the office of United States Lines. Not just someone. The president of the company.

Petzoldt arrived at the steamship office around noon. Feigning a confidence he didn't feel, he asked the receptionist if he could talk to the president about working his way over to England. The woman must have sympathized with the nervous-looking young man in the cowboy boots who had obviously come a long way. She told him the president was busy but the vice president might give him a few minutes. She directed him to another waiting room, where he registered with the secretary.

He had a short wait before the woman called his name and escorted him to the door of an impressive-looking office. A slender man who appeared to be in his mid-forties got up from behind his desk.

"So you're from Wyoming," the vice president said as he offered his hand and gestured to a chair. "How's the hunting this year?"

It turned out that the vice president was Kermit Roosevelt, the son of President Theodore Roosevelt, who had accompanied his father on safari to Africa and on many hunting and fishing trips in the West. He launched into an animated discussion of his favorite fishing holes in Jackson, the types of flies he used, and his experiences on the annual elk hunt. Finally, he asked Petzoldt how he could help.

"I would like to work my way to England on one of your freighters."

Roosevelt paused and slowly shook his head. "I'm afraid there are too many labor union restrictions to make that possible."

"I understand," Petzoldt said. He started to get up to leave.

The shipping magnate rocked back in his chair. "What takes you to England?"

Petzoldt explained his friendship with the Dean of Windsor, the phenomenal invitation, and how he had tried to save enough money to finance the trip.

"That's a pretty special opportunity."

Roosevelt opened a desk drawer and took out a shipping schedule. He ran a finger down the list and stopped in the middle of a page.

"Hmm," he said. "Maybe we can work something out, after all. The *American Farmer* leaves for England at three tomorrow afternoon. Do you have a passport? Could you make it?"

"Yes. I sure could!"

"I'll notify the captain. You'll be our guest. Good luck to you in England."

Petzoldt thanked Roosevelt profusely and fairly ran to the hotel to get ready.

He boarded the ship the next morning. As he stood on deck watching the mainland disappear into a world of water, he thought how far he was from the tepee at Jenny Lake. The distance could be measured in more than just miles. It was evident in his first-class cabin accommodations. The invitation to dine at the captain's table. Opportunities for conversations with people who had traveled the world. The voyage was a real eye-opener for a young man who the week before had been bumming rides on the railroad, and best of all at its end lay the prospect of Windsor and seeing his good friend Dean Baillie again.

But when they docked at Southampton and he sighted Baillie waiting on the shore, he scarcely recognized the clergyman. He appeared formal and severe in his black clerical garb and had little resemblance to the tweedy hiker at Jackson Hole. For a minute Petzoldt regretted coming and wondered what he would do with this seeming stranger in such a foreboding place.

His fears vanished as the Dean rushed up to him with a warm smile and hearty handshake. "Delighted to have you here!" he effused. "Let's get out of this dreary place."

The chauffeur put Petzoldt's suitcase in the car trunk, and they headed for Windsor. As they drove, the Dean pointed out landmarks while Petzoldt related his unusual travel arrangements and amazing luck in meeting Kermit Roosevelt. It was a fairly long drive before they finally reached the River Thames, passed Eton School, and wound up a narrow road from Windsor village to the massive stone castle on the hilltop. The royal guards waved them through the King George IV Gate; they wound past the famous round tower and proceeded to the deanery in the lower ward.

The Dean asked his "man," Dawson, to take Petzoldt's luggage to his room while he showed his guest the premises. He told Petzoldt he would have free access to any part of the deanery, including the huge library. Then sensing that the young man was travel weary, he left him alone in his room.

Petzoldt found himself in a large chamber with dark, massive furniture, huge ceiling beams that dated back to the fifteenth century, and a window overlooking a courtyard. Later, when Petzoldt would see American tourists wandering by, he was often tempted to surprise them by shouting, "Hi, everybody, I'm Paul Petzoldt from Jackson Hole, Wyoming."

His suitcase was nowhere in sight. Chagrined, he realized that Dawson had unpacked for him. He had hung and folded the clean garments and taken away a mountain of filthy socks and underwear that had collected during the long voyage. In his embarrassment he debated how he could gain control of his own laundry without offending.

Over the next few days Baillie gave him a tour of the castle and grounds. "Kings and queens have razed, renovated, and added wings to this castle ever since William the Conqueror first built it as a summer retreat," he said.

He showed Petzoldt the hundred steps that led from the deanery to the bank of the Thames and pointed out the lodging for the military knights and the royal apartments where the king and queen lived when in residence.

In St. George's Chapel he explained the heraldic display of swords and banners of the Knights of the Garter hanging behind the dark oak stalls.

They visited the tombs of Henry VIII and Jane Seymour, peeked into the Albert Memorial Chapel next door, and viewed the mausoleum in the garden, where Queen Victoria and Prince Albert were buried.

"When I was a very young curate, I once preached a sermon in Queen Victoria's presence," he said. "She was getting rather crusty in her old age and complained about 'terribly long services,' so I asked Sir Henry Ponsonby for advice on what I should say.

"'It doesn't matter much *what* you say,'" Ponsonby told me, 'because Her Majesty is too deaf to hear, and will probably go to sleep. But on no account let it last for more than five minutes.'"

One night during their customary late evening chat over cigars and Scotch whisky, Baillie asked Petzoldt if he would be interested in going to school. Having graduated from Cambridge himself, he thought there might be a chance he could arrange for his friend to be accepted there. It was a tempting prospect, but Petzoldt was not enthusiastic about structured classes.

"I've been reading John Dewey," he said. "He says education should begin with experience; it should come through activity rather than formal learning."

He told the Dean he wanted to do his own research in the fabulous Windsor library, continue their conversations, and get out around the country to see for himself what was happening in the world.

Baillie smiled and told him there were no strings. He was free to do as he wished. "You don't even have to go to prayers unless you want to," he added with a chuckle.

Petzoldt spent hours in the library reading everything he could find on economics and politics and then had long discussions with the Dean about current world affairs. Britain was in a slump. Mussolini and Hitler were flexing their muscles. The United States was still trying to recover from the Depression. Answers to his questions were elusive.

But as Christmas neared, Petzoldt's thoughts turned to that bright, funny girl he had met in the Campus Shop at the University of Wyoming a year before. He had not had any contact with Bernice McGarrity since leaving Laramie. He wondered if she would remember him. He wasn't strong on writing letters, but her address was still in his wallet. Maybe she would write him back, he thought as he picked up a pen.

Baillie was well aware that a young man needed more than mental stimulation so, when he noticed Petzoldt checking out the royal golf course, he arranged for him to play with some of the king's knights.

Petzoldt proved himself such an able partner that the knights invited him to the prestigious Stoke Poges course, which is near the graveyard memorialized in Thomas Gray's "Elegy."

Dean Baillie frequently invited Petzoldt for dinner at London's Garrick Club, or they planned an evening at the theater. One time after seeing Fred Astaire and Clare Luce in *The Gay Divorcée* they dined with the stars following the performance.

The Dean entertained at home as well. Petzoldt met authors, actors, educators from Oxford and Cambridge, and even royalty. Prince Rupert of Bavaria proffered an open invitation for him to visit in Germany, and Edward, Prince of Wales, was a dinner guest on three different occasions. Petzoldt talked to him about mountain climbing and heard about his visits to cattle ranches in the western United States. But he was careful to follow the Dean's coaching about protocol. It was all right to say, "Okay" and "You bet," but no profanity, and never open up a new subject during a conversation with royalty.

After Petzoldt bought a secondhand three-speed bicycle, the Dean arranged for him to spend several weekends on nearby estates. Once he rode way up north to visit the Dean of York.

But sights along the highways troubled him. Whole families limped over the roads pushing baby carriages and carrying bundles containing all of their worldly possessions. The contrast between the privileged life of the British upper class and the depressing sight of the poor was disturbing. He remembered the sadness in his own mother's face when she lost the farm and had to leave her family. He started to resent the snobbery towards the impoverished "low class" that he witnessed among the monied people.

One evening he talked to the Dean about his concerns.

"Today I played golf on a public course with a fine young man who was an excellent golfer," he said. "The guy was personable, well-mannered, and had one of the most beautiful golf swings I have ever seen.

"When we finished, I told him we needed a fourth to play Stoke Poges tomorrow. I asked if he would join our foursome. Well! He got the strangest look on his face. I was afraid I had offended him.

"'Oh no,' he explained to me. 'That's not possible. Those people are *gentlemen*!'"

Baillie took a long pull on his cigar before responding.

"I know what you mean," he said. "I'm Scottish. The upper crust English are very snooty about my people, as well. They don't think we're in the same class as they."

Then he chuckled. "But we get back at them. We tell them about the Englishman and Scot who were arguing about the relative merits of eating oatmeal.

"'In England we feed oats to our horses,' the pompous Brit said.

"'That's why you have such great horses and we have such great men,' the Scotsman replied."

After a hearty laugh and sip of port, he continued.

"And the Englishmen are always complaining that the Scottish have a reputation for thrift. Well, they don't compare with some of the wealthy English who count every penny.

"I knew a rich widow who sent her man and a chauffeur down to the local butchery to get a tuppence of liver for her cat. When they arrived at the store, the butcher said the lady had called to tell them not to buy the liver. Her cat had just caught a bird."

Despite Baillie's attempts to lighten the subject, Petzoldt could not get it off his mind. A few days later he asked if it would be all right for him to go to London for two or three weeks.

"Your friends have been very kind to me, and I have seen how British society lives, but I want to learn about the average Englishman and how he thinks. I want to see who are the people living on the dole and what it's like," he said.

"The dole is only twenty bob a week," the Dean said. "Five American dollars."

But he could see that the boy was serious. "Be careful," he said.

Petzoldt bicycled the twenty-one miles to London on a beautiful May morning. The Dean had given him directions to a slum area where he could find lodging. He located a narrow, two-story flophouse wedged between some high gray tenement buildings. Over a dozen indigents crowded into three small upstairs rooms, each crammed with eight simple cots. Nights were almost unbearable with the cacophony of snoring and fetid air aggravated by unopened windows.

Downstairs was a large sitting room with a coal-burning fireplace, where the tenants boiled water in little kettles to brew tea and cook sparse meals. Fish and chips purchased from a corner stall for fifteen cents was the staple diet. Sometimes Petzoldt bought bread and cheese or treated himself to a pastry.

During the daytime, he strolled through the city, often stopping to chat with storekeepers, cabbies, and bobbies. He lingered in the parks listening to soapbox orators as he had done in Long Beach, and in the evenings he struck up conversations with fellow tenants as they brewed tea. World problems were not the topics here. They talked about finding jobs and getting enough to eat. Petzoldt was amazed that they evinced so little understanding of England's economic woes. They showed no resentment and seemed to feel "the gentry" would set things right in time.

After two weeks in London Petzoldt wrote Baillie, who had suggested they drive to Scotland to visit his brother, and said he would like to bicycle up the east coast of England and meet him there instead of returning to Windsor. He peddled out of London and made his way along the rural roads through a series of villages before crossing the border and continuing on to Melrose.

Colonel Baillie was an exuberant country gentleman in his mid-sixties. He owned an estate in the Scottish lowlands, where fox hunting was a popular sport. When Petzoldt arrived before the Dean, the colonel outdid himself to make the boy feel welcome. He told wonderful stories about his frequent foreign travels and further delighted Petzoldt with his frank and uncustomary questioning of sacrosanct British tradition.

When Baillie arrived, the threesome set out for Edinburgh and drove on to Lochness to spend a few days at the Baillie homestead. From there they traveled to the west coast, where they stayed in the family's dank, unheated hunting lodge and Petzoldt learned the practical applications of warming up with Scotch whisky. He was amused when the Dean told the gruff, red-whiskered caretaker that the cowboys in the wild west where Petzoldt came from were just as tough as Scotsmen.

Once they returned to Melrose, Petzoldt hopped on his bike again. He took the long way back to Windsor and played a round at St. Andrews, where American Lawson Little won individual and paired matches in the Walker Cup that season. From there he rode to

Glasgow, Manchester, and Stratford-on-Avon, returning to the castle just in time to accompany the Dean to the Ascot races.

It was now midsummer of 1934, and Petzoldt had been in England for nine months. His friendship with the Dean had developed into true devotion, almost a father-son relationship. But he had never been able to settle in one place for long. The disruptions of routine that had been unavoidable in his younger years had now become a way of life. A natural bent for wanderlust did little to encourage him to sink roots. It was time to move on.

One evening as they were chatting in the study, Petzoldt told the Dean he wanted to make a bicycle tour through Belgium, Holland, Germany, and Switzerland before returning to America. As chancellor, Hitler was making overt moves to establish an absolute dictatorship in Germany under the tyrannical Nazi party, and Petzoldt hoped to get a firsthand look at how this was affecting western Europe. He thought he might do a little climbing in the Alps, as well.

Petzoldt probably did not mention it, but there was another reason he was bringing his grand tour to a close. Bernice McGarrity had not only answered his letter, but they had begun to correspond regularly. Their letters were long and frank, emulating the serious discussions mixed with humor that they had had in Wyoming. By late spring he had asked her to marry him. She answered immediately. Yes. But only after they had seen each other again to be sure of their feelings.

Baillie was visibly saddened by Petzoldt's announcement. With his wife deceased, one son in Africa and the other working on Fleet Street in London, he had spent many lonely hours over the past few years. Petzoldt was like family. But the young man's sense of adventure was stimulating, and he didn't want to stifle it. A few days later they said goodbye, sensing they would never see one another again.

Petzoldt cycled to London and then continued seventy-two miles to the chalk upland knifing between the sheer white cliffs of the Strait of Dover. He caught the overnight ferry to Ostend, Belgium, where he spent a few days strolling among the waterfront restaurants and seafood stalls, admiring and smelling the heaps of oysters, lobsters, and ocean fish that he couldn't afford to eat.

From Ostend he rode towards Brussels, stopping at Bruges, "the Venice of the North," where scores of bridges spanned numerous canals and motorboats dodged quiet flocks of swans. He stopped at Ghent to climb the 375-foot belfry and spent hours in Brussels's Grand Place, where the famous peeing boy statue stood in the midst of museums, art galleries, shops, and the ornate Hotel de Ville.

On the way to the German border, he went to Liège to see the battlegrounds of the Meuse-Argonne offensive where his brother Louie had almost lost his life.

He camped most of the time with a sleeping bag, a lightweight Egyptian cotton tent, and a "billy can" to cook in, hobo-style. When he reached Germany, pumpernickel bread, blood sausage, and cheese were so inexpensive that he seldom had to cook. And sometimes the farmers he stopped to talk with would invite him home for a glass of milk or a meal when they learned his name was Petzoldt.

He spent over an hour inside the magnificent gothic cathedral in Cologne, where there were fourteenth-century stained-glass windows, paintings, and a solid gold shrine said to contain relics of the Magi.

Upon leaving the church, he found himself in a game of dodge 'em with the deacon. The clergyman stood in front of him swinging a censer on the end of a chain. Every time Petzoldt would attempt to step around him the man would move back to block his path. His motive became obvious. There was a collection box for donations standing in the aisle. Petzoldt didn't have any coins to drop, so he suddenly dodged away, bolted past the cleric, and ran out the door.

As he made his way south down the Rhine River valley, he found that the nation was beginning to recover from the Depression and employment rates had risen. Hitler took credit for Germany's upturn. People smiled and exchanged the stiff-armed "Heil Hitler" salute. Pictures of "Der Führer" glared from every shop window. Often soldiers or youth patrols marched in city streets going through maneuvers while onlookers cheered.

He bicycled into France and followed the Rhône River valley, often hanging onto the backs of large trucks and letting them pull him up steep grades. Entering Switzerland, he peddled to Visp and Tasch, then shifted into low gear to peddle, or sometimes push, his bike over the mountainous hiking path that led to Zermatt.

The Swiss village was as quaint as the photographs in Lily's books. Colorful hand-decorated chalets bordered spotless streets and climbed up chartreuse hillsides, where the clanging bells of ranging cattle could be heard. Glacial streams cut through fields of wildflowers and the sharp, clear air was luminous and bright. Monte Rosa, Dent Blanche, and the Weisshorn towered nearby, and the magnificent 14,780-foot Matterhorn speared the sky like a massive granite shark fin.

Petzoldt found Bernard Bernard, a well-known climber and guide who owned a mountaineering shop, and asked if he could leave his bicycle with him. He wanted to climb the Matterhorn. Bernard, delighted to accommodate a fellow mountaineer, said he had heard of the "famous" American School of Mountaineering in the Tetons from mutual clients who had praised Petzoldt's skill.

Petzoldt strapped on his pack and started hiking toward the Hornli Ridge, which was wedged between two immense snowfields part way up the mountain. He traveled quickly and made camp on the Matterhorn Glacier above timberline by late afternoon.

As he was enjoying the sunset and preparing to settle down for the night, two French climbers appeared at his tent. They had seen him from the warming hut above, where they were taking shelter with their climbing party.

Didn't he realize that nobody camped in the Alps, they asked. That's why huts were scattered all over the mountain. And didn't he have a Swiss guide? Mountain climbing was a very dangerous sport!

In pidgin French, Petzoldt thanked them for their concern and tried to explain that he knew what he was doing. They shook their heads and left the crazy American to his folly.

A few hours before dawn, he was awakened by the sound of voices. He peeked out of his tent and saw a long string of trekkers carrying climbing ropes and flickering lanterns. The party tromped past him, casting derisive looks at the flimsy camp. Petzoldt had no intention of hiking in the dark like the Europeans. He slid further down into his bag and went back to sleep.

When the sun came up, he bundled his tent and sleeping bag and stashed them on the glacier. He traveled quickly and soon passed most of the group he had seen before dawn.

The legendary Swiss guiding technique that he expected to be of such high standard was nothing like what he had imagined. The clients were ill-equipped and too old or overweight to make such a strenuous hike. It was push and shove all the way. Furthermore, the guides showed lack of judgment in taking unnecessary chances and made no attempts to give instruction. It appeared to him that the primary concern was to haul people up and down the peak as fast as possible then hurry to the railroad station to sign up the next arrivals.

Later in the day, the skies became cloudy and the air grew chill. Light snow began to fall. Petzoldt saw that a climbing party ahead of him was having trouble. Conditions on the mountain had turned poor due to iced rock and a strong wind, and the people did not know how to belay properly. They were climbing dangerously, and he was relieved when they finally turned back. He decided to wait for them.

Two men and a woman eventually reached him after a slow and faltering descent. They were near exhaustion. One man said something, but Petzoldt had no idea what language he spoke. The climber smiled weakly and gave a hopeless shrug. Petzoldt nodded and held out a hand signaling for them to rest awhile. Then, with no words exchanged, the foursome started down the mountain with Petzoldt in the lead.

It was getting dark. He knew he would have time to hike back to his tent by himself before nightfall, but the others could not move fast enough to make it to the warming hut. Besides, they had put him in charge. He decided to stop. Between them they had a couple of candy bars, and he had a waterproof bivouac cloth. With some elaborate gesturing he was able to convince them that their only chance for survival was to huddle together under the one-man shelter.

No one slept. It was impossible to get completely under the sheet to escape the frigid air. By daylight, they were almost frozen. Petzoldt led the weakened hikers back down to the climbing hut, to which the large trekking party had retreated. Then he returned to his camp on the glacier, pitched his tent, and collapsed into his sleeping bag.

About one in the afternoon, he heard someone moving nearby. Speaking English with a "down under" accent, a man asked if he could talk with him. Petzoldt pulled on his boots and crawled outside.

The climber was Dan Bryant from New Zealand. He was traveling and climbing in the Alps and, although he was experienced enough to go without a guide, he wanted a climbing companion.

"I met the people you rescued last night," he said. "They said you appeared like a miracle and saved their lives. I guess you're something of a hero."

Petzoldt laughed and admitted that he was a guide in the United States.

Bryant said he had heard of him. He told him that snow and ice were his specialty because those conditions were typical of New Zealand mountains. With Petzoldt's expertise on Teton rock, he figured they would make a good team.

Petzoldt estimated Bryant was about his age, a bit smaller in stature, but strong and energetic. Impressed by the man's frankness, he agreed to join forces. They decided to traverse the Matterhorn over to the Italian side but to return first to Zermatt to resupply and start fresh the next morning.

At daylight, they proceeded up the mountain. They climbed well together, and their progress was so fast that they soon passed the large group that was making another attempt after failing the day before.

After two hours, they were on top of the Matterhorn. And looking at a dead body—apparently, that of a climber who had started from the Italian side the previous day and been benighted in the storm.

"There's nothing we can do for him," Petzoldt said.

Bryant agreed. The rescue unit would be coming to get him soon.

In spite of their unsettling discovery at the summit they were exhilarated. It was a glorious day and still early. Neither one of them was tired. So they decided to complete the traverse and spend the night in the Italian hut.

It was about one in the afternoon when they reached the shelter. They entered the small building and the stench almost knocked them over. A party had taken cover there during the storm and failed to go outside to relieve themselves. Besides human waste, the floor was littered with food scraps and paper. "We can't stay here," Petzoldt said.

They went outside to discuss the next move. Bryant suggested they continue on down into Italy, stay for a few days, and then do some more climbing together. Petzoldt said there wouldn't be enough time to do both before he planned to leave. They agreed to retrace their steps and spend the night at the Swiss hut.

Climbing quickly back to the summit, they passed the dead man and arrived at the hut by late afternoon. The place was packed with

1. Eldon "Curly" and Paul in costume after their missionary uncle brought two members of the Crow tribe to Iowa (around 1911)

2. Paul and dog Ranger in Twin Falls, Idaho

3. *Paul and his sister Lillian*   4. *Paul and his mother Emma*

5. *Snake River Canyon, Twin Falls, Idaho, where Paul had his first climbing experiences*

6. (above left) *Glenn Exum, Red, Tommy, Barbara Gray, Paul, Mrs. Gray, and the cook's baby at the Gray's ranch in Jackson Hole, Wyoming, July 1933*

7. (left) *Glenn Exum climbing in the Tetons*

8. (above right) *Paul and climbing party on the Bellyroll of the Grand Teton, 1933*

9. *Paul looking into a crevasse, 1933*

*10. (right)
Geraldine Lucas,
Paul, Ike Powell,
and two ranchers
from Kelly,
Wyoming, after
planting Old Glory
on the Grand Teton
summit, 1924*

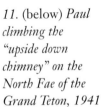

*11. (below) Paul
climbing the
"upside down
chimney" on the
North Fae of the
Grand Teton, 1941*

12. (above) *Paul belaying on snow in the Tetons*

13. (left) *Bernice Petzoldt rappelling in the Tetons*

14. (above right) *Camp V at 22,000 feet, 1938 First All-American Expedition to K2*

15. (below right) *Members of 1938 First All-American Expedition to K2 and their sherpas*

16. Paul on the upper Godwin-Austen Glacier, 1938 K2 expedition

hikers and a rescue party en route to evacuate the body. It looked almost as bad as the Italian shelter, so they kept on going and hiked all the way back to Zermatt.

Word spread fast through the Swiss guiding community that Petzoldt and Bryant had made a double traverse of the Matterhorn in one day. Their feat was so unusual that it was later recorded in London's renowned *Alpine Journal*.

Local alpinists mapped out several other challenging climbs for the pair to do in the area. They scaled Monte Rosa, Dent Blanche, and the Weisshorn and then continued further east to the peaks near Grindelwald. They bicycled over the pass to Visp, left their bikes, then hiked toward the sixteen-mile-long Aletsch Glacier. Making a number of camps along the way, they succeeded in getting to the top of the glacier and went on to climb the Jungfrau, the Eiger, and the Finsteraarhorn. By the time they got back to the Jungfrau railroad station, Bryant's vacation had run out. Reluctantly, they said goodbye and went their own ways.

Petzoldt was now completely broke. He had to get to the American Express office in Rotterdam, where his sister Gladys had promised to send money.

He retrieved his bicycle and struggled through the mountainous terrain along the Rhône River. A few days later he was in the Rhine River valley, subsisting on grapes and raw vegetables foraged from the fields and an occasional meal offered by a friendly farmer.

He joined a group of young German cyclists who spoke a little English. They told him that Hitler provided youth hostels throughout the country where they could get free meals, bathe, and sleep. They offered to get him inside with their group but warned him not to say anything and betray his foreign nationality.

All went well the first night. Petzoldt satiated himself with a real dinner, which tasted wonderful after so many days of near fasting. He took a hot shower and slept soundly on the simple cot.

But the next morning after breakfast, the guests were sent to make their beds. Petzoldt did a less than perfect job. Then a Nazi trooper stormed in to make an inspection, and all of the other youngsters snapped to attention. Petzoldt did the same. The trooper walked slowly down the aisle then stopped in front of him. He took a long look at the bed, then slapped Petzoldt across the face with the back of his hand.

"He's an American! He's an American!" the German cyclists yelled as Petzoldt pulled himself up from the floor.

The trooper glared.

"My name is Petzoldt. I'm a German from America."

One of the youngsters quickly translated and the inspector thrust out his hand.

"Passport!" he demanded.

Petzoldt showed him his papers. The Nazi spun on his heels and left the room, mumbling something about dumb Americans.

When Petzoldt reached the Netherlands border at Venlo, he was stopped and told he must pay a ten-dollar duty fee before entering the country because he was riding an English bicycle. The money would be refunded if he presented his receipt when he and the bike left Holland.

"I don't have any money," Petzoldt tried to tell the guard. "I will have funds waiting for me at American Express in Rotterdam, and can pay the fee then." The official refused to let him pass.

He was at a loss about what to do. There was a railroad station, but he couldn't afford a train ticket any more than he could pay the duty. It was too far to walk to Rotterdam. And he was anxious to be on his way back to America. He wandered around the customs house trying to think of a solution.

Then he got an idea. He asked the official how much a train ticket cost and then peddled back down the road, where he had passed a band of gypsies. After a great deal of gesturing, he managed to sell them the bicycle for enough money to pay his railroad fare and have a decent meal as well.

When he reached Rotterdam, there was no money waiting at the American Express office. But there was a Lykes Brothers freighter in the harbor. He decided his only option was to see if that company would allow him to work for his passage to America.

The captain's response was the same as Kermit Roosevelt's. Too many rules against it. But after Petzoldt said he was a student and elaborated on all of his experiences in England and on the Continent, the seaman relented.

"Could you pay your fare when we arrive in New Orleans?" he asked.

Petzoldt assured him that he could.

The captain checked his passport and smiled.

"Well, we're not carrying anybody, and you're a student," he said. "We'll take you for $75."

Petzoldt shook his hand and thanked him.

"You're flat broke?" the captain asked.

"Yes."

"Here's twenty-five bucks. You can get aboard tomorrow, and pay me back when we get to the States."

·
·
·
·
·
·

CHAPTER 4

Back Home

THE LYKES BROTHERS FREIGHTER CALLED AT CALAIS, THEN SAILED through the English Channel and down the west coast of Africa, docking several times to pick up or deliver cargo. While his shipmates labored, Petzoldt, the sole passenger, toured each port-of-call then returned in the evening for dinner in the officers' mess, and sometimes a game of poker.

When they left the Continent in the fall of 1934 for a lengthy North Atlantic crossing, he lounged in a deck chair with a book or observed flying fish cavorting in the wake. At night, he studied the constellations and watched phosphorescent light playing in the foam.

As the ship cruised into the weirdly calm waters of the Sargasso Sea, the bow sliced through bulbous tangles of gulfweed that superstitious sailors blamed for the mysterious disappearance of ships. Petzoldt wondered if the stories were true and if they, too, would be lost.

By the time the two-month voyage ended at New Orleans, he had won enough at poker to enable him to repay the captain's loan in full. He was out of debt but broke again until he could collect the few hundred dollars that Gladys had sent him. Jobs were scarce.

While Petzoldt was abroad, President Roosevelt had temporarily closed the banks, abandoned the gold standard, formed the Civilian

Conservation Corps and the Works Project Administration, passed the Emergency Relief Act, and taken a number of other measures in an attempt to help the nation recover from the Depression.

In Louisiana, Senator Huey P. Long staged a counterattack by espousing a "share the wealth" philosophy so "every man could be king." Friends of "the Kingfish" hailed him as the champion of the little man; Roosevelt and other detractors warned that he was the first American dictator. Petzoldt didn't know who to believe.

He found lodging in a federally sponsored shelter for the unemployed and homeless and tried to plan his next move. When he learned there was another government recovery program that provided college tuition, he enrolled at Louisiana State University in Baton Rouge. Reluctantly, he wrote Bernice McGarrity to tell her that his homecoming and their wedding would be delayed for awhile. He hoped she would continue waiting for him.

"Darling, you may have a hard time with me," he wrote. "I haven't much to offer you in the way of material things. I'm not even sure that you will always have enough to eat. But I know we'll have a wonderful life. There are so many interesting things for us to do together. Besides I love you."

Subsidized schooling helped, but the inability to find steady work led to desperation. He knew there was one way to make some money. Gambling. He figured he could make good use of what "Pop" Weiner had taught him about how to bluff at cards.

Just about this time, when he was playing golf at the local country club, a man took him aside. He said he was a left-hander, hit his ball right down the middle of the fairway, and shot a lot of pars but his tee shots didn't go very far.

"Paul, I could use you," he said. "Sometimes I have a game at a resort or a winter course, and I need a long driver like you. How would you like to be my knock-off man?"

Petzoldt had heard about such hustlers. There was nothing really crooked about sandbagging, although it was a little shoddy to hide your real ability on the course. But the man hinted that they would be playing for fairly high stakes, and he needed money. So he agreed to give it a try. A few days later the golfer wired him the bus fare to Little Rock, Arkansas.

When he arrived at the appointed golf course, he started practicing on the putting green. His erstwhile friend approached with two other players and, pretending he didn't know Petzoldt, asked if he would like to join them.

"Sure," Petzoldt said.

"We're playing for money," the man said. "Five dollars a hole, carry-over."

"That's all right with me," Petzoldt said.

They teamed beautifully. Petzoldt blasted 225-foot drives into the rough and his partner sent four or five straight shots to the pin for par. Then Petzoldt would settle down and shoot a birdie on the next hole.

By the end of spring semester he had enough money to go home. He caught a freight train from Baton Rouge to Casper, Wyoming, and then checked into a hotel to clean up for the rest of the trip. He didn't want his girl to see him looking like a hobo.

Bernice had dropped out of the university shortly after Petzoldt left for Windsor. She did not enjoy classes and didn't miss the social whirl on campus. She was content with the quiet life in her small hometown, where she lived with her parents and younger brother. She spent her days walking alongside the Wind River, lingering in the library, and chatting with the farmers and ranchers who came to town each Saturday. There were many times she thought that she and Petzoldt would never really be together. His letters were exasperatingly sporadic. Now that he was actually returning she panicked.

"It had been two years and a half since I'd seen him," she wrote, "and I was afraid that he might find me very unattractive and decide he did not want to marry me after all."

When he stepped out of the branch-line train at Riverton he saw her standing on the platform. She wore a white piqué dress and sandals. Her brown hair shone in the late afternoon sun and she was smiling. After a moment's hesitation, she ran to him.

Bernice, a Roman Catholic, wanted to be married at home by her parish priest, Father Morgan. Petzoldt had never subscribed to organized religion but had no objection to the ceremony if it pleased her, until Father Morgan told him he would have to take instruction in church doctrine and promise to raise any children in the Catholic faith.

"I can't do that," Petzoldt said. So, on June 16, 1935, with a couple from Dubois as witnesses, they were married by a justice of the peace in Thermopolis, Wyoming.

There wasn't time for a honeymoon before climbing season, so they went directly to Jenny Lake. Petzoldt purchased a huge canvas tepee that was about twenty feet wide and twenty-five feet high. He cut down lodgepole pines for support and left an opening in the top for a smoke hole. Rough-hewn log furniture, a Coleman lantern, and a small red Boston rocker made the home quite comfortable.

Petzoldt lost no time in getting back into the mountains. He explored much of the range that summer, seeking new routes for clients, retracing former climbs, and making several first ascents.

On June 26, with his brother Curly and William and Harold Plumley, he climbed the west face of 12,922-foot Mount Owen, the second highest peak in the area, which had resisted climbers until 1930. On August 2, he and W. F. Loomis pioneered the southeast face of the Grand Teton. They not only reached the ice-crusted summit in less than six hours, they descended on an untried route that followed a ledge to the skyline on the south side. There, the ridge narrowed to an eight-foot-wide parapet angled at approximately 60 degrees. Using two ropes, they had to negotiate six rappels to reach a safe notch leading to a clear exit.

Petzoldt claimed another first on August 12 when he led Exum and Elizabeth Cowles on a new approach up the East Ridge of the Grand. He and Ralph Herron had seen this southern traverse of the Molar Tooth when the smooth tower blocked them on their 1924 ascent. The party was able to successfully avoid the barrier by turning south and climbing a smooth 200-foot chimney to reach a sharp crest. The crest overlooked a great couloir which took them up to join the usual northern traverse.

On August 26, Petzoldt and H. K. Hartline completed the first ascent of the west ridge of Mount Moran, and two days later they joined A. Curtis Smith to do the northeast slope of Mount Owen, the most extensive snow climb in the park.

By this time, Petzoldt had perfected many innovative techniques to make his clients' trips safer and more enjoyable. Besides devising the voice signal system, he departed from the established European custom of having a climbing party tied into rope most of the time. He

71

concluded that the established practice of roping up the minute a party started up the mountain was dangerous. Walking along with loose rope invited accidents. He was convinced that it would be safer for clients to be independent of the rope, except in dangerous areas, so they could use their hands more freely. Another Petzoldt innovation was the "sliding middleman technique," which he devised for belaying three climbers over snowfields. If one person fell and didn't make a self-arrest with his ice ax, he could pull the others off with him. But belaying all three up one at a time was a very slow procedure, so Petzoldt organized a belaying method that was easy to learn, safe, and faster. The leader climbed as far as the rope would take him and stabbed his ice ax into the snow at an angle to create a sturdy belay point. Then, while the bottom climber belayed from below, the middleman tied a rope around his waist, clamped it on carabiners placed on the belay rope, and moved up to the top person. The low man followed to join the other two, then belayed the leader, who started the process all over again.

During that climbing season of 1935, while Petzoldt guided climbers, Bernice signed up new clients and maintained the office. But as summer ended, he knew they could not spend a rugged Wyoming winter under canvas. Besides, he was twenty-seven. It was time to find other ways of supporting his wife—and perhaps a child.

That October he had an opportunity to buy the 220-acre Ram's Horn Ranch on Ditch Creek, east of the Grand Teton. The sale price of $7,500 included three cabins, a barn, and a couple of horses. Petzoldt had enough money for a down payment, but he couldn't come up with the balance. So he contacted a wealthy friend from New Jersey, Ted Koven, who had climbed with him, and asked if he would be willing to finance the venture so that they could set up a dude ranch and hunting camp. Koven agreed.

As Jackson Hole was usually snowed-in during the winter and they would be unable to restore the buildings before bad weather hit, he and Bernice decided to board up the place and enjoy a belated honeymoon in Salt Lake City. But first, in order to appease the in-laws, they returned to Riverton for a wedding ceremony sanctioned by the Catholic church. In the presence of family and close friends, they repeated their vows before Father Morgan in the flower-filled McGarrity living room. That evening everyone celebrated the happy event with a picnic by the river.

They spent the early part of the winter in Salt Lake City. Petzoldt showed his bride the places he remembered from his university days there, and, when snow arrived, they took to the nearby mountains.

In those days few people owned cross-country skis. Homemade skis were made from long straight-grained pieces of lodgepole pine that were waxed with mixtures of honey and pine tar, or axle grease. Broken machinery belts were cut into straps for bindings, and the skiers wore common rubber overshoes. A single pine pole served as a brake or was used to push the skier through the snow.

The Petzoldts joined a group of friends for energetic weekends of Nordic skiing. Sometimes they drove up to the old mining town of Park City, took the mine train through a tunnel, and rode up the hoist to the surface. From there they skied over the Wasatch Mountains into Brighton Canyon, where they spent the night in a cabin maintained by the local mountaineering club. The next day they continued down the other side of the mountain to the Hot Pots Resort in Midway, where they bathed in steaming sulphur pools and feasted on fried chicken.

As Christmas approached they decided to try a winter at the ranch. They planned to take the train from Salt Lake to Victor, Idaho, where they could catch a ride on the mail sleigh over Teton Pass to Jackson. But when the train arrived at Ashton, Idaho, the tracks were blocked by a raging blizzard. They had to spend a week in the town's only hotel waiting for the storm to end. To make matters worse, the annual American Sled Dog Derby was taking place in town, and the hotel was alive with barking, scrapping huskies.

One day the snow finally stopped falling. The train still couldn't run, but the Petzoldts had their cross-country skis with them so they decided to set out on their own. Victor, Idaho, was almost forty miles away. Another thirteen miles over Teton Pass would take them into Wilson, Wyoming, and the Ram's Horn Ranch was twenty-five miles beyond that. It would be a lengthy trek, but Petzoldt assured his wife that he had friends along the way who would put them up nights. So they arranged for the hotel to send their bags to them when the roads opened and took off after breakfast.

The trip started out easily enough with Petzoldt following the railroad tracks and breaking trail across the flat fields. Bernice followed in his path. They stayed at a ranch that night and set out in calm weather the next morning.

But by seven o'clock that evening it started snowing again, and they were still wearily pushing their way through the heavy drifts. Two hours later they were struggling through a blizzard. Petzoldt could scarcely see to find his way, and Bernice was fighting to keep her balance in the strong wind. They didn't reach Victor until eleven.

The tiny town was pitch black. They passed the garage, gas station, cafe, and a couple of false-fronted buildings and finally found a sign advertising rooms for rent. Petzoldt hammered on the door until the proprietor begrudgingly answered and directed them to a shabby room down the hall. The only heat in the entire building came from a small coal stove in the sitting room. It was so cold that they had to sleep fully dressed—stocking caps, mittens, and all.

It was still dark when they got up to start again the next morning. Luckily the cafe was open to serve them a hot breakfast before they tackled Teton Pass.

A short distance from town the road became steep as it zigzagged to the 8,429-foot summit. They reached the top at six that evening, after almost twelve hours of uninterrupted climbing through snow that drifted five feet deep. The seven-mile descent into Wilson was a nightmare for Bernice, who was so exhausted that her knees buckled every few minutes.

"Many women have climbed mountains," she wrote. "A few have even fallen off and been killed, but I must be the only woman who has ever fallen all the way down Teton Pass and lived to tell the tale."

When they finally reached Gibb Scott's ranch in the valley, Scott warmed them up before the fireplace and filled them with hot coffee and fried elk steak. They stayed on a couple of days to recuperate before continuing to the Ram's Horn.

There were still twenty-five miles to travel. Refreshed after Scott's hospitality, they broke up the final leg of the trip by staying overnight at the Circle H Ranch. The caretaker didn't know them but was delighted to have company after weeks of being snowed in. He broke out some Scotch whisky, and they talked into the night. On the sixth day they made it the rest of the way home.

The ranch consisted of a two-room cabin for the kitchen and parlor and a couple of rustic log sleeping shacks. The snow had drifted higher than roof level, so the carpenters Petzoldt had hired to refurbish the place had had to shovel steps down to the doors. As the buildings were not designed for winter use, snow blew inside through cracks in the ceiling and windows.

With temperatures plummeting to fifty below zero, they piled blankets ten deep on the bed. In the mornings they had to scurry down an icy trail to the cookhouse, hoping a fire would still be smoldering in the woodstove. Melted snow provided water, and they heated water so they could bathe in a small tin tub. The closest store and post office was in Kelly, five miles away by ski. Petzoldt saw to it that they had an ample supply of firewood. There were plenty of good books to read and no lack of beautiful hillsides where they could cross-country ski and photograph wildlife.

Sometimes Petzoldt did more serious skiing with Curly, who had just retired as a jockey and was wintering in Jackson. Fred Brown, Petzoldt's closest friend in the valley and an accomplished skier, often joined them. They got a driver to take them to the top of Teton Pass then barreled down twelve hundred vertical feet to Wilson. They skied the bowls above timberline on Buck Mountain and spent whole days climbing four thousand feet to the top of Rendezvous Mountain and breaking trails though the powder where Teton Village Ski Area would develop some thirty years later.

One day the trio decided it would be fun to stand on top of the Grand Teton in winter. It would be a first-time adventure and could possibly lead to new avenues for the mountaineering school.

Petzoldt had learned the hard way in 1924 what it was like to be caught in an unseasonable summer storm. Temperatures of fifty below zero, aggravated by wind chill and the possibility of blizzards, were a realistic threat in December. He made preparations for the most severe conditions possible and packed extra woolen underwear, mittens, socks, bedding, and food. They brought a variety of waxes and borrowed sealskins to attach to the bottoms of their seven-and-a-half-foot skis for steep climbing.

When they started for Garnet Canyon early on the morning of

December 17, 1935, it was twenty-five below zero. Due to soft, deep snow and heavy packs it took them eight and a half hours to make the first leg of the trip—twice as long as it did in summertime. They arrived at the Petzoldt Caves exhausted but were relieved to find a dry, comfortable camping place after tunneling through snow under the overhanging boulders.

Surprisingly, at the higher elevation the thermometer registered a warmer fifteen degrees above zero. The cave afforded a natural fireplace as well, and Petzoldt had cached some wood in the shelter that fall. They decided it would be wise to rest there a day before tackling the more difficult terrain. Petzoldt and Brown used the extra time to take supplies to the Lower Saddle in preparation for the final assault. At seven A.M. on the third morning they donned their skis and started.

"We climbed at an angle of about 18 degrees in a series of switchbacks until we reached the glacier on the Middle Teton," Petzoldt later wrote. "Here we made one gigantic switchback high on the side of the Middle Teton itself, and then back to the highest point of the glacier on the north. We stuck our skis in the snow and took to the rocks. Instead of going directly to the Lower Saddle we traversed north along its base where the wind had blown a ridge bare. We struck the top ridge of the Saddle at its upper section where it meets the great couloir that leads to the 'Crawl,' a thousand feet above.

"We found the going easy for all the light snow was blown into the canyon and on the glacier. The day was so perfect and the climbing conditions so grand that we almost decided to take the South Side route since the ridge was free of snow. We reached the Upper Saddle at 10:40 A.M. Here the thermometer registered 12 above zero, but a stiff wind chilled us so after a council of war we decided to don all our clothes and leave our packs.

"The Crawl was blown clear of snow, and so was the first chimney. The second chimney, filled with ice in September was now clear. We left the unused rope behind and rushed to the summit—the first party to make a winter ascent in the Tetons."

It was almost Christmas when Petzoldt got back to the ranch, convinced that all of the Teton peaks could be climbed in winter on their southern and western routes. Bernice shared his excitement about the possibilities that winter mountaineering might trigger an untapped market for students and tourists.

But as winter dragged on, Petzoldt's buddies started dropping by the ranch. They came on skis or wrestled trucks through the snow and spent long evenings gambling and swapping stories of their exploits. By March, the routine had gotten old for Bernice.

"Every night the men played poker or sat telling goofy stories concerning their physical prowess," she wrote. "I'd notice a growing tendency on my part to sneer openly when one of them would tell for the fiftieth time about killing an elk with a pocketknife, or when another of them claimed to have killed a bull moose with his bare hands."

One March morning, Petzoldt returned from chopping wood to find her gone. "I've been homesick so I'm going home to spend a little time with Mother," her note explained.

She told him she was skiing as far as Kelly and would take the mail sleigh to Jackson and catch the stage to Rock Springs. "Don't worry," she wrote. "I'll be back when the snow starts to melt."

When she returned in April 1936, Petzoldt had a surprise for her. Ted Koven had suggested they drive to New York to promote the dude ranch. He had even offered to help with expenses.

The month-long vacation served as a second honeymoon. Bernice visited her sisters in Chicago and Manhattan whom she had not seen since she was fourteen. In New York they dined in small cafes, went to the theater, and strolled the streets to relish the big city excitement. The Kovens hosted parties for prospective clients, and Petzoldt showed movies he had taken of climbing, the wildlife, and the quaint cow town of Jackson. By the time they were back at the ranch they had enough reservations to wrangle dudes all season.

At the Kovens' suggestion they stopped in Denver on their way home to stock up on bedding, curtains, dishes, and other necessities for the summer season. By the end of May they were satisfied that the Ram's Horn was ready for business.

But when the first guests arrived in June the cook complained that the kitchen was woefully lacking in proper equipment. The springhouse used for refrigeration was inadequate. There wasn't enough water hauled from the well. Bernice struggled to appease her, control an untrained and often lazy staff, and still keep three square meals a day on the table for the ravenous visitors. And when the dudes weren't eating, they wanted to be entertained. That, too, was her job.

"Among our guests were several young prep school boys whose attitude toward the native people of Jackson's Hole was highly offensive to me," she wrote. "After all, who is to say who's a character? And then there was the college professor who was dreadfully shy but yet tried valiantly to be one of the gang, and the gray-haired motherly woman from New Hampshire whose husband was having an affair with his secretary, and the lonely spinster, and the young girl who was always in love with one of the wranglers and had to be watched."

In the meantime Petzoldt operated the mountaineering school. Besides a growing number of tourists, seasoned climbers started to congregate at the giant tepee to compare notes on their climbing exploits and techniques. They discovered several new routes. On July 28, 1936, Petzoldt, Karl Keuffel, and James Monroe combined a previously unexplored section of the southeast face of the Grand with the upper section of the East Ridge. On August 23, the famous German climber Fritz Wiessner, forester and mountaineer William House, and Elizabeth Woolsey, captain of the American Olympic ski team, developed a new route up the East Face of the Middle Teton.

Petzoldt had scoped the North Face of the Grand Teton at different times of day ever since he and Sterling Hendricks reconnoitered sections of it in 1933. He thought there was a feasible route up that side of the mountain. In broad daylight, it appeared perpendicular, but at sunrise or sunset, despite its vertical, overhanging appearance, it seemed to have a system of ledges, chimneys, and shelves that he thought might well be climbable. Surely it was one of the most difficult and hazardous of all Teton ascents, but he was bent on trying it. He and Wiessner talked about doing it together.

Late one afternoon Petzoldt had just returned from a climb with clients, when Curly, who was assisting with the guiding service that summer, told him that Wiessner, House, Betty Woolsey, and a few others had started for the North Face. Petzoldt was furious.

"I've looked at that route and told them about it and, by God, they didn't invite me along and they're not going to get up there first," he told Curly.

So the two brothers and Jack Durrance, one of Petzoldt's guides, gathered their ropes, pitons, and equipment, and took off for the Grand Teton in the dark of August 25.

"We left in the middle of the night and went up the trail to Amphitheater Lake," Petzoldt says. "We passed Wiessner and his party snoring in their tents."

They continued to the Teton glacier and climbed past a bergschrund up to the foot of the precipice. From there they scrambled over crumbling rock and up steep, difficult shoulders. Petzoldt and Durrance took turns leading, and Curly followed with the unenviable job of retrieving pitons. Falling rocks, exposed pitches, and downward slanting ledges threatened as they zigzagged from one sheltering overhang to another.

"The strain of the climb was beginning to tell on us," Durrance wrote in the *Jackson Hole Courier*. "I was fagged out pitifully, so was Eldon [Curly] who had carried a thirty-pound pack most of the way from the valley."

At the upper third of the cliff, Petzoldt crawled as far as he could on a ledge that finally narrowed to nothing and then turned back and said they would have to retrace their steps. They made a sixty-foot rappel to the North Corner, where a series of chimneys and couloirs brought the exhausted climbers to the summit by six o'clock. Wiessner's party had stopped far below.

That fall after the dudes left and the hunters arrived, the cook quit. Bernice sometimes had thirty or more people to feed all by herself. She fell into bed exhausted every night wondering how the ranch could once have seemed like such a grand idea. Staying at the ranch another winter was not a consideration. They boarded up the cabins and went to Riverton.

When the guests arrived in June 1937, they faced the same mix of problems. The new cook was no happier with the kitchen and springhouse than her predecessor. The business was not paying for itself, and the Park Service hinted that Petzoldt would lose his guiding concession if he tried to run a guest ranch, too. In July the Petzoldts turned the Ram's Horn back to the Kovens and moved back into the tepee.

That August Petzoldt invited Bernice to go on her first climb. He was guiding a party of four men up the difficult East Ridge of the

Grand. Although he had given her some basic training on practice cliffs, he suggested that she just accompany them as far as timberline, or perhaps Teepe's Glacier. It would require hiking over steep trails and some rugged terrain, but he told her she would not be doing any difficult or technical climbing. The rest of them would do that part on the second day, and she could wait for them in camp.

All the way up the mountain, Bernice expected Petzoldt to tell her it was time for her to stop. When she arrived at the timberline camp exhausted, he said nothing about the next day's hike to Teepe's Glacier. In the morning she tried to hide her surprise when he gestured at her rucksack and said, "All set?" She followed him up the steep hill to the glacier, thinking surely this was as far as she would go. Then he pulled crampons from his pack and told her to fasten them to her boots for the climb. Forty-five minutes later he led her past a deep, snow-filled gorge to an immense boulder jammed into a narrow gully. She felt dwarfed below the sheer wall that rose some hundred feet above her. Unpacking his climbing gear and tying into a rope, Petzoldt started to scale the cliff. He methodically felt for a reachable crack or a stony dimple that he could hang on to. Fastening his hands over tangible anchors, he carefully lifted a leg, feeling with his boot for that higher foothold he had spotted on the previous move as he inched up the rock. A half hour later he was on the top.

"On belay!" he yelled to her.

Bernice looked at the towering pinnacle in disbelief. Then, conscious of the climbers behind her, she checked to see that she was tied in properly. She took a deep breath and called, "Climbing!" Petzoldt slowly fed in the rope as she moved upward to the top of the wall. The others followed.

They traversed a snowfield to the East Ridge, a smooth, perpendicular face with a few faint holds in a zigzag crack. Petzoldt led off, driving pitons for the others to hang onto or to serve as belay points. The south side of the ridge was composed of huge overlapping granite slabs that were smooth enough to require friction climbing. Petzoldt, balancing himself with his fingertips, worked his way out to an overhang and swung himself up over the projection to the top. As he traversed each slab, he hammered pitons into the cracks.

"On belay!" he yelled to Bernice again.

"Slowly and tremblingly I rose to my feet," she wrote. "I heard him tell me to unbend my knees and stand up. The effort was almost more than I could endure. We were fearfully exposed here. There was a sheer drop of a couple of thousand feet on either side of the narrow slope."

She started up the slabs, balancing herself with her fingertips as she had seen Petzoldt do. Traversing slowly she got to within one hundred feet of the top when she suddenly lost balance and catapulted down the slabs. Petzoldt caught her up short with the rope, and she hung there, too panicked to move.

"Get up and start moving!" he yelled.

Too dazed to be mad she responded to the authority in his voice. She started to proceed upward and finally reached the top. "Well done," he said. "There's another tough section ahead."

Above them was a difficult gendarme that required three separate belays to circumnavigate and then a final large snowfield, where they had to hack steps into the ice en route to the summit. After ten hours on the rope, they were on top of the Grand Teton at four o'clock in the afternoon. Petzoldt swept his exhausted wife off her feet and swung her around joyously.

"Well, she's climbed it now," he said to the others as they all shook hands. "She won't have to climb any more. She can rest on her laurels."

Bernice, while not completely converted to mountaineering, nevertheless went on to climb both the Owen and Exum Routes before snowfall.

As the aspen turned golden and the air hinted at winter chill, summer visitors started to leave the park. The Petzoldts spent relaxing days hiking in the foothills, casting for trout in the Snake River, and visiting with friends who congregated at the Jenny Lake store.

They had been married two years. Although they hoped for a child, there were no signs of a baby on the way to tie them down. One day as they discussed potential plans for the off-season, they decided to spend the winter in Mexico.

It was a long, pleasant drive from Jackson through Colorado, into Texas, and on across the border down to Monterrey. They stayed a few days there in the shadow of the Sierra Madre, riding through the plaza in horse-drawn carriages, and savoring the ever-present music and spicy fragrance of the colonial town.

As they battled the noisy traffic on the way into Mexico City, a small boy jumped onto the running board of their car and talked them into renting a room in his family's house. They had come upon hard times and needed to find boarders in order for him and his sister to continue in school, he said. The Petzoldts were weary after a long drive and decided to take a chance. They were amazed to find a room in an elegant home filled with Oriental carpets, fine paintings, and antiques for a fairly reasonable price.

Then one night they were suddenly awakened by a massive jolt. The chandelier swung madly and they could hear a low rumbling noise. "It's an earthquake," Petzoldt yelled. "Get under a doorway."

They jumped out of bed and bolted for the French doors leading to a balcony that ran the length of the house. As they stood under the lintel, the Mexican family joined them and frantically crossed themselves and prayed. The side of a building across the street caved to the ground then the shaking stopped and an eerie silence followed. Only then did they notice the Mexicans staring. Petzoldt was completely nude.

When they decided that they were going to spend the entire winter in the city they moved to less expensive rooms in a building that was supposedly built on "earthquake-proof" steel pillars. For $28, plus $7 a month for a live-in maid, they had a living room, dining room, bedroom, kitchen, and bath. The apartment was ideally located close to the city center and had a balcony, from which Bernice watched children playing with their nannies in a lovely formal garden.

They settled in like locals, shopping at the open-air market, taking evening strolls, and betting on their favorite players at the jai alai games each weekend. Petzoldt won enough money gambling to take them on a two-week vacation to Acapulco in February and was able to arrange guest privileges for golf at the Chapultepec Country Club. He entered the Mexican championship golf tournament and made it all the way to the semifinals. He was defeated by a local businessman who later lost to the winner, Johnny Goodman.

But being near mountains that were higher than any in the United States was a temptation he could not resist. He was curious to learn about Mexican climbing techniques and wanted to test his own responses to high altitudes. So he made a project of checking out some of Mexico's famous peaks.

In the company of other mountaineers he had met, he made ascents of 18,696-foot Pico de Orizaba, 17,887-foot Popocatépetl, and 17,338-foot Iztaccíhuatl. Climbing these volcanic cones was different from his experiences in Switzerland or the Rockies, and the experience of looking down into craters when standing atop some of North America's highest peaks seemed odd. After some initial sloshing through volcanic ash at the base, very little hand-and footwork was necessary, and there were only a few places he had to rope up for dangerous exposure. The ascents were practically walk-ups, but there was so much scree that sometimes he would take two steps forward only to slip back one. He practiced his experimental system of pacing his steps with his breathing, so the altitude did not bother him at all.

Near the end of March 1938, as he was contemplating returning to Jackson to prepare for the climbing season, he received a telegram from Charles Houston of New York. Houston wrote that the American Alpine Club was sponsoring the First All-American Expedition to K2 in the Himalayas.

The famous German immigrant climber Fritz Wiessner had been asked to lead the trip but had had to turn the leadership over to Houston due to conflicting scheduling. In addition, another team member, William Loomis, had found it impossible to go. Loomis, who had climbed with Petzoldt in the Tetons, had offered to sponsor him to go in his place.

"The Himalayas!" Petzoldt shouted.

Bernice jumped up to read the telegram and threw her arms around him. "Paul, that's wonderful," she said.

He collapsed on the couch to reread the long message.

Then he jumped to his feet and started pacing the floor.

"They leave April twelfth. That's only a couple of weeks. I'll get Exum to handle the climbing school. You can go to your mother's in Riverton. Loomis said he'd sponsor me, and I have a few thousand bucks saved for personal expenses."

As Petzoldt spun into the ultimate mountaineer's dream, Bernice tried to stifle her fears. No Himalayan expedition had ever returned with all of its members unscathed.

"These mountains had not only taken a heavy toll in human lives," she thought, "but, when parties did manage to return, some of the members invariably suffered heart injuries, or loss of feet and hands, or at the least fingers and toes because of the long months of over-exertion, fatigue, and exposure. On one occasion an entire expedition had been buried by an avalanche."

"We'll have to pack up and start home right away," Petzoldt said. "I never thought I'd have a chance to climb in the Himalayas."

Bernice embraced him again and pressed her face against his chest so he couldn't see her eyes.

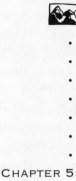

CHAPTER 5

K2: First All-American Expedition

ON MAY 8, 1938, PETZOLDT DISEMBARKED FROM A SECOND-CLASS CAR of the Frontier Mail railroad in Rawalpindi, India, where he and his climbing companions would launch their expedition.

The town was a microcosm of India at that time. The broad boulevards of the colonial British cantonment and the winding alleyways of old town were all clogged with sari-clad women and men in baggy, pajama-like *shalwar kansez* dodging bicycles, donkey carts, automobiles, and the ever-intransigent sacred cows. The air was thick with the smell of dung and steaming curry. Barking dogs and the calls of insistent merchants created a constant din.

Petzoldt had had only a short time to drive home from Mexico, arrange for Exum to manage the climbing concession, settle Bernice with her mother, and scrape up enough money for a train ticket to New York and incidental expenses for the months he would be abroad. Loomis had spared him any financial worries for the expedition itself.

When he joined his teammates in New York, the only person he knew was Bill House, a twenty-five-year-old Yale graduate and forester from Concord, New Hampshire. House had climbed with him in the Tetons, made several other ascents in the Rocky Mountains and Alps, and completed a successful first ascent on British Columbia's

Mount Waddington led by Fritz Wiessner in 1936.

New Yorker Charles Houston, at twenty-five a Harvard graduate and third-year medical student at Columbia University, was the expedition leader. When Wiessner had been forced to postpone his attempt on K2 for a year, the American Alpine Club, reluctant to give up the permit it had taken years to obtain from the Kashmiri government, appointed Houston to lead a reconnaissance trip on the mountain with the mission of discovering a route that would enable Wiessner to try for the summit in 1939.

Houston was renowned for his performance on snow and at high altitudes, having made the first ascent of 17,300-foot Mount Foraker in Alaska and participated in a combined American-British junket in 1936 that reached the highest summit climbed up to that time—25,645-foot Nanda Devi in the central Himalayas.

Houston had invited Robert Bates to join him. Bates, also a Harvard graduate, was a twenty-seven-year-old English instructor at the University of Pennsylvania. A mountain climber since he was a boy, he had climbed in the Alps and in 1933 had joined Houston on an ascent of Alaska's Mount Crillon led by Bradford Washburn. In 1935 he joined Washburn again on a National Geographic Society survey of the Yukon Territory's Saint Elias Mountains. A year later, the pair summited North America's highest unclimbed peak, 17,150-foot Mount Lucania, after which they trekked across a hundred miles of no-man's land in the Yukon.

The senior member of the team was Richard Burdsall, another Harvard alum from Port Chester, New York. In 1932 the forty-two-year-old engineer had reached the top of 24,900-foot Minya Konka in western China, which was the highest peak ever climbed to the top at that time.

Petzoldt, a Rocky Mountain westerner and stranger to the Ivy League, was the only outsider. And the only one not partially funded by his family.

In the 1930s, when there was little cross-country communication via airplanes and no television, many ill-conceived prejudices and stereotypes festered among the various sections of the United States. It was not uncommon for an easterner to think that women still wore poke bonnets and that cowboy-Indian clashes were commonplace in the "Wild West." Conversely, many westerners viewed their eastern counterparts as haughty, rich socialites who considered everything west of the Mississippi River uncivilized.

In a way, the American Alpine Club characterized these attitudes. Mountain climbing was not yet a popular sport in the United States. Many members of the small, exclusive organization were easterners who had climbed abroad and been indoctrinated with the British tradition which made specific distinctions between "gentlemen" mountaineers and their "hired" guides.

Mountaineering began as an activity of a select few and did not really blossom until Edward Whymper finally climbed the Matterhorn in 1865. Two years later the Alpine Club was founded in London by an initial group of twenty-eight members, and soon the sport swept into France, Germany, and other Continental countries with such great popularity that the Alps became known as "the playground of Europe."

Trailblazers pioneered climbable routes to other notable Alpine summits, and adventure seekers sought assistance from local Swiss, French, and Italian herdsmen and farmers who gave up their bucolic life for the more lucrative business of professional guiding.

"The climbers of the last century, if not necessarily rich men, were almost all unmistakably of what was then called the gentry," James Ramsey Ullman wrote in his book, *The Age of Mountaineering*. "And their standards were those of the time in which they lived. The line between employer and employee was hard and fast: on one side the amateur gentleman-sportsman and on the other the paid peasant-guide."

Petzoldt never subscribed to these perceptions when dealing with the greenhorns who came to the Tetons. But when he arrived in New York and was going over some of the expedition papers in the Alpine Club files, he made a disturbing discovery. He found a memo questioning whether "this Wyoming packer and guide" would be able to adjust himself socially to the rest of the party or dress and transport himself properly when they were guests at the British and French Alpine Clubs.

"Well, that was a little shock to me," Petzoldt said later. "Not that I'm not a packer and guide, but that sort of puts you as a guy that's maybe been to fourth grade or something. Of course they didn't know that I'd attended the queen's garden parties, lived in Windsor Castle, and been wined and dined with the Prince of Wales."

But when he met his fellow teammates at the farewell banquet, his discomfort was allayed by their welcome. "We had put together a group of friends. Petzoldt was the unknown," Houston remembers. "We thought Paul was great when we saw him. He was outgoing, a very warm and friendly person."

Houston announced that the estimated $9,000 cost of the expedition had been raised through contributions and loans based on future income from lectures and published articles the team members would produce. He reiterated that the official mission was to reconnoiter a route for Wiessner's attempt the next year but allowed that they would push as far as they could anyway. Their primary objective would always be safety. They would take every precaution to avoid joining the deadly roster of climbers lost or severely injured in the Himalayas.

As he would be forced to delay his trip two weeks and sail alone on the *Queen Mary*, he wished them good luck and promised to meet them in May at Rawalpindi.

On the morning of April 12, House, Bates, Burdsall, and Petzoldt boarded the S.S. *Europa*. Their Atlantic cruise took them to London, where they spent a couple of days before crossing the English Channel to Paris. It was there Petzoldt discovered that Houston had ordered very little climbing hardware to be put in the supply crates.

After receiving the invitation to join the expedition, Petzoldt had pored over photographs of K2. He could see that no matter where they reconnoitered a route, there would be rock as well as the proverbial glaciers.

Houston and Bates were experts on snow and ice mountaineering, but Petzoldt knew rock well. He was experienced in the granite mountains of the American West and used hardware freely. But in Paris, the other climbers talked about Houston's aversion to mechanical devices and said that practically no hardware had been packed for the highly technical climb. Houston subscribed to the old British school of climbing that disdained using "ironmongery" to "take advantage of the mountain."

English climbers considered reliance on snapping oblong steel rings (carabiners) into the eyes of pointed spikes (pitons) that were hammered into rock and strung with rope to secure fellow climbers to be unsporting, more an act of engineering than mountaineering.

The fact that the Germans had invented hardware and the techniques for using it further denigrated its use. In those pre-World War II days, German mountaineers were considered summit collectors who took foolhardy risks to conquer mountains "for the glory of the Fatherland and honor of the Führer." Purists claimed that reckless Germans had "driven spikes in all the peaks of Switzerland."

"My God! We hardly had a piton or a carabiner," Petzoldt said when he discovered the omission. "And hell, you could look at K2. That's rock! And there's places on it, if you fell you'd go down 10,000 feet before you would land."

So Petzoldt found a Parisian mountaineering shop and bought some pitons and carabiners. Knowing Houston's philosophy, he hid his purchases among the expedition materials.

After a few days, the group left Paris and took the train to Marseilles, where they caught a P & O ship to Alexandria, Egypt. From there they passed through the Suez Canal to the Indian Ocean and on to Bombay and a dusty three-day train trip to Rawalpindi.

As promised, Houston joined them on May 9. The others had already met Captain Norman R. Streatfield, a black-haired, blue-eyed Scotsman who had served in the Bengal Mountain Artillery and would be their official transport officer and liaison with the Indian authorities. He brought with him six Sherpas from Darjeeling, who had been specially selected by William Tilman, leader of the 1938 British attempt on Mount Everest. The small, wiry porters of mixed Tibetan, Indian, Nepalese, and Mongolian blood were noted in Himalayan mountaineering circles for their strength and dependability.

That evening over dinner Houston reviewed final details of the trip. In the morning, the Sherpas and the crated supplies would leave in a couple of lorries while Streatfield and the five Americans traveled the 180 miles to the Vale of Kashmir in two passenger cars.

It was difficult to sleep that night. Visions of the mountain no one had ever summited fed Petzoldt's dreams. Everything he had read, all of the photographs of the Karakoram Range that he had studied whirled in his mind.

This was the longest, highest rampart of forbidding peaks in the world. The inaccessible pyramid of K2's rocky summit soared some 12,000 feet above its icy glacier. The changing, violent weather patterns were legendary and poorly documented. The climate in the Karakoram could alternate suddenly between balmy days, temperatures plummeting far below frostbite range, and periods of whorling winds, snowstorms, and drenching rains. There was an ever-present threat of thundering avalanches and killing rock falls. And with thirty-three peaks exceeding 24,000 feet in elevation, the danger of severe altitude sickness was a dire reality.

K2 had been discovered in 1856, when Captain T. G. Montgomerie, who was conducting a survey of India, sighted a distant cluster of massive peaks in the Karakoram Range. He took measurements of the mountains and logged them by numbers with the prefix of K. K2 was the highest.

Other British scientists who continued the Great Survey attempted to identify local names for the peaks. They learned of Masherbrum (K1) and Gasherbrum (K3, 4, and 5) but found no local name for K2.

Five years later, when Captain Henry Haversham Godwin-Austen was conducting the survey, he struggled to within seventeen miles of the mountain before being forced to retreat. For many years, cartographers mistakenly attached his name—Godwin-Austen—to the massif.

Since its discovery, only two expeditions had made attempts on K2. A group of English, Swiss, and Austrians were the first to tackle the giant in 1902. They were thwarted a short distance up the northeast spur.

The next effort was in 1909 when Prince Luigi Amedeo of Savoy, the Duke of the Abruzzi, led the largest and most elaborate expedition ever launched in the Himalayas. The seasoned explorer, who had climbed and surveyed mountains in Alaska and Africa, failed to bring his customary brass bedstead on the Himalayan junket, but his entourage included ten companions, one hundred porters, and 13,280 pounds of cookware, food, camping goods, photographic gear, surveying equipment, and scientific measuring instruments.

The Duke was unsuccessful in his attempt to reach the top of K2, but he gave his name to a ridge that he explored on the southeast side of the peak just above base camp. He climbed to just over 20,000 feet there before retreating from the deep snow and rocky slabs he encountered.

He then moved the expedition back down onto the Savoia Glacier on the west side to explore a pass at its head for a possible route to the summit. He made three attempts on the pass and spent twelve hours cutting steps in hundreds of feet of blue ice before giving up again at 21,870 feet. Finally, after being thwarted on several other attempts to find a passage, he pronounced the mountain unclimbable.

Twenty-nine years later, as they began their drive from Rawalpindi to Srinagar in the Vale of Kashmir, the 1938 American team was determined to prove Abruzzi mistaken.

It was a two-day trip. Their short caravan left the sere, sun-baked plains and zigzagged up into cool forests of blue and Himalayan pine. They surmounted Murree Pass, then descended through terraced rice paddies into the narrow Jhelum River canyon where an immense gorge knifed between towering rock walls.

Gradually the vista opened, and they drove into a vast, verdant valley that once contained the waters of a prehistoric lake. Mist hung over irrigated fields which stretched behind rows of Lombardy poplars bordering the road. They could see the Pir Panjal mountain range encircling the city of Srinagar, and once they caught a quick look at the chalky summit of Nanga Parbat far in the distance.

They crossed the muddy Jhelum, where moored houseboats lined the banks, passed the maharajah's polo field, and finally pulled up in front of Nedou's Hotel. Houston advised them to rest well that night. Their entire supply of gear would have to be repacked the next morning. Everyone would have to pitch in to get the job done in time to leave on schedule.

Tea chests carrying food and equipment had been carefully packed in New York. Houston, Bates, and Bostonian Art Emmons had masterminded the shopping list: 100 pounds of biscuit mix, dried vegetables from Massachusetts, chocolate, dried fruit from California, cheddar cheese from Liverpool, malted milk tablets from Wisconsin, 50 pounds of pemmican from Denmark. They had also brought hard candy and fruit drops, tea, dried milk, cereal, rice, and pasta. They even included a few delicacies like kippered herring, caviar, and plum pudding.

And a special treat furnished by Houston's father—a bottle of Hudson's Bay Demerara rum.

Specialized equipment added to the bulky load. Besides their personal boots and high-altitude clothing, there were double eiderdown sleeping bags lined with flannel, 12-pound two-man tents with collapsible bamboo poles, larger tents and sleeping bags for base camp, crampons, gasoline and stoves with decompression chambers suitable for use in rarefied air, flashlights, cookware, repair kits, and a medical chest.

"Nearly everything had survived," Bates wrote in the official expedition book, *Five Miles High*, "though a tin of red pepper had become blended with some cocoa, a 5-pound can of jam had been pierced with a nail, so that its contents decorated every single object in a 120-pound case, and a large tin of honey had soaked the contents into Houston's fur-trimmed, wind-proof suit. Otherwise all was well."

But an unanticipated problem surfaced. The state of Kashmir was divided between Hindus and Muslims, and the porters belonged to both religious groups. Cows were sacred to the Hindus, and the followers of Muhammad reviled pork. Streatfield explained that transporting tins of camp meat could cause trouble. Houston solved the dilemma by directing the men to relabel offensive cans with wrappers reading "corn," "sauerkraut," and "beans."

Houston had anticipated that the tea chests shipped from New York would be too heavy for portage by pack horses and porters. Loads would have to be redistributed and restricted to 55 pounds apiece. Knowing that the leather *yakdans* usually carried by the local porters were not only weighty but also too expensive, he had brought along thirty knocked-down plywood boxes to be assembled on site.

While the others unpacked the chests and weighed out 55-pound loads, Petzoldt became foreman of a makeshift container factory with the six Sherpas as his crew. While he made certain that materials were distributed in such a way that all of an essential food or type of equipment would not be lost if one crate disappeared, the Sherpas sawed, hammered, and squealed over the "magic" of a screwdriver that automatically bedded the screws with a push of the handle.

But soon after the packing started they discovered that the new crates could accommodate much more than the measured parcels.

It was imperative that the contents fit snugly to withstand the un-avoidable jostling on the trail. Petzoldt called a halt to his production line and told the Sherpas they would have to start over. Delighted to have another turn with the hammers and screwdriver, they emptied the filled boxes, sawed them in half, and reassembled them. The job was completed in three days.

On the evening of May 12, with their work accomplished, they enjoyed their last taste of leisure for many weeks to come. They hired a *shikara* and paddled along the beautiful canals past mosques, Hindu temples, and the elegant palace of the maharaja. Their boat floated down the Jhelum River, where hundreds of swimmers splashed and played in the moonlight. In the distance, a wedding celebration filled the night with sounds of laughter and pounding ceremonial drums.

They started their 330-mile trek the next morning, leaving Srinagar's watery maze to jolt along bumpy roads in their honking lorries. The trucks fought their way through tangles of vehicles, peddlers, and bullocks along the shores of misty Lake Dal and into the foothills of the Pir Panjal Range.

Upon reaching the Sind River, they unloaded the gear, left the trucks, and mounted men and baggage on twenty-five ponies for the five-day trip to Dras. The trail passed through meadows and stands of fir trees where tall, swarthy nomadic herders and sari-clad women wearing gold in their ears and noses, tended horses, cattle, water buffalo, and goats.

After a long, dusty hike, they made camp on a grassy field along-side the Sind. Ahdoo, the cook, produced a spicy curry for dinner, and the climbers selected their personal Sherpas who would attend to their needs for the rest of the journey. Houston selected Pasang Kikuli, who had been his orderly on Nanda Devi. The captain chose Tse Tendrup, who had been with him on the French expedition to Hidden Peak. Kitar, who had been shadowing his western idol since the miracle of the screwdriver, became Petzoldt's official helper. House asked for Pempa, Phinsoo joined Bates, and Burdsall was served by Sonnam.

The convoy funneled into a narrow canyon cut by the river and filled with the melting remains of spruce-littered avalanches. A series of narrow switchbacks through the steep-walled valley led to the village of Sonamarg and on to the foot of the mountain pass that was their initial destination. The mountainsides were brilliant with edelweiss and yellow crocuses, and the air played a symphony of cuckoo, eagle, skylark, and dove calls.

They were to cross the 11,230-foot Zoji La at night. The fabled pass, traveled for centuries by trade caravans from Turkestan, western Tibet, and Ladakh, would not be officially opened for two more weeks. Some years deep snow closed the route to travelers for six months. Streatfield suggested they start across the mountain at 12:30 A.M. in order to complete the steepest part of the journey before the morning.

The frosty pass resembled a highway that night. In addition to the expedition, caravans of traders wearing prayer patches sewn on their sleeves were also attempting to cross while snow conditions remained favorable. It was a hazardous trip for the heavily burdened horses, who slipped and strained over the ice crust and floundered in deep drifts. There was little light in the black canyon, and both men and horses had to feel their way along the narrow path. In places, they had to kick steps up steep snow chutes that stabbed between towering walls. The party was relieved and thankful to at last be safely in the U-shaped valley of the Dras at dawn.

Now on foot, for another week they followed the Dras and Shingo Rivers, which chiseled through a series of deep canyons and led to the muddy Indus. Small villages, sculpted with curving steps of rock-walled terraces, dotted the hilltops. The natives laboriously hauled up basketloads of soil from the river bottoms some thousands of feet below to plant apricot trees, wheat, and barley in fields irrigated by ditches filled by high melting snowfields.

A narrow trail hugged the rocky walls bordering the Indus. Occasionally they passed waterfalls and cozy grass coves where they lunched or camped for the night.

One evening Ahdoo served the party a special pilaf with raisins, bits of cinnamon bark, fried onions, and fruit seeds blended into the steaming rice. Petzoldt expressed his satisfaction with a hearty yodel every time his plate was refilled and became so elated that he initiated a knot-tying contest among the Sherpas.

Everyone was amused as the eager porters tried to mimic Petzoldt's demonstration of tying a bowline with the rabbit (rope end) coming out of his hole (a loop), going around a tree (the rope length), and then popping back down the hole. The rope session was so successful that Petzoldt started organizing informal mountaineering lessons for the Sherpas. Certainly they knew how to climb in snow. One of the men, Pasang Kikuli, had even been on Mount Everest with an English party.

But the Sherpas knew nothing about belaying or handling rope. Petzoldt figured they should get some rock experience before they were confronted with the real thing. So one night he pulled out the pitons and carabiners he had purchased in Paris. Houston smiled but said nothing when he saw the hardware.

Petzoldt demonstrated how to rappel by using the rope as a body sling. Then he made a game of it. Tying a sling to a rock and inserting a rope through it, he told Kitar to turn his back to the slope, straddle the rope, then reach back with his left hand to grasp both sides of the rope, bring them around his left leg and up over his left shoulder. Then he instructed him to grip both ropes with his right hand and hold them near his right hip. With his left hand holding the high end of the rope, he should spread his feet slightly and brace them against the wall of the practice rock, then lean back, and let the rope slide up through his right hand, over his left shoulder, around his left leg and through his crotch as he backed down the cliff.

Kitar looked a bit shocked when Petzoldt told him to step backwards off the cliff. Urged by his cohorts, he took a tentative step, cautiously let the rope slide, and smiled as he realized that he could brake himself and regulate his speed. Gaining courage, he allowed the rappel ropes to lower him to the bottom. Another volunteer followed and soon the athletic little men were scurrying down cliff faces like acrobats.

On May 25, the caravan reached Skardu, the capital of Baltistan, where tall hills stratified with violet, red, gray, and ocher sandstone surrounded the desert valley of the Indus River. They stayed there two days to prepare for the final leg of their journey to base camp.

One evening the Americans were invited to the villa of the wazir (governor) of Baltistan. Streatfield was singled out as a special guest, and Petzoldt, probably due to his size and possibly the fact that his beard had grown in red and resembled the hennaed whiskers of local men of import, was offered the other seat of honor.

When the party was comfortably settled around the table a whole roasted lamb was carried in and laid on a mammoth bed of rice. With great ceremony the host reached over and plucked out the sheep's eyes. He served the delicacies to Petzoldt and Streatfield and smiled in anticipation of their compliments. Petzoldt didn't see what Streatfield did, but he popped the eye in his mouth and downed it with a hefty gulp of wine.

Soon after leaving Skardu the party crossed the Indus, which was no easy feat with the river in flood. They crowded into a big barge that the Sherpas claimed was like the one used by Alexander the Great. The awkward craft had a flat bottom and square sides fastened by homemade iron clamps. Everyone aboard rowed frantically with flimsy-looking willow sticks and rude paddles, while the load of three horses, five sheep, seven goats, seventeen people, and a steersman hurtled downstream through the thundering water. Once safely across, the barge had to be pulled back upstream to risk a hazardous return trip with the baggage.

As the team approached the village of Askole, the last outpost of civilization, the terrain became more difficult so they left the horses at Yuno and journeyed the rest of the way on foot, with porters carrying the baggage.

The route steepened, and the sun bore down relentlessly as the men trudged to an altitude approximating that of Zoji La. Their thirst became almost unbearable, but the streams were so heavy with mica particles that they dared not drink.

On the descent, they dodged falling rocks as they gingerly made their way two thousand feet down a precipitous talus slope. In places landslides had bared smooth slabs that had to be negotiated by friction holds.

Petzoldt was unnaturally quiet during the ten-hour traverse. Shortly after they started he had begun to feel sick. He fought back nausea and tried to steel himself against a severe back pain that worsened as the trail deteriorated. Soon he was chilled, and it was all he could do to put one foot in front of the other.

When Houston became aware of Petzoldt's condition, he stopped and made camp, even though they were only about six miles from Askole. He took Petzoldt's temperature. The thermometer read 103 degrees. By then the back pain was excruciating, he was dizzy, extremely weak, and his pulse was racing.

Houston ruled out sunstroke or food poisoning but feared Petzoldt might have pneumonia, which could prove fatal at an altitude of 10,000 feet. Feeling rather helpless, he gave Petzoldt a heavy dose of aspirin and checked him periodically during the night.

Petzoldt awoke in the morning drenched with sweat. The fever had lowered a bit, and he claimed he felt much better. He insisted that he could continue on to Askole. Houston reluctantly agreed.

By the time they reached the tiny terraced village of mud huts, Petzoldt's temperature had risen again. Shivering and in a lot of pain, he crawled into his sleeping bag as the others busied themselves paying off the first group of porters and hiring fresh ones for the rest of the trek.

By the next morning, Petzoldt's temperature had soared to 104.4 degrees. Houston, with only two years of medical school to his credit, had no idea about the cause of Petzoldt's illness, but he announced he would stay with his patient while the rest of the party continued on to establish a base camp.

"If he dies, I'll bury him and go on to meet you," he said. "If he recovers, we'll both try to catch up with the expedition." "That was a very unselfish act," Bates remembers. "He had put everything into this; he'd been living it intensely for two years. But he felt as a doctor, whatever happened, he couldn't leave Paul."

That evening, Petzoldt's temperature hit 104.6, and he became delirious. When the others left the next morning, he had rallied enough to make a few weak jokes but was still unable to travel. He was keenly disappointed that he might miss the attack on K2 but urged Houston to leave with the group. The doctor refused. When Petzoldt's fever finally abated two days later, he insisted that he was strong enough to make double marches and try to rejoin the expedition. Houston cautiously agreed to give it a try.

On June 8, Bates, Burdsall, House, Streatfield, and their Sherpas were resting at a 13,200-foot-high camp near Urdukas. Sitting on a flower-sprinkled slope in the midst of spearing peaks, they looked down upon the moraine of the Baltoro Glacier, which wormed through the canyon below them.

"While we were lazing in the grass of this delightful oasis, and looking for ibex (whose sign was everywhere) the greatest surprise of the expedition took place before our eyes," Bates wrote in *Five Miles High*. "Pasang suddenly shouted from the slopes above camp, 'Sahibs, sahibs, look see!'"

There, in the midst of fallen boulders and melting snow, were four moving dots. Petzoldt's red plaid shirt was unmistakable.

"'Why it's Petzoldt!'" [Burdsall] shouted. 'Petzoldt and Houston! How in the world did they do it?'"

Petzoldt, arriving pale and thin, had made the thirty-five-mile trek in record time. His illness was diagnosed later as dengue fever, a virulent disease transmitted by mosquitoes.

Reunited, the team prepared for the ascent. The porters gathered at small wormwood fires and wrapped unleavened dough around hot rocks to make the *chapatis* that would serve as rations during the lengthy traverse over the glacier. Petzoldt waded into a few pints of hot tea and mountains of cheese and crackers, while assuring everyone that his illness had been caused by hunger.

It took three days to travel nineteen miles across the Baltoro Glacier. The mornings began with each climber's Sherpa tapping on the tent flap to offer steaming mugs of "bed tea." After a breakfast of flat bread, camp was dismantled, and the journey over the ice continued. With the gutteral thundering of avalanches in the distance, they circumvented gaping crevasses and forded glacial streams. They glimpsed ice pinnacles 150-feet high that resembled freestanding sailing ships. Biting winds and pelting rain made their progress slow and cautious.

On June 12, they established base camp at 16,600 feet near the junction of the Savoia and Godwin-Austen Glaciers. "Before us the valley was dark with sullen clouds," Bates wrote later, "but directly ahead of us a rift in the vapor suddenly disclosed, not ten miles away, though high in the air, the glittering apex of a ghostly summit. It was like something from another world, something ethereal seen in a dream. For a few stunned moments we stared at the peak we had come so far to see; then it was gone. The glacier stretched ahead for miles into a void of blank, swirling mist." The tents were strangely silent that night as the men contemplated their first glimpse of K2, the aloof giant that would be their target.

In the morning, they emptied the crates again and sorted the contents. Streatfield paid the porters and sent them back to Askole. He gave the head man a leather pouch containing forty-five stones. "Throw away one rock every day," he said. "When they are all gone, come back to meet us."

They made camp. The Sherpas laid rock floors for tent platforms, constructed a stone dining shelter with a tarpaulin roof, and built food storehouses from empty boxes. Once the home base was organized, the mountaineers planned their attack.

The west, south, and east sides of K2 were accessible from base camp. There were five ridges and several rock faces rising from 10,000 to 12,000 feet above the glaciers to reconnoiter.

Two main ridges could be reached from the Savoia Glacier to the west. The northwest spine that rose from Savoia Pass above the glacier's cirque looked promising, although the Duke of the Abruzzi had declared there was "no hope" on that side of the mountain. The west ridge was unexplored.

Immediately above base camp the 23,330-foot Angelus peak led to a ridge heading northwest toward the summit. Eastward up the Godwin-Austin Glacier were the southeast ridge, where the Duke had turned back, and the northeast ridge, where a treacherous mile-long shelf hung at 22,000 feet.

On June 14, the entire group started toward Savoia Pass. Many of the crevasses were blanketed with layers of soft snow that appeared to be solid. The lead climbers broke through the veneer and had to be caught by the rope attached to their companions. To make matters worse, the afternoon sun burned down, further weakening the snow underfoot and penetrating the cream protecting their faces. The team decided they would divide into two- and three-man exploration parties to save time and energy.

After an exhausting climb, Petzoldt, Houston, Burdsall, and House set up a temporary camp, while the others returned to base to organize their own reconnaissance. Unfortunately, the exertion renewed Petzoldt's fever, and he spent the night shivering in his sleeping bag as the blazing sunshine suddenly turned into a blizzard.

The frustrating explorations, the changeable weather, and Petzoldt's fluctuating health continued for another week. There didn't seem to be any natural route. Photographs and maps of the northwest ridge and Savoia Pass made that approach appear promising, but only a few hundred feet above base camp two exploratory parties were turned back by precipitous cliffs and snowbound ice slopes.

Bates, Burdsall, and Houston explored the northeast ridge from several sides. No likely route was visible, but they felt the area might have possibilities.

Petzoldt and House climbed a thousand feet up the southern wall of the valley to scope out a possible route on the ridge that had foiled the Duke of the Abruzzi. Petzoldt had a lot of experience judging distant heights in the Tetons, and he felt he could get a pretty good idea of the size and pitch of cliffs and pillars. Using powerful binoculars, he soon spotted a series of ribs that formed a ridge to about 13,000 feet and culminated in a massive snow and ice plateau at about 25,000 feet. The summit cone rose some 2,200 feet above the top of the snowfield. Halfway up the pyramid an immense hanging glacier hovered over the upper northeast ridge and a corner of the Abruzzi Ridge. The two men thought the plateau could be reached and the overhang underpassed with care. The route might possibly lead to the top. But they couldn't be sure. The summit was covered by clouds.

They decided to set up Camp I on the Godwin-Austen Glacier at the foot of the Abruzzi Ridge. Then everyone would return to base camp to resupply and compare notes.

"The expedition spirits were now at very low ebb," House wrote in *Five Miles High*. "From one side of the mountain to the other we had been unable to find a route. Two weeks had been spent apparently to no other purpose than to convince us that no way we had seen was possible. We remembered rash statements we had made back in the United States to the effect that we were prepared to spend the whole summer reconnoitering and would do so until we found a way up the mountain. Two weeks of continual discouragement made the prospect of a whole summer of the same depressing to say the least. Every one of us would have liked to be clear of the whole business right then."

Houston called a planning conference. It was obvious that the Savoia Pass was out, but the men couldn't agree on the best attack to make. Houston and Burdsall were convinced that they should all concentrate on the northeast route. Petzoldt and House favored the Abruzzi Ridge as it looked safer than the other, and they knew it was climbable for some distance.

After a lengthy and animated debate, they compromised. They decided to move all supplies to Camp I and further investigate the Abruzzi. If that ridge proved hopeless, they would follow Houston and Burdsall's suggestion and check out the northeast. If neither route proved feasible, they would give up the idea of climbing the peak altogether and settle for making further reconnaissance for Wiessner's expedition.

Meanwhile, Streatfield would remain at base camp to supervise the distribution of food and supplies for the Sherpas to carry up to the higher camps as they were placed. Burdsall figured that the mountain was too much for him, so he volunteered to forego the high attack and stay below to help the captain and conduct scientific studies.

But locating suitable places for camps became difficult. As the mountain became steeper, finding flat spaces large enough for tent platforms was a problem. The campsites had to be close enough together to allow for both the transport of heavy loads in a single day's round trip and safe retreat in case of storms.

The party made its way up the peak in relays. On July 1, Petzoldt and House established themselves at Camp I. The next day they reconnoitered a second campsite while the others moved up to the first. On July 3, everybody packed up to Camp II.

Petzoldt, now feeling better, reconnoitered for Camp III with House on July 4. Encountering a ragged stone outcropping that paralleled a vertical ice wall, they had to set nine hundred feet of fixed rope to use as a handrail for the porters who would follow with full loads. Houston had to admit that the hardware came in handy, but using it made for lively camp discussion.

"When time lagged on our hands and we were tired of playing chess or reading, it was considered good sport to stir up a debate between Houston and Petzoldt on the use of pitons," House wrote. "The former held that their use mechanized mountain climbing to a point where one might just as well use a cog railway. He had been against their use from the start and had been aghast when he learned that the 10 which he thought sufficient had been augmented by an assortment of 50 purchased on our way through Paris. Slowly, under Petzoldt's pontifical arguments, he was won over to recognizing the protection they gave when natural belays were lacking. Even after they had proved indispensable for safeguarding the route higher up, however, he still could not condone their use and referred to them apologetically as 'iron ware.'"

The going got tougher as they climbed higher. Petzoldt and Houston battled steep walls and frozen slopes as they tried to locate a position for Camp IV. They picked their way through a ridge of broken rock that was bonded by snow and ice until they were blocked by a huge vertical pinnacle. Petzoldt laboriously edged up the tower into an overhanging crack, finally managing to reach the ledge. After he belayed Houston up to him, the pair worked their way over a narrow sloping shelf. Then an immense block of russet-colored rock stopped them. They turned back to the pinnacle, later christened "Petzoldt's Gendarme," and decided a small clearing above it was the only suitable location for the camp.

Like precarious landings on a flight of stairs, higher camps were established. The degree of climbing difficulty increased exponentially as the altitude increased.

On a mission to site Camp V at 22,000 feet, Bates and House were charged with finding a route over a reddish brown cliff that posed a giant obstruction above Camp IV. It took over an hour of chopping steps up an ice slope leading to the base of the cliff to reach their target. Once there, they found the ledges small and sloping, the cracks shallow and too narrow to insert fingers into. But there was a deep diagonal slash that looked promising.

About a foot from the base of the crack was a spur of rock about a yard high that Bates tied onto to belay House. House then made a tricky traverse into the crack, but the surface was so friable that for the first fifty feet he was only able to pound one piton in a tiny fissure to fix a rope.

The walls above that point were smooth as paper and the sides sloped inward. House rested for awhile, then, knowing Bates's belay would be useless as he climbed higher, he pressed hands and feet against the walls and friction climbed up the chimney.

After twenty feet, the smooth sides suddenly flared outward. House wedged his back against one side of the crack and his feet against the other to hitch his way up a few inches at a time.

Finally he could resume his vertical spread-eagle position to reach a ledge forty feet up the crack. He rested before tackling the pitch where the chimney iced over and narrowed to eighteen inches. Despite the monumental effort required and the enervating effects of high altitude, he succeeded in emerging from an opening eighty feet above Bates. This major obstacle of the Abruzzi Ridge was later named House's Chimney.

And so it went for two more weeks. While two men went ahead to find the next camp spot, the Sherpas and other team members hauled enough gear up from base to the last location to provide it with a ten days' supply of food and fuel in case of emergency delays due to inclement weather.

As they moved from 17,700 feet to 19,300, 20,700, and 22,000 feet (at Camp V), it became more and more difficult to handle the extreme altitude. Every step took extra effort, and, with their final goal seeming increasingly elusive, the men were easily depressed.

A raging blizzard held the climbers in camp on July 17. They snuggled down in their sleeping bags all day as violent winds shook their tiny tents and snow freezing on the canvas chilled even the inside air. But as fast as it had struck, the storm abated the next day. Petzoldt and Houston decided to pack up to Camp VI, which they had located two days before. Once the others hiked up to join them, they hoped to finally determine if the Abruzzi Ridge was climbable.

"Soon Petzoldt and I had passed our high point reached the day before and were well on our way up the famous Black Pyramid which caps Abruzzi ridge," Houston wrote in *Five Miles High*. "This was to be the crux of the climb for, ever since our first examination of it, we felt that the last thousand feet leading onto the great snow shoulder was by far the most difficult and inaccessible stretch of all."

Petzoldt led the way as they kicked steps up a steep snow gully that he had studied earlier from below. He was convinced that the route would lead to the top of the pinnacle. It did. At noon the two men shook hands at the top of the 24,500-foot Black Pyramid. They had mastered the Abruzzi Ridge and located a way to the snowfields on the mountain's shoulder.

Energized by their success, after a brief rest they cut eighty steps to traverse a steep slope leading to a jumble of ice chunks that had fallen from the shoulder. They threaded through the gigantic blocks of the ice fall and continued up to the top of the 30-degree snow slope. They could not see the summit past a small curving hill, but they felt they had found the key to K2. They turned back to Camp VI to tell the others.

The support party had their trials, too. After wrestling 35-pound packs from Camp V up a slope covered with loose stones, they struggled all afternoon to chop rocks from the ice to use as platforms for three tents. The difficulty of their task was aggravated by the fact that the only possible campsite was an uneven shelf that scarcely had room for one shelter. They were disgruntled and uncomfortable but stoic when Petzoldt and Houston arrived with their good news.

It was July 19—ninety-eight days since they had left New York. The rigorous climb, adverse weather, excessive altitude, and twinges of homesickness were taking their toll on the four Americans.

After reaching Camp VI, Houston wrote, "Our thoughts were frequently with our friends and families. We all felt that could we only be home for a few days, our energies and enthusiasm would be greatly strengthened, and we would attack the last few thousand feet with renewed vigor. Our nearest contact with home consisted of letters which we could be writing, but, alas, never seemed to do."

That evening they held a council of war about whether to make a bid for the summit or call it quits. Bates reckoned they had with them about ten days' supply of food and fuel. Houston figured they would probably have to pitch two more campsites in order to make a try at the summit. They agreed that would necessitate at least an additional two-week supply of rations, which would require several days of tedious transporting up from below.

On the other hand, they all knew that the lower encampments still had plenty of supplies. They wouldn't have to take along the tents and food in order to retreat to the base.

The salient point was the weather. There had already been a couple of severe storms. If the current clear skies continued, making a try for the summit would be no problem. But should the monsoon break in a few days, they could be stranded with little margin for safety. A French expedition in 1936 had been weathered in by snow and wind for two weeks. And an attempt to descend House's Chimney and Petzoldt's Gendarme, a route that was treacherous under prime conditions, would certainly lead to frostbite, or worse, in a storm.

From the onset, the first priority of the expedition was to get the six climbers and their Sherpas back down to the valley safely. Since conquering K2 without incident appeared questionable, the group decided in favor of caution.

After a lengthy debate, they took a vote. Two men would take a three-day supply of food and climb as high above Camp VII as they could in one day. If they didn't make the summit but thought there was a potential route for future parties the expedition could be deemed a success. Since Petzoldt and Houston had reconnoitered the route and were better acclimatized to the extreme altitude, they were chosen as the most likely to succeed.

As the morning sky ripened to a pale purple hue, they left Camp VI. Bates, House, and the Sherpa Pasang Kikuli volunteered to help carry supplies and establish Camp VII so the summit climbers could conserve their energy.

They retraced the route up to the Abruzzi Ridge where Petzoldt and Houston had climbed the day before. The five men roped up to cross a large snow gully and performed some tricky rock work to get themselves over a ledge leading to the top of the massive Black Pyramid. Once there, they stopped for a quick lunch.

But then they came upon the 45-degree snow slope where Petzoldt and Houston had painstakingly fixed ropes and chopped steps for a traverse. It was already three o'clock. The afternoon sun had melted the ice that had anchored the pitons that held the ropes. It would be slow going without the makeshift railing for support. If the others were to return to Camp VI before dark, they had to retreat at once. Petzoldt and Houston waved them good-bye and shouldered the extra packs. Transporting all five loads for their new camp, they struggled to a small site 3,550 feet beneath the summit. They dropped their gear and dug a platform for their tent in the deep snow.

When they were finally settled under flapping canvas, they were famished and cold. Petzoldt assembled the stove, fueled it with gasoline, and placed a piece of solidified alcohol called *meta* on the bottom to warm the burner and vaporize the gasoline. Houston scooped snow into the aluminum pot to boil water for tea and pemmican, the compressed patties of dried beef, fruit, and suet they would have for dinner. But, when Petzoldt dug into the food pack for matches to light the fuel, there were none.

"My God," he said. "They forgot to pack the matches."

Both men knew this oversight could spell success or failure for the expedition. Without the ability to light a stove and melt snow for food and water, they would have to scuttle any attempt on the summit.

"I think I might have some," Houston said, digging into his pocket.

He pulled out nine scruffy matches. Four were in a book of safety matches that had to be struck on a chemically prepared friction surface. He had bought them in Kashmir. They were extremely fragile.

The other five were the wooden strike-anywhere variety which had survived the two-and-a-half month trip from New York. These had been wet and sun-dried numerous times, and it would be only after much rubbing and greasing that they could be coaxed to spark above an altitude of 20,000 feet, where the air is thin and oxygen scarce.

Houston and Petzoldt had been higher than 20,000 feet for the last sixteen days. Now at 24,700 feet and in sub-zero temperatures, the nine unreliable matches were all they had to keep them going.

Petzoldt grabbed an ever-strike match stick and struck it. It flared, fizzled, and died. Houston pulled off a safety match and flicked it across the friction pad. The head broke off.

Petzoldt forcefully struck another wooden match. It burst into flame. With relief, he lit the stove and started to boil a pot of snow.

"This neglect must have been an evidence of altitude effect," Houston later said.

The possibility wasn't unlikely. The Americans had been over 17,000 feet for forty days, since they left base camp. People were known to go berserk and chase after one another with ice axes at such high elevations. Excessive fatigue, dizziness, and nausea were common symptoms. Disorientation, loss of memory, and personality changes were frequent complaints on mountaineering adventures. Forgetting to pack matches, though a critical oversight, was understandable. But the men melted an extra supply of water for morning in case the remaining matches were faulty.

They crawled into their warm bags early in anticipation of an exciting day. Houston later reported their conversation:

> "I think the weather looks settled," said Paul.
>
> "I'm sure of it," I replied, feeling all the while that the clouds had looked rather ominous, and wondering if *he* had the same doubts.
>
> "If only the wind holds off, the cold won't be too bad."
>
> We each thought for a moment about numb fingers and toes on other mornings before the sun reached us.
>
> "Are those matches safe?" from Paul.
>
> "They're here in my sleeper."
>
> "We'd be out of luck with no matches."
>
> Silence.
>
> "Well, tomorrow's the big day. Let's get some sleep."

A warming sun welcomed them next morning. It took three more matches to light the stove, but they were able to enjoy a warm breakfast before starting.

They clamped crampons onto their boots, tied into a sixty-foot rope, and plodded up a shoulder of knee-deep snow, finally reaching the high point of their previous reconnaissance trip, where they stopped to take pictures.

From the top of the shoulder the slopes gentled, but the consistency of the snow became irregular and alternated between deep powder, ice crust that was barely penetrated by their crampons, and frost feathers formed by tempestous winds and extreme low temperatures. These mountains of soft snow drifted into massive ice shelves that could break into huge pieces and crash downhill with a single misstep.

They made a cautious crossing over a narrow snow bridge that took them to a higher slope. The soft snow swallowed them up to their hips. Every step took monumental effort. Houston began to feel the effects of the altitude, and his legs felt strangely weak.

As tired as he was, Petzoldt fell into the conscious rhythmic breathing pattern that he had been perfecting since his climbs in Mexico. Instead of pushing forward as fast as possible until his lungs ached and he was panting for breath, he took even breaths and adjusted the number of steps to the steepness of the terrain. On flatter places, he took one breath per step; as the elevation increased, he changed his pace to two or three breaths per step, maintaining the same breathing rhythm. He was convinced that this new method, along with additional salt in his diet, was what was keeping him stronger than the others.

By one o'clock they stood atop a massive snowfield leading up to what appeared to be the final cone, which rose beyond an ice cliff, barely 300 yards away. But the frozen shelf, littered with ice fall from above, augured avalanche danger. They would have to cross swiftly. They had lunch and rested before coiling their ropes to dry in the sun while they were gone.

Although the climb had been strenuous, Petzoldt was back to peak condition and handling the exertion and altitude well. He took the lead and kicked steps up the slope.

Houston was struggling. "My progress was ludicrously slow," he wrote. "Every inch I gained in altitude was an effort. My legs were so weak I was forced to rest every five or six steps, and soon fatigue made me forget all danger from above."

He gave up at the base of the final cone. "I've reached my limit," he shouted to Petzoldt.

Petzoldt later remembered the ensuing events. He had stopped climbing and turned to look at his partner. Houston was slumped against a giant boulder. It appeared that his legs had given out at 26,000 feet. He was so fatigued that he had unconsciously rested where there could be danger of ice falls from above. Despite the four Shetland sweaters, flannel shirts, and a windproof glacier suit, the wiry climber was huddled into himself against the frigid, windless air. He was pale and breathing heavily. Petzoldt knew that the exhausted man should not continue.

"Why don't you rest there and I'll go on a bit further," Petzoldt called. "I want to go on and get over to the left side of this ice cliff to see if there's a climbable route to the top. We could go home claiming our expedition a success!"

Petzoldt thought Houston muttered something about damned German daredevils. Houston has no recollection of making such a statement. He only remembers staggering back to where they had left the ropes and lying down to rest in the sun.

While Houston struggled to safety, Petzoldt walked up the slope, traversed under the ice cliff, and climbed a short way up the gully that led toward the summit. There was broken rock and snow, but it did not look too difficult. At the pyramid base, there was a large flat area suitable for camping. It appeared that climbing onward toward the summit itself would not be as tricky as much of the lower part of the ascent had been. He was convinced that a way to the top would prove to be direct and relatively easy. He stopped to take notes and photograph the evidence. Then, tearfully, he clung to the rock and stared at the mountain for a long time.

Starting back toward the platform where Houston waited, he finally felt his exhaustion. All he could think about was a cup of hot tea and the warmth of a sleeping bag. He pushed himself across the ice fall then gave a victory whoop and stumbled into Houston's arms. Any earlier disagreement was forgotten.

"The whole world was deathly still," Houston later wrote, "not even the clatter of rock falls broke the calm. All the peaks about us seemed breathlessly awaiting our descent. We trudged down to Camp VII in a deepening twilight. About us the mountains turned first pink, then lavender, then purple. We reached camp safely, exhausted and cold, but curiously content."

The specter of altitude sickness seemed all the more real that night. Houston admitted that this illness was probably responsible for his collapse and inability to continue up the final pyramid.

"I counted my pulse," he said. "It was 135, whereas normally at sea level it is 50. I thought of all sorts of notes to write in the little book I carried, but somehow didn't have the mental energy to put them down."

Petzoldt, in turn, allowed that the altitude might have affected his judgment, leading him to decide to climb alone. Nothing was said about the flaring tempers.

Anxious to get their meal and settle down for the night, they carefully unwrapped the last three matches that remained after cooking breakfast. They dried each one and waxed the tips before attempting a strike. Again, it was the third match that finally flamed. Too exhausted for conversation, they ate quickly but were careful to melt extra snow so they would have water for the morning.

Later, before turning off his flashlight and going to sleep, Petzoldt decided to test his faculties for the affects of altitude. If he could write a poem, he wasn't nuts yet, he figured. He picked up pencil and notebook and wrote:

> *In early dawn, in aching cold,*
> *I stopped a moment to behold*
> *The sun, and saw it paint in rainbowed glow*
> *Endless mountains, ice and snow,*
> *In Karakorum's windswept dawn.*

"Okay, so far," he thought.

Petzoldt felt satisfaction in having discovered a route to the summit, but he was haunted by the suspicion that the expedition's chance for real success had been curtailed by poor planning. He had sensed it at Camp III but didn't admit it to himself. He thought at that time they had not packed enough food to the higher camps to allow time for a proper assault on the peak.

He tried to stifle his doubts the next morning as they breakfasted on cold water, crackers, and jam. His spirits picked up as they packed up camp, traversed to the Black Pyramid, and hiked toward Camp VI.

The reunion with Bates and House was filled with congratulatory hugs and back-slapping, and camp was broken quickly. They hoisted all of their equipment and headed down to Camp IV, and on to base camp next day.

"There was a big celebration when we got back to camp," Petzoldt remembers. "We had extra gasoline, so heated up some water and had our first bath in two months. We changed into clean clothes. And we got out the Hudson's Bay Demerara rum. It's the one that's 150 proof. If you take it straight it would burn your tonsils. We poured it with water and had a couple of drinks, but in our condition at that altitude, one drink was equal to about three. So we were singing and having a great time."

The weary men hoped that the porters who were coming to get them would bring mail. And soon. Some of the climbers played chess, Petzoldt lounged on an air mattress with a copy of *Blackwood's* magazine, and Houston composed his official press release and dispatch to the American Alpine Club.

"The high clouds had grown thicker and there was an ominous ring around the sun, which we photographed from all angles, as if to justify our abandonment of the attack," Houston wrote later.

Petzoldt never agreed with what Houston had written, and the debate continues to this day.

"Jesus Christ," Petzoldt later said. "We weren't turned back by bad weather. We made up our mind not to climb the mountain. If we'd have brought up a little bit more food and planned to get to the summit, we could have gone back as conquerors of K2!"

But according to Houston, "Our mandate from the American Alpine Club was to find a feasible route. We never expected to summit. We never expected to get as high as we did.

"So we were feeling pretty pleased with ourselves for having done what we did. I don't think we ever seriously considered regrouping and trying again. The weather did deteriorate—not dramatically—but it deteriorated. So the decision in terms of the ethic of those days was correct. In terms of today, we were chicken."

In the book about the expedition House contributed his opinion,

> Ten days after leaving Base Camp the region around K 2 appeared to be still in clouds. This observation was made from about 13,000 feet on the edge of the Deosai Plains above Skardu. What we had been able to see of the interior of the range during that time suggested continued storms. Our crossing of the Skoro La (16,700 ft.) was in a storm which seemed confined to the N. or K 2 side of the pass. Whether the apparent continued stormy weather would have been serious enough to prevent climbing, there is no way of telling. It is possible that in character it was no different from what had been experienced on K 2—namely a succession of good and bad days. From the generally low observation points in the valleys it is quite possible that the clouds which seemed to be covering the whole of the interior of the Karakorum were only on the tops of the outer, lower peaks and did not represent a continuous storm at all. This would fit in with what was often observed from K 2, namely clouds on surrounding outer mountains, but good weather on K 2 itself.
>
> It seems safer, therefore, not to regard it as a definite break in the weather, but rather as a temporary break which might have

been followed by stretches of good weather such as were experienced on K 2 during June and July.

A few tempers flared on the final retreat as the men attempted to rationalize their actions. But officially Houston reported to the *Himalayan Journal*, "Ours was a united party in every sense; our shared experiences can never be forgotten. Our purpose, reconnaissance, was completely accomplished, and a way was found by which, with the smile of good fortune, a second party may reach the summit."

On August 10, the group returned to the capital city of the Vale of Kashmir. Srinagar, built on the shores of the Jhelum River and Lake Dal, was reminiscent of Venice. Rows of ornate wooden houses with elaborately carved balconies jutted over the water, where houseboats and large flat-bottomed *dongas* served as hotels and homes for Europeans, who were not allowed to own property. The American team rented a houseboat named *The Royal Family*, where they officially closed the expedition with a high tea. They spent a few days boating on Lake Dal, visiting the fabled Shalimar Gardens, and sorting out equipment before sailing back to America.

Then one evening, while they were sipping cocktails, someone said, "It seems foolish to have come this far and then sail directly home without seeing more of the Far East."

"Why not hire a bus and driver?" another chimed in. "Drive from Rawalpindi up through the Khyber Pass and then tour Afghanistan and Iran on the way home."

Everybody thought this was a grand idea and decided to cash in their return tickets. Except Petzoldt. There was no way he could afford such a trip. The ship ticket money wasn't even enough to pay for the food and incidentals he would need to get him back to the United States. Unlike the others, he couldn't wire home for a couple of thousand dollars if he needed it. But he was damned if he'd admit it.

So when the time came to collect the tickets, Petzoldt cashed his in but said he wouldn't be joining the excursion.

"I'm going to stay on in India awhile," he told them. He wasn't sure how he would manage, but he knew something would turn up. It always did.

CHAPTER 6

Intrigue in India

DURING THE WEEK THE TEAM SPENT ON THE HOUSEBOAT, PETZOLDT DID some exploring on his own. Just as he had done on his trip to Windsor and Europe, he mixed with the local people in order to learn more about their customs and way of life.

He was particularly interested in eastern religions. He had never been religious himself. His parents' piety had not rubbed off on him, and he was inclined to dismiss organized religion as "hocus pocus." He considered himself a realist and had trouble understanding those who based their lives on blind faith.

"There's a pattern that people follow that go for this sort of thing," he says. "There are people that believe that there's something out there with some sort of mind that knows all. So if you believe in a God that watches every sparrow or whatever, then it's easy. All you have to do is click a switch to change to Karma, the Great White Master, ancient philosophy, the Golden Age, Shangri La, and the whole thing that people have been arguing since the ancient Greek philosophers. What is real! The whole thing is based upon a belief that out there somewhere is reality, and life is only a shadow of reality."

Since coming to India he had been impressed by the pervasiveness of theology. Muezzins sang from minarets to call the faithful to prayer.

Hindu *sadhus* would fall into trances and will their minds to control their heartbeat, exist for days without food, stop breathing for long periods of time, and moderate other bodily functions.

Ecstatic crowds celebrated death at funeral pyres and purified themselves in rivers flowing to the Ganges. Jains refused to kill a bug in case it was someone reincarnated, and sacred cattle snarled traffic at will. The fanaticism eclipsed that at the "Holy Roller" camp meetings he had witnessed as a child, and he wanted to learn more about the mysticism that triggered it.

One day he struck up a conversation with Dr. and Mrs. Johnson,* who were spending the summer in a rented houseboat near *The Royal Family*. The doctor was slight of build, wore a long white beard, and adopted the immense turban and loosely woven cotton suits of India. He told Petzoldt that he and his wife were in Srinagar to escape the awful heat of the Punjab, where they made their permanent home in a little village.

Dr. Johnson was a retired physician and surgeon from Sutter City, California. He first came to India as a young Baptist missionary but became disillusioned after a few years and returned to the States to study medicine at the University of Chicago. After earning his degree, he practiced in California, where he successfully opened his own little hospital.

Later the doctor renounced the Baptist faith and yearned to find a true path to salvation. He tried Catholicism to no avail. Finally, after studying books on Indian mysticism, he read about the Radhi Soami sect in the small village of Dera Baba Jaimal Singh near the city of Amritsar in northern India.

The spiritual leader of the cult, S. Sewan Singh, claimed to be "one with God." Within ten years, the shrewd and charismatic guru had transformed a modest ministry serving a handful of poor people into a highly respected following of 250,000 converts, many of them prominent Indians. Johnson corresponded with the master, and in

---

*Petzoldt cannot recall Dr. Johnson's first name, nor is it mentioned in the official letters and reports. Possibly because of this fact, or as legal precaution, Patricia Petzoldt changed Johnson's name to Barker in her book *On Top of the World*, in which she used fictitious names for other people and places as well.

1932 he returned to India and became a follower.

The doctor and Indian master became close friends. Johnson established a tuberculosis sanitarium and small clinic and spent many hours writing books and articles with the hope of attracting more American converts.

Two years later he married former San Franciscan Elizabeth Bruce, who served as his nurse and had a small business selling cosmetics which she compounded from local herbs. Bruce, a rather severe-looking woman in her mid-forties, had straight brown hair and wore sacklike cotton dresses. Having lived in India for many years, she had become radical in her mysticism.

Although Petzoldt was not a "seeker," he related intellectually to the doctor's grasp of philosophy and his inquiries into various religions. They spent hours debating.

"All religions have a right and wrong," Petzoldt would say. "When you've got God on your side and God says you're right, then look out. Because if you're right, everybody else that thinks differently from you is wrong.

"All down the ages we've had religions killing one another. They're still killing one another. Maybe it's hopeless. Maybe this ideal that some way people can live in peace and get together to have a workable system is impossible."

Johnson argued that what happened in this world was unimportant because the master's lessons held the true key to peace. He had performed many miracles to prove it.

"If we join the master and do as he bids, our Karma will be forgiven," he said.

Followers of the master would not have to pass through the endless cycles of reincarnation to reach Nirvana that were prescribed by Mahatma Gandhi and other sects, he explained. They would achieve perfection sooner.

"The express route to paradise," Petzoldt quipped. The doctor allowed him his joke, but his wife didn't smile.

It was nearing the end of August, and the Johnsons were preparing to leave Srinagar about the same time the K2 party was taking off for their final tour. Johnson saw that Petzoldt was in a bind, being alone in India with not enough money to get him all the way home.

He was impressed with the depth of his curiosity about the sect and privately hoped he could lure the young American into the fold. He invited him to drive down to the colony with him and his wife to meet the master.

"I'm getting old," he said. "Practicing medicine and running the clinic is getting to be too much for me. And my wife has more than she can handle with nursing, the cosmetic business, and managing the sanitarium. If you will stay on and take over some of our responsibilities, we'll give you a third of our earnings."

"I'm afraid I can't do that," Petzoldt said. "I've been away from my wife for more than three months."

"Well then how about coming as an employee? We'll pay you a monthly salary for helping manage the hospital and being Elizabeth's salesman and business manager. We'll even send for your wife and take care of her passage to India," the doctor said. "We need you."

Petzoldt promised to think about it. The idea of remaining in India and having an opportunity to really understand the people and their religion intrigued him. And it would be a relief not to be as stranded and broke as he anticipated he would be after the K2 team left. The next day he told the doctor he would accept the invitation, at least until he heard if Bernice was willing to join him.

Bernice had been looking forward to his coming back to Wyoming so they could make a proper home and settle into a normal life. The prospect of a trip to India all by herself was exciting but frightening. She had never traveled alone. And being a Catholic, the idea of living in the commune of an Indian guru was interesting but a bit disturbing.

Yet she could tell that Petzoldt was too immersed in India to leave right away. After the exchange of a few letters, they decided they would give the doctor's offer a try, with the understanding that if they didn't like it, they could quit any time and go home.

Bernice sailed from Seattle in November of 1938 on the freighter *Hikawa Maru*. After several one- and two-day calls at ports in Japan and China and a transfer to the *Suwa Mara*, she spent a lonely Christmas in Singapore before continuing to Colombo, Ceylon, where Petzoldt was to meet her.

But the ship arrived a day early, and he was not at the dock. Bernice spent an anxious night in a hotel then headed for the Thomas Cook offices the next morning to leave a message of where she could be reached.

On the way to the travel bureau, she saw "a tall, thin man wearing a light blue cotton suit and the usual sun helmet worn by most Europeans in those parts." It was Petzoldt. She ran to catch him by surprise.

"I was shocked at how thin he'd become," she wrote. "He had lost thirty pounds since I'd seen him, and for a moment this big rough husband of mine seemed almost fragile." The next morning they boarded a steamer for a one-day cruise to India. Six more days by train brought them to the railroad station in Beas on the night of January 3, 1939.

Johnson had dispatched a two-wheeled cart called a tonga to meet them. After a bumpy five-mile ride through the dark countryside dotted with fields of wheat and maize, they arrived at the village of Dera Baba Jaimal Singh and stopped at the Johnson compound.

The complex consisted of several masonry buildings—a small hospital, a central residence enclosed by a fence, and a long, white, two-story sanitarium, which was where they would stay. "Home," Petzoldt said as he helped Bernice out of the cart.

They climbed a steep flight of stairs to an open veranda which ran the entire length of the second floor. Their apartment was one of three that opened onto the balcony overlooking the Beas River.

Petzoldt and the driver carried the luggage into the bedroom and lit the oil lamps to reveal an attractive room with a high ceiling, twin beds, and a couple of armchairs. A small marble fireplace at one end of the room crackled with burning wood chips and charcoal. A modest study was on one side of the room and a peculiar bathroom on the other. The plumbing fixtures consisted of a freestanding tin tub and a toilet-seat stool placed over a china bowl. Pails of water, soap, and towels were close at hand.

They met Mrs. Johnson on the way to breakfast the next morning. Bernice thought their hostess seemed to be in a rather trancelike state as she slowly approached them in the garden. When Petzoldt introduced them, Mrs. Johnson stared at Bernice, then said, "It is just as I thought." Then she escorted them through the gate to her residence.

The main house stood behind a large enclosed courtyard. French doors opened onto the patio from both the living room and dining room. The kitchen, where Mrs. Johnson spent many hours concocting beauty potions and vegetarian meals, was in the rear. She and her husband lived upstairs.

The other residents had already gathered at the table: Mr. and Mrs. Harry Remsten, wealthy Californians who were potential converts; David Elliott, a forty-year veteran of schoolteaching in Kansas who had embraced the cult; Indomati, an Indian princess being treated for tuberculosis; and Bhagat Singh, an attorney who was slated to become the next guru of the sect.

Earlier while they were dressing, Petzoldt, remembering his wife's bent towards sarcastic humor, had cautioned her. "Now remember, these people are going to seem strange to you, and you will be equally strange to them. It might be better if you kept quiet for a while until you understand their way of thinking a little better. Just sit back and listen for a few days."

After breakfast, Bernice agreed that the people were certainly different. And she asked Petzoldt why there was a double-barrel shotgun leaning against the living room wall.

"Rabid dogs," he said. "We have to shoot them from time to time. It's my job because nobody else wants to harm their Karma by killing an animal. We keep the gun loaded so if someone reports a mad dog I can grab it fast and run out to shoot it."

That afternoon he gave her a tour of the village. They passed a few small stalls displaying food and household goods, then strolled to the town center, where the master's residence stood. A high rock wall isolated the two-story masonry home from the daily hubbub. The spiraled marble towers of two Radhi Soami temples dominated the skyline and loomed as an anomaly among the hovels clustered around them.

"How do the people live?" Bernice asked. "Some of them have patches or small fields of grain and vegetables they cultivate on the outskirts of town," Petzoldt said. "They live in the village but each morning they go out to their fields. In the evenings they return about sundown, in time for evening worship. They gather near the temple and listen to the master speak." "Tell me about the cult," she said.

Petzoldt explained the unconditional obedience to the master that was required to attain Nirvana without completing the thousands of life cycles mandated by many eastern religions. Members of the master's commune must place all of their money in a common fund, eat the same food, gather each night at the temple to worship and listen to the master speak, and meditate to free their minds from their bodies and reach another plane.

"Several of them claim to have talked with Christ and Buddha and other ancient philosophers on these excursions to higher realms," he said. "The old doctor told me he would go there and here was the whole gang—Jesus Christ, Confucius, Muhammad, Plato, Aristotle, the whole bunch of them."

"Have you tried meditation?" Bernice asked as they walked back to the apartment.

"Of course," he said. "I tried it every day for awhile. One time I think I was on the verge of achieving the state I've been instructed to watch for."

"I think concentration as they describe it would be a cinch for me," she laughed. "I've never had any trouble throwing my mind into a blank."

"They have a little hocus pocus system," he said. "You close your eyes and they put their thumbs in your ears, which gives you a funny, drifting-off feeling. Then you're supposed to cut off every idea and everything that comes into your mind and try to be a blank. You concentrate on nothing. You can't concentrate because if you do concentrate on something then you're having ideas and stuff flowing through your mind. You get so it's nothing. Nothing. Then you're fading out, something like going to sleep in a car and not hearing the motor."

"What happened to you when you almost reached this trancelike state?"

"At first I didn't think that it happened. I thought these thousands of people were pretending. Then I had this experience.

"I had a preconceived idea in my mind of a Shangri La, so that's what I went through. I was sort of floating around in this beautiful land with the most pleasant sensation. Much more pleasant than anything I've ever had before or since—sex, the marijuana I smoked once in college, nice alcoholic glows that I've had, standing on top of mountains, moments of triumph—any of those high spots in my life have never compared. It was beautiful, good, a complete release.

"Then I brought myself back to reality. I stopped because I was afraid of it. I feared that I could get hooked."

That evening he took Bernice to the temple so she could see the master in action. It was almost sundown and hundreds of people spread their blankets on the ground and waited for the holy man to appear.

When Singh finally arrived, he climbed to a raised platform while the entire crowd prostrated themselves before him. He was a handsome man, taller than most Sikhs, and about fifty years old. He made a striking picture in his flowing robes as he stood silently for a few moments gazing far into the distance. The crowd sat motionless.

He spoke in Urdu, a literary form of the Hindustani language. His voice was low but commanding, and the words sounded rhythmic and melodic, like poetry. Petzoldt, who was studying the language, could understand a little bit, but Bernice had no idea what he was saying. Still, the effect of his presence was profound.

At one point during the evening, Bernice felt the other worshippers staring at her as if she were some sort of negative influence.

"I had a queer feeling when the crowd of people turned and looked at me," she told Petzoldt later.

"These people are difficult for me to understand and I've been around them longer than you have," he said. "But try to remember that all people are alike. These people are normal enough. Remember how serious people at home can get about their religion?"

Over four months at the colony had taught Petzoldt not to be surprised at anything. Mrs. Johnson ran the compound like a boot camp, and everyone from the Indian princess to the wealthy Americans was slightly afraid of her.

Johnson was kindly and professionally competent, but some of his medical practices were alarming. Although Petzoldt officially functioned as a bookkeeper, advisor, and cosmetic salesman, the doctor taught him how to administer anesthetic and treat the everyday sores and wounds the local villagers suffered.

Then about three o'clock one morning, he was summoned to the hospital. When he arrived, Johnson told him they were going to perform an emergency operation. An Indian had been brought in with what appeared to be a ruptured appendix. Petzoldt was to give the anesthetic.

Petzoldt knew that the villagers used their ancient folk remedies for everything and only came to the doctor as a last resort. When he saw the patient and started to give him ether, he didn't think the man had much chance to survive.

Just as Johnson was about to begin the surgery, he suddenly stopped and handed the scalpel to Petzoldt.

"My hands are too unsteady tonight," he said. "Cut here."

Petzoldt looked at the doctor in disbelief. Johnson nodded. Petzoldt took a deep breath and made the incision. What happened next almost knocked him over. Since there had not been enough time to boil water, the doctor told a servant to hurry to the well, pump a bucketful, and bring it back fast. Then he instructed Petzoldt to pour water into the open incision while he plunged his hands into the patient's belly and sloshed off a handful of intestine. When the deed was done, he carefully replaced the innards, inserted a drainage tube, and sewed up the patient. The Indian recovered.

It was more difficult for Bernice to assimilate into the colony. While Petzoldt worked on the accounts or was out selling creams and lotions, she often stayed in her room to read. But she missed having friends and chatty phone calls. Other than Petzoldt, the only person she could talk with here was the doctor.

Sometimes, when Johnson was not busy at the clinic, she had long conversations with him. The doctor talked of nothing but the master, yet he never pushed her to commit to the sect.

Mrs. Johnson, however, often seemed withdrawn and suspicious. She treated Bernice civilly but didn't go out of her way to make her feel welcome.

As for the other followers, Bernice noticed "some fishy glances now and then." No one said anything to her about being a negative influence, but the discomfort she felt at the master's prayer meeting stayed with her.

"They want to try and convert you," Petzoldt said when she expressed her concerns. "Just try to have an open mind. Who knows, maybe you will decide to retire to a cave in the hills and meditate for a few years."

One evening at dinner, her composure broke when the Johnsons and the other tenants swept into an animated discussion of "the serpent power" at the base of the spine.

One of the principles of hatha yoga, which is predicated on a physiological theory, is that in each individual there exists a dormant divine potency called a *kundalini*. The *sushumna*, a vein running up the backbone, passes from the *kundalini* through six psychic centers called *chakras*, or wheels, and terminates at the supreme psychic center atop the skull, the *shasrara*.

To achieve complete enlightenment, a believer must develop his will so intensely that he can bring all his automatic body processes under the control of his mind. By raising the feminine *kundalini* up the *sushumna* and through one *chakra* to another until it unites with the masculine *shasrara*, he may achieve salvation.

All through dinner the cultists talked of nothing else. As the minutes ticked towards an hour, they became more and more excited. Bernice became more and more amazed that grown people could believe that a person who mysteriously "raised" some invisible thing at the bottom of the spine would automatically become all-powerful and one with God.

"Perhaps a swift kick in the rear end would do the trick as well," she said.

Dead silence.

Petzoldt blanched. "It's getting late," he said nervously. "Would you excuse us?"

When they got to their room, Bernice apologized for her blunder. "You'd better tell Mrs. Johnson," he said.

The next morning, Mrs. Johnson, standing stoically by the stove stirring a pot of herbs, nodded and smiled unconvincingly when Bernice said she was sorry about her remark. Bernice persisted with a one-way conversation until she finally got a rise from the woman by admitting that she had attempted meditation.

Mrs. Johnson turned to face her. "You will know when you are getting close," she said.

"How?" Bernice asked, relieved that the atmosphere had thawed.

"One day you will hear bells. At first they will be far away. Then they will come closer."

A few days later, Bernice noticed a strange ringing in her ears. She also felt dizzy and nauseated. The symptoms were sporadic at first, and then she began to throw up after every meal. One morning she was too ill to get out of bed. Petzoldt went after Johnson.

> "Do you remember when you first had the ringing?" he asked as he prepared a medication.
>
> I answered unthinkingly, "Well, it was always after meals that I felt the worst."
>
> I was suddenly shocked and frightened and cold. I sat staring at Paul and Dr. [Johnson].
>
> Dr. [Johnson] said, "I see." He left some medicine for me to take.
>
> When he was gone I looked at the breakfast tray.
>
> Paul also looked at it, and I could see he was thinking the same thing I was.
>
> "We may be mistaken, of course," he said, "but we won't take any chances. Don't touch the food on the tray. I'll go to the market and get something to tide you over, then we'll see what we can do."

Although Bernice's fertile imagination convinced her that she was being poisoned, Petzoldt thought it far more likely that Mrs. Johnson tainted the food to make her a little sick and teach her a lesson. The chance that his wife suffered from the typical intestinal problems endured by most newcomers to India was also possible. Nevertheless, he thought it wise to control what she ate for awhile.

By January 25, after three days of living on fruit that could be peeled, which was all her husband dared purchase at the village market, Bernice felt much better. She was even hungry. That evening Petzoldt offered to bring her a hot meal from his own plate at dinner.

He arrived in the dining room just as the Johnsons, the Remstens, Elliott, the lawyer Singh, and Indomati were seating themselves. He took his seat and waited to be served. When the servant brought his plate, he picked it up, stood and gathered some silverware, then excused himself. Bernice later described what happened next:

> Mrs. [Johnson] said, "Where are you going?"
> "I'm taking this to Mrs. Petzoldt," Paul replied.

"Let me have it," Mrs. [Johnson] said, "and I'll send one of the servants with it. Or better still, I'll have a plate fixed in the kitchen and sent to her room."

But Paul held on to the plate of food. He said, "No thank you, Mrs. [Johnson], don't bother. I'd rather take it to her myself."

By this time Mrs. [Johnson] had risen and stood clutching the table in an agitated manner. As Paul started toward the door, she screeched, "Give me that plate!"

Paul paused and said coldly, "Perhaps you have something you'd like to add to it?"

Mrs. Johnson wailed, pushed her chair aside, and bolted for the courtyard. While everyone watched in stunned disbelief, she ran from the yard back into the room. Petzoldt saw her going for the shotgun.

He dropped the plate and rushed through the door connecting the dining and living rooms. Just as he reached Mrs. Johnson, she aimed the gun at him point blank. He grabbed the stock and twisted it sideways, but the hysterical woman fought him off, and it was all he could do to keep control of the weapon.

While Petzoldt struggled with Mrs. Johnson, Dr. Johnson rushed up behind his wife and tried to convince her to release the gun. Recognizing that she was beyond reasoning, he hurried into the courtyard, probably intent on summoning servants for help.

Meanwhile, Elliott and the attorney Singh ran into the room and jumped on Petzoldt's back, pummeling him on the head. Petzoldt shrugged off the two men and wrenched the shotgun from Mrs. Johnson's hands. Then he threw the gun out of an open window and bolted into the dark courtyard just as Dr. Johnson returned.

Not seeing who it was, and intent on his escape, Petzoldt collided with the old man. He heard someone fall to the stone floor but didn't dare stop to investigate who it was. He could hear screaming behind him as he fled.

Bernice, alarmed at the commotion, threw on some clothes and hurried out to see what was causing the disturbance. She met Petzoldt on the stairs.

"Oh God! Something terrible has happened!" he said.

He told her about Mrs. Johnson's fury over the plate, how she had threatened him with the shotgun, his desperate escape.

"I knocked someone down in the courtyard," he said "I think he might be hurt."

Petzoldt didn't dare return to the main house yet. He asked Bernice to find out who he had bumped into and check his condition.

By the time Bernice got to the Johnson residence, the gate was locked. She talked a servant into letting her in. When she entered the living room she saw the other guests milling about somberly. Johnson was lying unconscious on the couch. He was bleeding from the nose, streaks of blood stained his long white beard, and his breathing was labored. Mrs. Johnson, looking dazed, bent over him.

Bernice watched them for a few minutes then returned to the apartment. She put her arms around Petzoldt and told him it was Johnson that he had run into.

"How is he?" he asked.

"I can't tell. He's bleeding some. Perhaps he's dying."

Finally Petzoldt said, "Go back in and come out every so often and tell me how he's getting along."

A few hours later she came back to tell him Johnson had died at one o'clock in the morning.

They sat by the fireplace trying to figure out what they would do next. Someone knocked on the door. It was Bhagat Singh, the attorney. He wanted to talk with them before the police arrived.

Singh explained that one of the main tenets of the Radhi Soami cult was peace and passive resistance to attack. Scandal and publicity, which could result from revealing that Mrs. Johnson had brandished a shotgun in a quarrel with other inmates of the colony, would be extremely damaging.

He told the Petzoldts that he had fabricated an official explanation of the accident and instructed all of the other witnesses to testify accordingly. If Petzoldt would go along with the statement and plead guilty, they would get the charge of culpable homicide reduced to one of simple hurt. If he didn't cooperate, the cult would make a very bad case against him.

"You are aware, I'm sure, that Mrs. Johnson is in complete control of everything said or done at the complex," he said. "It is especially evident that the elderly gentleman, Donald Elliott, is under her influence and apparently afraid of her.

"We will say that you tried to attack Dr. Johnson and Elliott attempted to protect him. You were so infuriated that you took a swing at him, but missed when he ducked. Instead, the blow struck Dr. Johnson full in his face and knocked him down, the back of his head striking the concrete door sill as he fell."

As Bernice told the story later, he then elaborated further:

> "Nothing must be mentioned of the quarrel, or the reasons for the quarrel, or the gun, or the struggle. It is much better this way for all of us. Don't you think so? Mrs. [Johnson] just gets confused at times. That's all. She's not a bad woman, and she is suffering now from the loss of her husband."
>
> Petzoldt said, "But why did you jump on my back tonight?"
>
> The Indian attorney batted his eyes, and looked suspiciously about him. "It was for the best," he explained in a soft voice. "You see, if you had gotten the gun you might have killed us all. Mrs. [Johnson] cannot shoot. I have seen her try to shoot the mad dogs and she cannot. She misses."
>
> "Oh, God," Paul muttered, rubbing his hand over his face.

The Criminal Investigation Department operatives from Amritsar arrived around three o'clock the next afternoon. Singh related his concocted version of events, Petzoldt pled guilty as advised, and, according to one of the official reports, "the police had no reason to smell a rat." Petzoldt was taken to Beas.

The following afternoon, Petzoldt sent Bernice a note saying that the English chief of police had taken him home instead of booking him in jail. He told her not to worry. Then he suggested she visit the master and try to determine his attitude about the situation.

She set out for the master's residence about nine the next morning. Hoping to avoid attention, she draped a black scarf over her head and wore a long robe and native sandals. She met Petzoldt's Urdu teacher when she was almost at the village. She asked the friendly old man for advice.

"He said gently, 'Do not be perturbed Mrs. Petzoldt Paul. The master understands all. Only remember this, do not speak to him unless he first speaks to you. You must also not leave the chamber until he precedes you.'"

The teacher escorted her to the master's residence and instructed a guard to open the gate and announce her. She followed the servant up winding marble steps to a large golden trough, where she removed her sandals and washed her feet. Then she followed him down a hall and into a magnificent room.

"The master was seated in a chair at the far end of the room. He didn't appear to see me. I prostrated myself at his feet and, after what I considered a decent interval, raised up, crossed my legs under me, and sat waiting. I remembered that the Urdu teacher had told me not to speak until the master had spoken to me.

"I sat and sat and sat. A couple of hours passed and he hadn't spoken. Another hour passed. I seemed to have relived my whole life in these three hours. Not that the experience was unpleasant. It wasn't. I simply remembered practically everything that had ever happened to me.

"Finally the master rose and left the room. I untangled my stiff aching joints and limped back to where I had left my shoes."

That afternoon Petzoldt drove up in a tonga to get her. He quickly briefed her on current developments in the case. A postmortem showed that Johnson's head hit the pavement and he suffered a concussion. Apparently, the blow was not a hard one and the skull was not cracked. The autopsy concluded that the old man suffered from hardening of the arteries and died from a ruptured blood vessel.

Petzoldt, however, was charged with manslaughter. Stories about the young American mountaineer circulated quickly. Articles about him and his difficulties appeared in *The Civil and Military Gazette* of Lahore and the Delhi *Statesman*. When the postmortem results were published, someone posted a two thousand–rupee bond and he was released. He had no idea who paid the bail.

He told Bernice he had wired Charles Houston to ask Loomis if he would send funds for their return passage. In the meantime, he thought there was still potential danger for them at the sanitarium. They had to leave at once. They would return later to get their bicycles, books, and other belongings.

As they started for Beas, he asked Bernice about her experience with the master. She told him about her three hours of silence.

"According to his followers it isn't necessary to talk to him," Petzoldt explained. "They insist he reads their minds."

"Oh, Lord," she muttered, "is that what he was doing?"

She tried to recall what she had been thinking. "I wonder if the master *forced* me to relive my past," she said.

Then it hit her. "Paul, the master put up the bond. I know he did."

"I guess maybe he did," he agreed.

On February 4, Petzoldt followed up his cable to Houston with a letter describing the accident and the lawyer Singh's "official version."

"They fabricated an entire new story about the affair and came to me saying that unless I told the story they ordered me to tell, they would all testify in such a way as to make a very bad case against me. Knowing the corruption that exists in Indian lawyers, being without funds to fight the case, and realizing I had little chance with so many against me, I could do nothing except to agree to their fabricated version of the accident."

The same day he wrote to Edward M. Groth, the American consul in Calcutta. Houston was a friend of Groth's and had notified him that Petzoldt might look him up when he passed through Calcutta en route home.

The day after receiving Petzoldt's letter, Groth got a cable from Houston alerting him to Petzoldt's problem. Groth immediately wired Petzoldt in care of the Thomas Cook Agency, instructing him to go to Lahore to meet with C. E. Macy, the American consul from Karachi, who would be in the city on business. He arranged a meeting for them at Falleti's Hotel at one P.M. on February 7.

The Petzoldts, appearing "very upset, despondent and worried," met with the consul at the appointed time. They repeated their story and Petzoldt executed an affidavit giving a chronological account of his movements in India from the time of his arrival with the K2 expedition up to the time of Johnson's death. The consul promised to do all he could to help.

Prior to their meeting Macy had interviewed A. V. Askwith, the Home Secretary of the Punjab Government, who showed him the preliminary police report on the case. He also telephoned the district magistrate at Amritsar, who confirmed Petzoldt's guilty plea when the charge of culpable homicide was changed to one of simple hurt. The lesser charge carried a maximum sentence of one year in prison, a fine of one thousand rupees, or both.

After his meeting with the Petzoldts, Macy cabled Groth.

> NO MURDER MOTIVE PETZOLDT CASE MERELY TRAGIC
> ACCIDENT RESULTING SCUFFLE AND ILL ADVISED PLEADED
> GUILTY **STOP** ARE TWO YOUNG AMERICANS IN TROUBLE
> NOT ENTIRELY THEIR FAULT **STOP** URGENTLY RECOMMEND
> FRIENDS EXTEND FINANCIAL AID **STOP** PLEASE CABLE
> LOOMIS CARE HOUSTON FIFTY HAVEN AVENUE NEW YORK
> EXTREME URGENT PROVIDE SUFFICIENT FUNDS FOR IMME-
> DIATE REPATRIATION PETZOLDT AND WIFE **STOP** IF CAN GET
> ASSURANCE THESE FUNDS FORTHCOMING BELIEVE CAN
> MOVE GOVERNMENT SUCCESSFULLY SUSPENSION SEN-
> TENCE UPON ASSURANCE LEAVE INDIA AT ONCE **STOP**
> MAILING HIS AFFIDAVIT.

But Macy still felt Petzoldt's outlook appeared rather hopeless. In his official report he wrote: "even though Petzoldt's statements in his affidavit about what had happened at Dera Baba Jaimal Singh on the evening of January 25, 1939, might be accepted as correct, his plea of guilty had more or less effectively stopped any effort in court to help him, for of course, an appeal can not be made from a sentence imposed following a plea of guilty. All that can be done is to apply for a reduction of the sentence imposed. The third difficulty was, that even though by some means not then apparent, opportunity might be given in court to argue the case on its merits, bringing in the story about the gun in Mrs. Johnson's hands, at that late date by Petzoldt alone, with no corroborative evidence, would not be particularly effective. It would appear to be merely a concocted tale thought up by Petzoldt after he had seen either his attorney or the Consul."

On the evening of February 7, Macy attended a dinner party at the home of Sir Douglas Young, Chief Justice of Lahore. One of the guests was Ambrose E. Chambers, an American attorney. Chambers, concerned over the plight of his fellow countryman, spent the greater part of the evening describing the events of January 25 in minute detail. He asked the Chief Justice if there was anything he could do about Petzoldt's predicament. Young offered to contact Bhagat Ram, a prominent Lahore lawyer.

On February 8, Ram called Macy and agreed to take the case. "I'll pay you Rs. 200 plus Rs. 15 for travel expenses to Amritsar," Macy told him. "If the fine imposed is not more than Rs. 200, pay it. If it is more than that, or if a prison sentence is imposed, report back to me and we will see what can be done."

Petzoldt and Ram went to Amritsar at once. They returned to Lahore on February 9 with news that they had prevailed. The magistrate finally acceded to Ram's persistent arguments and permitted Petzoldt to change his plea to one of not guilty.

"This was a bombshell in the opposition's camp, whose observers in the courtroom immediately sent messengers out to report developments to the headquarters at Dera Baba Jaimal Singh," Macy wrote in his official account.

The hearing for cross examination of the prosecution's witnesses was set for February 11. But to Petzoldt's surprise, Mr. Saini, a wealthy Indian electrical contractor who was a member of the Radhi Soami cult, put up a bail bond that allowed him to remain free until the trial.

Macy suggested they take advantage of the intervening days before the hearing to retrieve the Petzoldts' belongings at Dera Baba Jaimal Singh. Since it could be dangerous for Petzoldt to go, he offered to drive Bernice to the sanitarium. While she packed, he could look over the scene and interview the other Americans. Petzoldt agreed.

But when Macy went to pick up Bernice the next morning, there was a note from Petzoldt. They had taken the early train to Beas and planned to slip into the apartment quietly, get their things, and leave immediately.

Macy left at once by car. When he arrived at the compound, the Petzoldts had already left, but he found Mrs. Johnson, Elliott, and Harry Remsten at the main residence "all very much upset."

"Discreet questioning brought out quickly that the story told at the trial had been a concocted one," he wrote in his report, "but those concerned persisted in asserting that they had told it with the best of motives, i.e. to save Petzoldt from being indicted for murder. It was brought out that a gun had been brandished, as Petzoldt asserted, but Mrs. Johnson kept reiterating that the weapon was not loaded."

Macy didn't find Mrs. Remsten with the others. "She was reported to have a severe headache," he wrote, "but it seemed quite apparent that she was in the ill graces of Mrs. Johnson for the same reason that the Petzoldts had been, namely refusal, or at least disinclination, to whole-heartedly embrace the tenets of the sect, and particularly to fully subscribe to the principle of donating everything to the common fund."

On the pretense of examining the Petzoldts' quarters, Macy maneuvered Harry Remsten to his apartment. His private questioning of the nervous couple revealed that they were bored and disillusioned with the cult. They wanted out.

"The principles of the sect might be well worthy of living up to by persons past the prime of life, such as Elliott, who had apparently embraced the faith as an escape from a life of frustration," Macy told them, "but it hardly seems worthwhile for a young American couple to throw away their future in Indian religious immolation."

Macy urged them to leave the colony before they lost everything. He told them they could also set things right for Petzoldt by changing their story at the prosecution's hearing the next day.

"How can we do that without committing perjury?" Remsten asked.

"Simply tell the truth," said Macy. "No matter whom it hurts, or whatever might be the consequences."

Remsten said he would think it over.

Macy returned to Lahore that night and told Petzoldt what had happened. He didn't know whether or not Remsten would come forth at the prosecution's hearing the following morning. He did not. The judge set a trial for March 10.

Since Petzoldt was free on bail, he and Bernice decided to pass the month before their court appearance as pleasantly as possible. They booked a room at a tiny inn in Amritsar, where the trial would be held, and took to their bikes.

Amritsar was a large city situated on a level plain drained by the Ravi and Beas Rivers. The rivers formed a natural dividing line between the English cantonment, or military side, and the native section.

Renowned as the center of Sikhism, the town was noted for the magnificent Golden Temple, the Sikhs' principal place of worship. The elegant building was surrounded by a series of walkways and a moat of white marble. A brilliant gold-leaf dome was reflected in the "Pool of Nectar," built by Ram Das, the fourth Sikh guru. Nearby, a seven-story octagonal tower overlooked the spacious Jullianwala

Bagh park and the neighboring marketplace.

One day they rode their bicycles across the river to explore the bazaar and visit the Golden Temple. As they pushed their bikes through the narrow lanes into the crowded, debris-littered market, they tried to dodge the traffic and stay close to the stalls. It was dirty and noisy, but they had fun bartering a few pennies for glass beads, cobweb scarves laced with silver threads, and gilded shoes with pointed upturned toes.

They wound through the bustling streets, thoroughly enjoying the exotic scenes, and soon found themselves deep into a maze of alleys. The air grew foul and the din of unintelligible voices surrounded them. They lost all sense of direction.

Petzoldt stopped someone and tried to ask the way to the Golden Temple. The man shook his head. He tried getting directions from other locals, but no one seemed to understand him. People watched them intently as they pressed further into the bazaar. Some started to follow.

"I don't like their attitude," Petzoldt said, sensing hostility in the followers. "Something must be wrong."

They pushed their bicycles faster, and the crowd behind them grew. Petzoldt kept saying the Indian words for Golden Temple and the people pointed straight ahead.

Finally, some men motioned them onto a side street. As soon as they turned, Petzoldt realized it was a blind alley. He told Bernice to turn around and head back out, but the crowd refused to let them through. Someone spit at them. "This is it," Petzoldt said. "If you can smile, for God's sake, do."

By then they were surrounded, and there was low, angry muttering among the mob. Petzoldt smiled and talked as if nothing were the matter, while they vainly attempted to push their way back onto the main lane.

Just then a tall Sikh came running and shouting through the throng. Petzoldt recognized him as a man he had met in Lahore. The man shook his fist at the Indians and ordered them to disperse. The people waited a few minutes and then, one by one, sullenly turned away.

"What did you tell them?" Petzoldt asked, greatly relieved.

"I explained you are Americans," he said. "That you did not know."

"That we did not know what?"

"That you should not be walking in this place. They mistake you for English."

He explained that several hundred Indians had been killed at the site in 1919 when British troops fired on a subversive political meeting. They were near the area where the massacre occurred. The site had been declared a national monument, and foreigners, especially Englishmen, were not welcome.

The Sikh escorted them out of the bazaar to the Golden Temple. Later, he led them back to the bridge, where they crossed safely to the cantonment. Petzoldt promised that they would be more cautious on future cycling excursions.

On March 10, the Petzoldts appeared at court. Bhagat Ram, who had made eight trips between Lahore and Amritsar during the month to prepare his case, sat with them. Mrs. Johnson, the attorney Singh, and the three Americans were on the opposite side of the room. A bewigged English judge called the proceedings to order.

The prosecution presented its case as expected. Mrs. Johnson took the stand and testified that Petzoldt knocked her husband down through sheer malice. Elliott swore that when he attempted to interfere in the scuffle, Petzoldt took a swing at him, he ducked, and the blow struck the doctor full in the face. The Remstens were mute. They claimed they had remained at the dining table and could not see or hear what was happening in the adjoining room.

Ram called the attending physician. The doctor presented proof that the blow to Johnson's head was not severe enough to cause death. There was no skull fracture, only a concussion. He determined that the doctor died from a hemorrhage caused by the fall and aggravated by advanced age and hardening of the arteries.

The trial dragged on for three days. Volunteer helpers at the sanitarium and other cult members were questioned. Conflicting testimonies appeared to hinge on the speaker's degree of subjugation to Mrs. Johnson. Mr. Saini, who had posted Petzoldt's bail and later invited him and Bernice to be his house guests, vouched for Petzoldt's character. Elliott vowed that he overheard Petzoldt planning to hit Johnson with a brick.

Then, in the last hours of the trial, one of the servants at the colony came forward. Averting his eyes from Mrs. Johnson's glare, he testified that he had been in the courtyard when his mistress ran out of the dining room. He said he hid in the dark and watched her rush into the living room for the shotgun. He detailed the ensuing struggle for the gun, Singh and Elliott's attack on Petzoldt, the doctor's appearance in the yard, and Petzoldt's frantic flight and accidental collision with Johnson.

This first admission of a gun in Mrs. Johnson's hands caused a stir among the spectators. The judge pounded the gavel for order.

Ram used the excitement of the moment to recall Harry Remsten to the stand. He asked the American if the testimony of the preceding witness was true. Remsten, relieved that the facts were finally in the open, said that it was and told about Singh's fabricated story.

The attorney then asked Mrs. Johnson to return to the box.

"Is it true that you threatened Mr. Petzoldt with a shotgun?" he asked.

"The gun wasn't loaded," she said weakly.

On March 12, Petzoldt was acquitted.

According to Macy's report, Bhagat Ram waived his normal attorney fee of around 1,500 rupees and accepted the 200 rupees that Macy originally advanced to pay Petzoldt's fine. Ambrose E. Chambers and John Schulman, another American attorney who was concerned about the case, each donated 100 rupees to reimburse Macy for his out-of-pocket expense.

"In conclusion, there remains but one other point, and that is the manner in which funds for the repatriation of Mr. and Mrs. Petzoldt were obtained," Macy's report stated. "Through Dr. Charles Houston, leader of the K2 expedition of the American Alpine Club, the members of the expedition guaranteed the cost of return steamer passage for the couple, and telegraphed to Consul Groth at Calcutta $550 to be used for that purpose."

Petzoldt, however, claims he was never informed about his friends' financial aid. "I never knew that they sent money there," he says. "If they sent money to the consul, I never got it. The fellow who was an engineer [Mr. Saini] gave me the money and I suspect he got it from the master, who wanted to clear things up. I know it was from the master because he gave Bernice a solid gold bracelet."

Unfortunately, the $550 has been the source of ill feeling among

134

members of the K2 expedition for almost sixty years. Houston, House, and Bates claim it was difficult for them to scrape up that amount of money in those days when they were young and not established. They expected, and contend that Petzoldt promised them, that on his return to the States the loan would be repaid.

Petzoldt counters that he was not only unaware of their loan, but that he had never seen Macy's report proving his innocence of a crime against Johnson until shown copies of it by this author.

"For fifty-seven years I have not known of the existence of this letter," he said in a telephone interview. "Had I known of [it], life would have been different for me because I would have proof that the story concerning this escapade was a deliberate frame-up against me—This has been a tragedy of my life because rumors were circulated all during this time—that I was guilty of murder in India and had been kicked out of India and told never to return.

"So I'm glad to get this information, even at this late date," he says. "Let the dead bury its dead."

CHAPTER 7

The Mountaineer

THE TETONS LOOKED STRANGELY SHRUNKEN WHEN PETZOLDT RETURNED to the tepee at Jenny Lake. As he stood on the banks of the Snake River and saw the summit of the Grand impaling the clouds so visible above him, he remembered the final pyramid of K2 that revealed itself only after an exhausting three-month attack. Those moments when he had viewed the mountaintop and breathed the rarefied air at 26,700 feet, where no other man had stood, seemed even more significant in memory.

They had been able to put the unpleasantness in India behind them. On March 21, 1939, he and Bernice sailed on the *Kasima Maru* from Ceylon to Naples and spent the next six weeks bicycling through Rome, Genoa, Pisa, Turin, and over the Italian Alps to Paris. Bernice had never been to Europe and Paul, sensing the military buildup, felt it might be his last chance to show her those countries before war erupted. Besides, it would complete her trip around the world.

The next few years were busy ones for the guiding service. Petzoldt continued charting new climbing routes and on July 6, 1940, he, along with Joseph Hawkes and Bernhard Nebel, made a first ascent on the west couloir of 9,550-foot Cube Point, a prominent tower east of the popular Symmetry Spire.

In September the Petzoldts struck their tepee and reentered the University of Wyoming at Laramie. Petzoldt managed the sporting goods department of the Holiday Department Store to support them, and they spent their spare time skiing. But by year's end, Bernice decided school was not for her, and Petzoldt, almost thirty-three years old, still lacked enough credits to graduate. They headed back to Jackson.

That winter Elizabeth (Betsy) Cowles invited Petzoldt to join her and Elizabeth Knowlton in February on a trip to the Sierra Nevada de Santa Marta mountains, an isolated range in Colombia, South America. The region had been explored by German climbers but attracted few Americans. And there were a number of high peaks that had not been attempted.

Cowles was a young New Yorker who had climbed in the Alps and made the second ascent of the north ridge of Mount Moran with Petzoldt, Glenn Exum, Macauley Smith, Bill House, and Bob Bates the previous summer. Knowlton was a reporter for the *New York Times* and had authored *The Naked Mountain* after joining an expedition to Nanga Parbat in 1932.

The women confided that there was more to the trip than mountain climbing. According to Petzoldt, they secretly told him that their expedition was partially supported by the U.S. State Department because it was suspected that German fliers were being sent to South America to spy on the United States. There were unexplained sinkings of ships in the Carribean, and the feds suspected that the Germans received reports on our naval activity from the coastal mountains of Colombia, where a number of their countrymen had immigrated.

"On a clear day with a glass you could see the smoke from ships from the Panama Canal to the Carribean," Petzoldt said later. "They suspected that these people had radioed U-boats so they could find the ships and sink them. We were supposed to go to this place and climb mountains and also look around to see if these people were there."

The threesome sailed from New York on the S.S. *Jamaica* on February 5, 1941. Five days later, after a stop at Jamaica, they landed in Barranquilla, a major seaport and industrial center. But when they disembarked from the ship, they were unable to collect their luggage from customs. Every time they attempted to get through the line, the officers would give another excuse for delaying them.

Luckily, they were met by Juancho Ujueta and Max Eberli, a Swiss expatriate, who came to their rescue.

"Let me tell you a story," Eberli said. "I have a friend who got his brother a job as a customs agent. After the man's term expired, he went to my friend and asked to borrow some money. 'What?' my friend asked. 'You mean you were there four years and didn't end up independently wealthy?'"

"How much do you think it will take to get our stuff out of here?" Petzoldt asked, understanding the message.

"Oh," Eberli said, "let me try it for a couple hundred American."

They retrieved their gear and got a photography permit without further delay.

A noisy drive through streets clogged with traffic finally brought them to the inexpensive Astoria Hotel, where they spent three uncomfortable nights sleeping on wooden beds that afforded neither mattresses nor springs.

Arrangements for the expedition kept them busy during the daytime. The enervating heat and language barriers were frustrating as they exchanged money in the banks and shopped for supplies in the local market. The sound of whistles from steamboats on the Magdalena River, transporting coffee and petroleum from the interior and cotton from surrounding regions, mixed with a cacophony of shouting and honking in the crowded street.

In the evenings they treated themselves to a last taste of luxury by dining at the elegant Prado Hotel. They celebrated Lincoln's birthday with a special anniversary dinner at another fine restaurant. In the midst of all of the toasts and festivity, Max Eberli became so excited about the upcoming adventure that he asked to join them.

On February 13, Petzoldt departed with the luggage aboard a craft suspiciously nicknamed the "flea boat." The others met him at Santa Marta the next morning. They boarded an open-air train to Fundacion, then took a bumpy, dusty bus ride to the village of Valledupar. On February 15, they continued by Ford car to rendezvous with their pack train at El Salado.

The long caravan of mules and horses then wound through a dense jungle filled with exotic flowers and birds, plodded over Monte Grande Pass, and descended into Pueblo Bello by nightfall. A German family, also named Eberli, offered a sleeping room, where the guests lined up in cots four in a row.

The next evening an English-speaking neighbor invited them to a birthday celebration where the drinking was prodigious and toasts rang loud as a juicy conglomeration of chicken and vegetables was dumped from a large pot onto shiny green banana leaves spread on the table.

Their trek continued through the San Sebastian valley to a "Clean! Cool! Bugless!" boardinghouse owned by the Richter family. During a five-day stay, their suspicions were aroused by fellow boarders Helmut Schmidt and his wife.

"He is a German aviator," Cowles wrote in her diary. "Why is he here?"

On February 22, they started again. The trail, bordered by alpine rose bushes as big as trees, was slippery and steep. They got their first view of the distant Santa Marta range the next day and arrived at base camp in Gloomy Gulch on February 24. That was the end of the line for the pack train, which turned back to the valley with a promise to return and pick them up on March 19.

Petzoldt established a basic routine for the expedition. He encouraged the team to maximize their health and energy levels by setting aside days of rest, taking daily doses of salt pills and vitamins, eating plenty of good food, and taking advantage of opportunities to read and relax. Although he himself often carried packs weighing up to 100 pounds, he advised each person to make a self-determination as to the size load he or she could handle.

They agreed to move up the mountains in relays in order to conserve energy. He would go ahead to scout a high camp and cache a ration bag, then return to help the others carry supplies to the new site. He urged them to hike slowly, stop to take pictures, and enjoy the experience.

"Paul is in his element here, works hard, also adds enormously to the fun of camp life with cheerfulness and jokings," Cowles wrote in her journal.

Taking off alone to reconnoiter a site for Camp 2, Petzoldt picked his way down the barren, rocky gulch and hiked out of sight over a high pass at the end of the lake. His distinctive yodel echoed over the rock cliffs long before he reappeared at base in the late afternoon.

He told the party he had found a spot for the second camp not too far away at about 14,000 feet. It was the dry season at that altitude, and the skies were so clear that one could see hundreds of miles and watch the frequent rainstorms and lightning flashes over the jungle below. The camp overlooked high valleys and numerous lakes, and there was a good view of the unnamed peaks that they would try.

They established the highest climbing camp on March 4 at about 16,700 feet. It was on a rocky point between ice and snowfields, so they dubbed it the Condor's Nest. They named the peaks they hoped to summit La Reina (18,160 feet), Pico Ujueta (18,060 feet), and Guardian Peak (17,180 feet).

As the native people were traditionally afraid of the high snows, no one had ever approached these mountains. So they felt it was fitting for them to christen landmarks as they trekked—Gloomy Gulch Lake, Sunset Lake, Lake of the Two Little Islands, Blue Heaven Lake, Red Lake.

"Being the first ever to be here gives us the right to christen," Cowles wrote.

They made a first ascent of La Reina on March 5. "Terrible breakfast, cold, ice in our water pail," Cowles wrote. "Started off. I led for an hour, then Elizabeth. Tried the snow ridge on the right but couldn't make it because of icy conditions and no crampons (left behind). The snow face, steep, went all right. A crevasse (bergschrund) to cross. Ticklish. On top, Petzoldt's yodel took 11 seconds to echo (from our #2 peak, next door)."

The first ascent of Pico Ujueta came two days later. The climb started on rock then traversed an icy slope and three long snowfields. Cowles reported that "rocks and scree piled every which way," and "the drop to the north [is] astounding."

"Clouds come up with wonderful lights and colors," she wrote. "A fine view of La Reina, just south of us, a great snowy pile like vanilla ice cream. ('Pass the chocolate sauce,' said someone). To the north the Caribbean Sea, right at our feet. The mountain ridge to the east is like a necklace, a peak between each strand."

On March 8, they began their descent back to Gloomy Gulch. After a few days of rest, Eberli left the group, and the others focused on the third unclimbed peak. Knowlton decided to remain in camp while Petzoldt and Cowles made a reconnaissance.

A short distance from camp they reached a lake and mistakenly made a left turn. They spent hours struggling around chains of lakes, rock buttresses, and steep rises and drops in the terrain. They crossed a main watercourse with difficulty, "then slopped around in a morass," sinking thigh-deep in mud like quicksand. Hoping to locate the main valley leading to the third peak, they confronted a succession of hills. Finally, exhausted, they camped for the night.

They studied maps and photographs. But every time they climbed over a ridge, another appeared in front of them. After several arduous hours of hiking, they saw their peak, at last. Far in the distance.

"We're further away than when we started," Petzoldt said.

They didn't have the time, food, or energy to push on so they returned to camp. At least they knew the direction to go for a second attempt.

On March 16, Petzoldt and Cowles succeeded with a first ascent of the 17,180-foot, ice-crusted mountain they had named Guardian Peak. They hurried back to Gloomy Gulch to tell Knowlton the good news. Three days later, packed and reunited with the mule train, they left a note for future expeditioners: "Have a good time in this wonderful region."

The reunion at the Richter home in San Sebastian occasioned another celebration. There were many hugs and much storytelling as Richter poured his customary rounds of hearty drinks. Sitting at a table to eat and sleeping between clean sheets was a welcome luxury to the weary travelers.

Petzoldt and Cowles learned that the Schmidts had moved into their own home in the village. They visited them the next day with some groceries left over from the expedition. Schmidt told them that his family had to leave the country.

"Mystery," Cowles wrote. "He is re-called to the German Air Force? Or being expelled from here by the Colombians? By influences from the USA?"

With the conundrum unsolved, they left for the States on March 27. Petzoldt, with all of the equipment, went by ship, while Cowles and Knowlton traveled to New York by plane.

"On returning to the U.S., we were interrogated by the State

Department about the Schmidts and other Germans seen in the high country," Cowles wrote. "Sometime later, they [the Schmidts] were held temporarily at Ellis Island en route for Germany."

Bernice drove across the country to meet Petzoldt in New York that April. They visited friends in Long Island before heading for Wyoming to prepare for the season.

On June 25, 1941, Joseph Hawkes, Earl Clark, and Harold Plumley joined Petzoldt to make the first summit of the CMC route on Mount Moran. The following month, with Betsy Cowles, Mary Merrick, and Frederick Wulsin, Jr., he pioneered a route that became known as the Petzoldt Ridge.

That August Hans Kraus, a New York doctor and accomplished climber, hired Petzoldt and Exum for an attempt on the North Face of the Grand Teton. The difficult wall had only been scaled once when Petzoldt, Curly, and Jack Durrance conquered it in 1936. Bernice convinced Petzoldt that she should join this second party and become the first woman to perform the feat.

When they started out the next morning, Petzoldt cautioned her to conserve her energy for the tough pitches. They reached timberline by late afternoon with no problem. But when he pointed out a perpendicular wall of smooth granite that loomed in the distance and told her that was their target, she began to have serious misgivings.

By daybreak the surrounding cliffs looked insignificant in comparison to the North Face. The early light that usually delineated irregularities in rocky surfaces revealed a slab as flat as a piece of paper.

"You said that when you got close to the face it didn't look so smooth," she said.

He assured her that there were plenty of projections to hold onto and that she had proven her ability and was up to the climb. Then he told everyone to put on their crampons.

It was cold and the gathering clouds looked threatening when they kicked steps up the snowy slope of the Teton Glacier. Near the top of the ice field Petzoldt told everyone to tie into a rope and move one at a time while he belayed them around and over a maze of crevasses. The last few yards were so steep and solidly frozen that he had to hack steps the rest of the way to the base of the north wall.

The four climbers clung to the precipice, resting against the damp granite before tackling the final ascent. Petzoldt tied into a rope with Bernice and instructed Exum and Kraus to do likewise. He started climbing. The other couple followed. They moved slowly and deliberately, seeking hand- and footholds in small frozen cracks. The rocky tower hid them from the sun and a chill wind drained their endurance.

Petzoldt worked his way about two thousand feet up the pitch. About eleven o'clock he stopped. A few hundred feet above them was a ledge that could only be reached through a huge crack formed by a large slab of rock extending over the cliff face, something like an "upside-down chimney" that emptied into thin air. He told Bernice to wait while he drove two pitons where she was standing. Then she was to belay him while he maneuvered into the crack.

He proceeded cautiously. Bernice slowly fed out the line. She watched as his hands and feet massaged the wall for holds, and he slid into the chimney. Then suddenly he swung around, facing downward with his feet braced on one side of the chimney and hands on the other. He inched upward like a spider.

"Fiercely I watched his rope, guarding it with every fiber of my being!" she wrote. "It must be free with just the right amount of slack. But not too much The slightest tug would have thrown him off balance."

As he neared the top, the chimney narrowed, and he was able to swing upright again and reach the ledge. Bernice shook with relief. Then he yelled for her to climb.

"I was astounded!" she wrote. "There was nothing to climb on the wall! Nothing! The wall was damp and icy and as smooth as glass! And bulged in the middle!"

"Climb!" he yelled again.

He belayed her firmly as she entered the chimney. She clawed halfway up the slippery walls and then began to lose traction. Her hands slid on the rock and her feet stabbed for a shelf or nodule to hold her. Then she fell. The rope caught her. She tried to regain purchase with the rock and fell again and again until her waist burned from the rough fiber tightening around her. On her fourth attempt she made it.

The other climbers joined them, and they rested before continuing on a series of vertical rope leads up to the summit.

At seven P.M., they stood on top of the Grand Teton. It was snowing and the wind was vicious. Their hands were so numb they could scarcely sign the register. Petzoldt reluctantly told them that it was too late and stormy to savor the moment for more than five minutes. They retreated down the Owen Route to their timberline camp.

In October Teton National Park ranger Harold Rapp arrived in Petzoldt's hunting camp and told him that a parachutist was stranded on top of Devils Tower National Monument. Petzoldt was needed to help get him off the 1,280-foot monolith.

DEVILS TOWER RISES 1,280 FEET ABOVE THE BELLE FOURCHE RIVER WITH a columnar vertical shaft towering 865 feet from its sloping foundation. It was formed eons ago when a mass of molten rock forced its way upward through a succession of sandstone layers until it reached a resistant mantle that stopped its progress. The dome-shaped mass cooled under the blanketing surface, contracted and cracked into huge, multi-sided columns, and crystallized into a granitelike rock. In time, the gradual forces of erosion from rain, heat, cold, and wind, wore away the overlying mantle and exposed the tall central shaft.

Wyoming ranchers Will Rogers and Willard Ripley had made the first ascent of the tower in 1893. Hoping to attract a crowd and raise some cash by an act of derring-do, they pounded handmade wooden pegs into a vertical crack up the side of the formation to create a ladder that would take them to the top. Rogers, decked out in a red, white, and blue suit, carried an American flag to the summit on July 4. Ripley, who had actually gained the top after completing the upper section of the ladder, did not make his first ascent public until later. Babe White, "The Human Fly," made another unsuccessful attempt in 1927. But it wasn't until ten years later that Fritz Wiessner, Bill House and Laurence Coveney became the first serious climbers to reach the top.

The trapped parachutist was George Hopkins, a wing-walker and stunt pilot, who parachuted from burning planes in motion pictures and collected U.S. sky-diving records. His 2,347 jumps were the most ever recorded, he had made the highest jump from an elevation of 26,400 feet, and he held the world's record for the longest delayed jump of 20,800 feet. He had made a $50 bet that he would become the first person to reach the top of Devils Tower by parachute.

Hopkins had left Rapid City, South Dakota, at daybreak on October 1 in a two-passenger plane piloted by Joe Quinn. The morning had dawned clear and cold with a ground wind blowing about 35 miles per hour. When Quinn reached the appointed jump off point, his passenger bolted from the aircraft, taking careful aim at a small area he had pinpointed for a landing. But part way down, worried that he might overshoot the target, he partially collapsed his parachute to check his drift. Instead, he plummeted faster and faster. Skimming near the tower, he thrust out a foot in an attempt to anchor himself on a raised rock, and catapulted against a protruding boulder.

Hopkins had worked out a paper plan to climb down to the ground by pounding a sharpened Ford axle into the rock with a sledge hammer, attaching a hundred-foot rope to the axle through a hayloft pulley, and then adding another thousand feet of rope. He had calculated that he could scramble the rest of the way to the bottom freestyle.

But when Quinn dropped the axle and rope, the package hit the summit with a bounce and fell about fifty feet to snag on bushes growing out of the tower's side. Quinn winged away toward Rapid City and it was not until late afternoon that Clyde Ice, a pilot from nearby Spearfish, was enlisted to make another attempt to drop a rope.

Ice had evacuated many flood and forest fire victims and had flown numerous mercy flights to hospitals. He figured a tower drop posed unique problems due to sudden updrafts that could ravage his 65 horsepower plane. So when he flew in with a second rope, he cut the motor, glided about six feet above the monument while his partner tossed out the line, then restarted the engine. The loosely coiled rope landed in a hopeless mass of tangles.

Hopkins had to spend the night on the rock. Ice returned just before dark to drop food, blankets, a tarpaulin, and a note promising they would get him off the next day.

Then it started to storm. Fog enveloped the top of the monument, and Hopkins crept into his make-do shelter to pass a miserable night in rain and sleet.

At dawn, Hopkins threw down a note stating that he intended to parachute to the ground. The National Park Service quickly squashed the notion. Instead, they sent for Rocky Mountain State Park ranger

Ernest K. Field and Colorado climbing guide Warren Gorrell to do an alpine-style rescue. In the meantime, Ice airlifted the stranded daredevil a bearskin-lined flying suit, a megaphone, and a medium rare T-bone steak.

By the time the sky cleared that afternoon, over a thousand sightseers, photographers, press and radio reporters had gathered to watch the loner stranded on his "sky island."

Field and Gorrell arrived early on the third morning. The two rescuers examined the routes that had previously been climbed. Deeming them too difficult, they explored a number of alternative passages in various directions to no avail. When one of them slipped and was narrowly caught by the rope, they retreated to the ground.

People from all over the country called with suggestions that they lasso Hopkins or shoot a rope up to him by cannon, and it was rumored that the Goodyear blimp, *Reliance*, was on its way with a special pick-up basket.

Late on the afternoon of October 3, Jack Durrance, who had successfully climbed the tower, telegraphed from Dartmouth that he was coming to help, along with a few other experienced climbers.

Day four. A new storm with rain and snow boiled over the Black Hills. News wires buzzed with the saga of "Devils Tower George," and the episode was featured in *Time* and *Newsweek*. Planeloads of curiosity-seekers circled overhead, and local motels and grocery stores tried to keep up with escalating hordes of tourists. Field and Gorrell muscled a thirty-foot extension ladder onto the top of one of the columns, and a Park Service mechanic pounded heavy iron spikes and a few two-by-fours into the upper portion. All was in readiness for Durrance to scale the rock.

But the Dartmouth climber failed to appear when expected. Storms in the Midwest had canceled all flights out of Chicago. Durrance was on a train headed for Denver. He would have to come the rest of the way by automobile.

About noon on October 5, after driving all night, Petzoldt and Rapp arrived in a snow-covered car.

"When we got to Devils Tower, a sleet storm had gone through the area," Rapp remembers. "The tower was nothing but a sheet of glass."

Petzoldt opened the car trunk to get his climbing gear and was deluged by reporters. Rapp put on his felt-soled shoes, and they pushed their way through the mob to the base of the monument. Buffeted by wind, they climbed to the top of the fixed ladder to investigate the route. The tower's deep cracks were choked with ice all the way to the summit.

Hoping for a change in the weather, they climbed back down to the valley floor. When they reached the ground, a man handed them a note that Hopkins had thrown to the crowd.

"I do not want to be rescued by mountaineers," the message said. "I'm not a mountaineer. I got up here by air and I'm going to get down by air."

About midnight, with screaming sirens and flashing lights, Durrance and three other climbers arrived in a cavalcade of police and highway patrol vehicles. He conferred with Petzoldt and the rangers, and the rescue was set for daylight.

They started at 7:30 A.M. Durrance took the lead, tied into a 125-foot rope with Petzoldt and Rapp. Field, Gorrell, and Chappell Cranmer were on a second rope, and Merril McLane and Henry Coulter on a third.

Durrance "climbed facing the wall, utilizing friction holds on the sloping column faces, and jamming his right foot into the larger crack when width permitted," wrote Field in an article for *Trail and Timberline*. He hammered wooden pegs and pitons into the rock as he progressed. The string of climbers followed him to a point about 150 feet below the summit. Then, leaping from one sloping ledge to another over a crevice 500 feet deep, they gained a shelf that gave access to the top.

When they were within voice range of Hopkins, he peered over the edge. It was almost four o'clock. It would soon be dark.

"Well, George," Petzoldt said, "we hear you got up here by air and want to get down by air. You've got ten seconds to make a decision because we want to get down off this thing. It's cold as ice."

"For God's sake, come and get me," said Hopkins.

The rescuers, who had been climbing for eight hours, pulled themselves over the ledge.

Hopkins, ever cognizant of records, told author Dale M. Titler,

"This was the greatest moment! I knew for the first time I was really safe! The others followed until the largest assembly of men—nine in all—were gathered on top of Devils Tower."

Durrance asked Petzoldt to get Hopkins down. Petzoldt tied Hopkins into a safety sling and demonstrated how to use the rappel rope, reassuring him that he would be belaying him securely until his feet touched the ground.

They started their slow descent at 4:45 P.M. In the gathering dusk, onlookers pinpointed them with spotlights, blinding them with the glare and making their progress more difficult. While the others followed, Rapp and Durrance stayed behind to clean up debris, then joined their teammates at 9:30 amidst a loud roar of approval from the crowd.

Hopkins, ever ready with quotable comments, declared, "This was not exhibition jumping. It was partly to let people know just what a person can do with a parachute if he really knows one."

"It was the damndest example of human nature I've ever seen," Petzoldt told Bernice when he returned to Jackson next evening. "I had a friend from Wyoming who was out in that crowd. Some of the comments this guy heard! One guy said, 'What's the goddam fool fooling around with that rope for? Why don't they go off?'

"Somebody else said, 'Aw, hell, it's getting cold. Let's go home. Nobody's going to fall!'"

That autumn of 1941, Petzoldt signed a two-year contract with New York agent W. Colston Leigh for a lecture tour to show movies of K2, the Tetons, South America, and Mexico. He was heavily booked for several months, appearing before audiences at Stanford University and other West Coast colleges, private schools, organizations, and even the New Tribes Mission, an evangelistic group from Chico, California.

Then one lazy Sunday morning in December, while he and Bernice were in Sacramento visiting her brother, someone switched on the radio. The Japanese had just bombed Pearl Harbor.

CHAPTER 8

Wartime

WHEN THE PETZOLDTS ARRIVED IN WASHINGTON, D.C., IN THE SPRING of 1942, the shock of Japan's attack on Pearl Harbor still shuddered through the city, which roiled with people rallying to the military crisis. Ralph Olmstead, a friend from Twin Falls High, who had worked his way up from law school to the U.S. Department of Agriculture, offered Petzoldt a job in the department. Petzoldt's expertise in outfitting and organizing provisions for the K2 expedition qualified him for tracking the millions of items stored for shipment abroad in the government's Lend-Lease program. Olmstead directed him to feed the information into a new punch-card filing system.

"They had millions of tons of stuff stored in four or five venues and didn't know where it was," Petzoldt remembers. "And they had this great new miracle machine that had cards with holes in them, but they had to know where to put the holes. I said I think I can do that."

He started by interviewing the department heads to find where items were located and what they were shipping to whom. Then he organized placement of the card holes. One hole was for the type of food, such as meat. Then other perforations specified if it were beef, pork, chicken, etc.

What container was it in? A box? Cardboard or wooden? Cans?

What size? Where was it warehoused? There had to be a hole for everything. It was not much different than organizing supplies on the K2 expedition, and Petzoldt soon had the mountain of information catalogued on punch cards so requests could be processed quickly.

But sometimes the well-organized system was not enough. "One night I got word that we just had to get some food to the Caribbean," Petzoldt remembers. "There were a couple of ships coming into Puerto Rico that were filled up with commercial cargo, much of which was food. One was sunk on the way, and the other in view of the port.

"The situation was pretty desperate down there, so suddenly I was in charge of giving orders to fill up ships with food that we had going to the army or to the Russians. The only place we could get ships were Liberty ships coming off the manufacturers on the West Coast.

"So we had the best advice we could get within twenty-four hours on what they ate in Puerto Rico. But it didn't happen to be quite the right stuff. They eat beans, but they don't eat just *any* beans. They eat red kidney beans, but at that time they wouldn't touch a pinto bean from Texas. And they ate a lot of cornmeal, but it had to be of a certain grind and texture so after they boiled it it would stick on meat fillings.

"My office was in charge of doing this and we loaded up maybe 20,000 tons of food—zip—in two days. The wrong stuff. Some of it sat down there and nobody would eat it."

Bernice got a job as a clerk for the U.S. Maritime Commission, and they subleased an apartment close to Petzoldt's office and searched for a permanent home.

One day that fall as they were driving through the Virginia countryside looking at houses, they spotted a boxy old derelict posted with a "For Sale" sign. Intrigued, they got out of the car to investigate.

On closer inspection, Bernice announced the place "an architectural monstrosity" but admitted there was a touch of charm in the climbing roses encircling the front porch and the rickety old windmill that flapped and fluttered in the yard. Petzoldt eyed a forest of black pine crowding right up to the back door.

As they were strolling about, an old lady suddenly appeared and launched into a well-rehearsed monologue. She told them she was only the second owner since the house was built before the Civil War. She pointed out a depression in the ground where a trench had been dug during the Second Battle of Manassas, a tree where a Yankee had been hanged. No one had ever cultivated the 112 acres of woods, she told them. She lived in a small cottage tucked in the pines. Would until she died. They could have the whole farm cheap if they would let her stay in her woods. After she passed away, they would get the cottage.

Half amused and half interested, the Petzoldts followed the woman inside. Upstairs there were three bedrooms and one antiquated bathroom, featuring an immense footed bathtub. The lower level consisted of living and dining rooms heated by battered coal stoves and a rear kitchen with an old-fashioned sink fastened to the wall. It would take a lot of work, Petzoldt reckoned, but the price was right, and he always had trouble passing up a bargain. Bernice agreed. They moved in during a bleak December snowstorm.

Bernice quit her job to become a full-time homemaker, while he made the daily twenty-five mile commute to the Department of Agriculture.

The Lend-Lease program had been sending the Soviet Union flour, oils, beans, and various foods for some time, but the people in charge of negotiations found the Russians difficult to deal with. They often requested massive amounts of supplies, many times more than they knew they would realistically receive. Personnel in the Department of Agriculture became frustrated and tempers sputtered. Finally, Petzoldt got the assignment.

"Before I took over the operation, they had an awful time because nobody really knew how to handle the Russians," Petzoldt says. "They couldn't understand these horse traders, and that's what they were. You'd talk to them just like you'd talk to some rancher out west."

Petzoldt called their bluff. "You sons of bitches come in here asking for all that and you're just cooking your goose," he would say. "You're not going to get this so why ask for it? We'll get you all that we can, but your demands have to be reasonable."

If the Russian needs were not met, he tried to direct excess rations apportioned to the U.S. Army to them. He personally went to department heads to check the requests against existing inventory. The Russians responded to his common-sense logic and requested that Petzoldt be their liaison on all dealings.

But as the war worsened, supply ships could not get through to Murmansk. Only one or two ships in big convoys made it. So Petzoldt devised a plan to send Russian icebreakers from Murmansk to New York, where they were serviced and dispatched to the Panama Canal and on up to Seattle. From there, about fifty ships loaded with oil and other cargo followed the icebreakers up through the Bering Strait and on to Murmansk. The freighters could then cruise the major rivers and drop materials at cities along the route. The top-secret plan earned Petzoldt a presidential deferment.

Still, since he was thirty-four, married but without children, the draft board in Laramie questioned his exemption from service. The army contended that a government position held no more priority than the work of boys being taken from the farms and ranches where they were so badly needed.

Petzoldt had a horror of being compared to Jack Dempsey, who had been branded a slacker for not fighting in World War I. He felt that the people back home wouldn't think that Paul Petzoldt had any special qualities that should prevent him from going to war like the rest of their young men. So he resigned from the department, enlisted in the U.S. Army, and reported to Fort Dix for induction.

PRIOR TO LEAVING THE DEPARTMENT OF AGRICULTURE, HOWEVER, HE had received a letter from a ranger at Grand Teton National Park. The ranger was considering joining the ski troops and wondered what Petzoldt knew about them.

America's first mountain regiment had been activated on November 15, 1941. The unique army infantry division was created by President Roosevelt after a two-year lobbying campaign spearheaded by Charles "Minnie" Dole.

Dole was one of a handful of Americans who had become a skiing fanatic after the sport was introduced to this country in about 1930. A graduate of Yale, he spent many winter days with long wooden skis clamped to his feet with Mason jar rubber bands, climbing hills herringbone-fashion and making short downhill runs.

One day in 1937, Dole fell and broke his ankle. Alone in a mountain of deep snow, he painfully dragged himself down to a doctor in the valley. His ordeal convinced him that, considering the growing popularity of the sport, there was need for a method of mountain rescue. He rallied a group of skiing enthusiasts and created the National Ski Patrol.

By 1939 Dole had new concerns. The situation in Europe was worsening, and Dole and his friends were concerned that America would be brought into the conflict sooner or later.

Dole was impressed by the success of the Finnish soldiers who repelled Stalin's troops during the war between Russia and Finland in 1939. Skiers from the small country would ambush the enemy in the mountains and then escape through the woods, exchange their skis for ice skates, and flee on the frozen rivers. He felt that the United States would need mountain troops if they had to defend high terrain in Germany, Italy, France, or Austria. He rallied the ski patrol and members of the Sierra Club and the American Alpine Club to help him convince the army of this fact. Then he started pestering the president. Roosevelt finally made it happen.

Skiers from all over the country flocked to enlist in "the army's greatest sports school." College coaches, captains of ski teams, famous athletes, mountaineers, daredevils, and even photographers and falconers signed up for the new "fraternity." They bunked at Mount Rainier's Paradise Lodge in Washington the first year, then in November 1942 moved to their own special facility at Camp Hale, Colorado.

Petzoldt understood the Teton ranger's interest in the mountain regiment but discouraged him from joining because he felt that the fledgling ski troops lacked trained leadership and organization. He knew from personal experience on K2 that planning and directing lengthy outdoor expeditions in high country required special knowledge and procedures.

"I wrote him back saying no because, even though they had some good skiers in there who knew something about the outdoors, all of the officers were fresh from West Point and they didn't know a thing [about specialized outfitting and conditioning]," Petzoldt says.

The ranger sent Petzoldt's letter to a friend, who channeled it to the powers in Washington, and one day Petzoldt got a call from an officer in the War Department asking him to lunch. The official quizzed him on his climbing experiences in Switzerland and on K2, as well as his guiding concession in the Tetons. In the course of the conversation, he also told Petzoldt that the three experimental ski regiments had been combined into the Tenth Mountain Division, the only infantry unit specifically trained for mountain warfare.

After the lunch date, Petzoldt received a packet of material offering him a captaincy if he would sign on as an advisor to the ski troops at Camp Hale. It was tempting, but at that time he still felt his presidential deferment indicated that his duty was at the Department of Agriculture, so he declined the commission.

When he later resigned from the government job and was inducted at Fort Dix, Petzoldt applied for the Tenth Mountain regiment. He was rejected. The officer in charge told him the battalion was "only for people of experience," and that they were sending him to the medics. Petzoldt called upon friends in the American Alpine Club and Sterling Hendricks, a former climbing companion who was influential in the Department of Agriculture Experimental Stations division, to vouch for his mountaineering expertise. He finally gained the assignment. But as a private, not as a commissioned officer.

Camp Hale was the antithesis of a desk job in Washington. Tucked into the Colorado Rockies about halfway between Leadville and the area that was later to become Vail, it stood at an elevation of 10,000 feet and was surrounded by gigantic mountains and cliffs.

The ski troops were composed of ski instructors from winter resorts like Sun Valley, Ivy League downhill racers, mountain climbers, outdoorsmen—adventuresome, strong-willed athletes who were impatient with red tape and indifferent to matters of rank. Officers and enlisted men all learned together and developed as a team, improvising and devising their own training programs.

"Having never had mountain soldiers before it was pretty hard to find experienced ones, so you had to make the best of the unknown," Friedl Pfeifer, a renowned skier and founder of Aspen Ski Area later said in a televised documentary about the troops.

On his second day at Camp Hale Petzoldt was on floor-scrubbing duty when a Canadian medical officer approached him.

"You're Paul Petzoldt?" he asked.

Petzoldt said he was.

"I've heard of you. Come with me."

154

He followed the man to his office.

"We've got to get someone to work out a standard operating procedure for mountain evacuation," he said. "We don't have anything in place. You're in charge."

He promoted Petzoldt to the rank of sergeant, assigned him three squads, and ordered him to experiment on the project until he developed a safe and reasonably foolproof system of rescue.

Most of the troops were accomplished downhill skiers but were not accustomed to cross-country skiing over roadless backcountry for weeks at a time carrying all of their food, sleeping bags, tents, and army gear with them. Ernest "Tap" Tapley was an exception. He drew duty as Petzoldt's assistant, special guide, and winter skills instructor.

A nineteen-year-old from Amesbury, Massachusetts, Tapley made his mark as a skier in 1940 when author and radio commentator Lowell Thomas saw him barreling down the famous Tuckerman's headwall on Mount Washington. Thomas offered to get him a job with the Sun Valley ski patrol the following season, but war broke out and Tapley enlisted in the Tenth Mountain Division instead.

Petzoldt met Tapley on the ski hill. It didn't take long for him to realize that the young man was one of the most accomplished all-around outdoorsmen he had ever met.

Josh Miner, founder of Outward Bound USA, agrees. Tapley, one-eighth Passamaquoddy Indian, "was a contemporary mountain version of renaissance man," he wrote. "He could live in the wilderness with nothing but a knife. He was a skilled hunter, tracker, trapper, fisherman, and expert axeman, a fine outdoor cook, a virtuoso with ropes and knots. A master of all trades, he could make anything and engineer anything. He had the greatest manual intelligence I have ever seen, could do the most minute things with his hands. He was a forester, fire fighter, mountaineer, canoeman, mule skinner, dogsled-team driver, navigator, meteorologist, avalanche expert, cliff evacuation expert, survival adept. He played the violin, and painted. He was a born athlete, a deadly horseshoe pitcher blindfolded."

Tapley, in turn, admired Petzoldt. "We camped together," Tapley remembers. "I made the fires and coffee, kind of waited on him a little bit. I knew that he was the mountaineer that he is, and I tried to learn what I could from him."

Little was known about the equipment and skills necessary for existing in the outdoors for long periods of time at high elevations and in all kinds of weather. The U.S. Army's winter war gear had not been updated since 1914. The service provided excellent clothing, yet attacks of frostbite and hypothermia were common.

Petzoldt had learned on K2 that the best protection against cold was to wear wool next to the body. Dampness in wool moves through progressive layers away from the skin, keeping a person fairly warm and dry. But many of the ski troops complained about allergies to the fabric and wore cotton socks and undershirts beneath heavier outerwear.

One day Petzoldt proved his point. He asked several GIs to put on various combinations of socks—cotton-cotton, cotton-wool, wool-cotton, wool-wool—and then told them to double-time around the field for half an hour to work up a sweat. Then he had them remove the socks. All of the socks were damp, but the men wearing two pair of wool socks had dry feet and a wet outer sock. Those wearing cotton under wool had clammy, pink feet and both pairs of socks were wet.

Petzoldt's primary assignment was the prevention of injuries and illness. The Tenth Mountain Division often skied twenty to twenty-five miles per day and spent the night in snow huts. The training culminated with the dreaded D-series, in which vast numbers of troops climbed to 13,000 feet and spent six weeks conducting war games in all kinds of weather. When someone floundered under the extreme conditions, it was Petzoldt's job to get him to the first-aid station.

"This was entirely new for the army," Petzoldt says. "They didn't have anybody who could lower wounded people over cliffs or down mountains or go out and rescue them in a blizzard."

There was no set system of evacuation at that time. In the Tetons, Petzoldt had developed a method for building makeshift litters by chopping down slim pine trees, strapping them front and back to backpacks, and carrying the injured off cliffs and exposed areas to trails where horses could meet them. Sometimes they slid victims down snow chutes in canvas wraps or carried them piggyback.

But in the army he had to devise ways for large numbers of troops to stage evacuations off high peaks or through deep drifts of new-fallen snow. The army already had aluminum body baskets with chicken wire around them which could be carried like stretchers. Petzoldt went a step further and invented a kind of sled by placing the baskets on wedges attached to skis; this kept them above the snow and made it possible to control their descent with ropes at the rear, much like today's ski patrol toboggans. In heavily wooded areas, the toboggan could be belayed and guided around trees blocking the path. The patient could be tucked into a sleeping bag for warmth on cold or lengthy trips.

When it was necessary to get someone off a cliff, a taut "zipline" would be fastened from the top to a rock or tree at the bottom so the basket could hang from it by slings and carabiners. Then someone would feed out a belay rope tied to the basket to control the descent. It was a hazardous procedure, but fast, and fulfilled army dictates for minimum treatment on site and quick evacuation to a first-aid station.

Petzoldt and Tapley also organized a way for whole units of soldiers to get over steep cliffs in quick succession. In a rather dangerous procedure, each man tied a sling around his waist and fastened two carabiners onto its long tail. Then, lining up on the edge of the precipice like paratroopers, each man clamped his carabiners [with gates reversed so the rope couldn't slip out] over a double zipline and then jumped into space, hanging onto the sling tail for balance. A topside belayer controlled the jumper's speed and stopped him before he reached the end of the 120-foot zipline.

"We might have bruised a few people," Petzoldt says, "but we never so much as broke a bone."

One blizzardy night when the temperature plummeted below zero, they had to make an actual rescue of a man who had suffered a ruptured appendix while on a high mountain maneuver. Another time a fellow fell off a cliff and broke his leg. Cases of frostbite and hypothermia requiring evacuation were legion.

In the summer of 1944, Petzoldt had a special assignment to go to Camp Carson, which was over the mountains near Colorado Springs, to train some medics headed for Burma. That is where he set up the first real mountain-climbing camp. While he was there, Camp Hale was suddenly closed. In an unexplained move, the skiing soldiers were marched onto a train headed for hot, flat Camp Swift in Texas.

It didn't make any sense to Petzoldt to train and acclimate troops for 40 below zero conditions and then send them to temperatures exceeding 100 degrees. He applied for a transfer and used his influence in Washington to obtain an assignment to officer's candidate school at Fort Benning, Georgia. He graduated as a second lieutenant and was asked to stay on as an instructor. Later, he was transferred to Camp Croft, South Carolina.

As it turned out, the Tenth Mountain Division put their alpine training to good use. In 1945, the troopers engaged experienced German forces on Riva Ridge in Italy. Their esprit de corps and hardened physical condition enabled them to liberate much of the Po Valley. Of 14,000 men, 992 were killed and 4,000 wounded in the campaign.

A few months after the war with Germany ended, Petzoldt was recalled to Washington and given orders to fly to Paris for indoctrination. He was assigned to the Unified Control Council of Allied Nations in Berlin.

The Control Council was set up by Allied leaders at Yalta to take the reins in Germany until a stable government could be established. When Petzoldt got to Berlin, authority over the city had already been split between the Americans, the British, and the Russians. The business and government sections were reduced to rubble, and everything was under military jurisdiction.

One of his first jobs was to locate German Agricultural Department officials and bring them back to Berlin so they could reconstruct records and help determine what facilities were still intact and what supplies needed to be sent from America. Petzoldt was issued a small plane with a pilot and interpreter and sometimes flew as far as Italy and France to track down the missing persons.

He approached the Nazis cautiously, and with a .45 revolver strapped to his side. Most of the Nazis were contrite and gave him little trouble. He told them that the Allies were there to help Germany rebuild, and they needed the records in order to feed the people. The Allies would either have to put German agriculture back together or send hundreds of thousands of tons of food to keep the people from starving to death.

He told them that if the Germans raised crops themselves, the United States would send them new tractors and other farm machinery. That being the case, they could reopen the coal mines and steel mills to manufacture parts for the equipment and repair bridges and railroad lines in order to restart the economy. His arguments convinced the Nazis.

"Then I was given the dirtiest job they had in Berlin," Petzoldt remembers. "I had to go around and pick billets for members of the Control Council.

"I'd ask a German where were the best homes where the most Nazis lived. He said Dahlem, a ritzy residential section. So we went there and I'd look over a home to see how it would do for us. If I found a lot of Nazi pictures and insignia in their drawers, I'd just give them my papers and say you have four days to get out. They could take their personal things but had to leave a certain amount of dishes, bedding, and such. And out they went. This was war!"

Petzoldt selected a beautiful home for himself and three roommates. The large house had four bedrooms, a massive library, a totally equipped kitchen, and a wine cellar and was surrounded by a lush lawn and gardens.

But the wine cellar was empty. So Petzoldt, who had accumulated substantial winnings from poker games, decided to fill it.

The U.S. military forbade troops to send more than the amount of their wages back to the United States. If they sent additional cash, they were accused of getting it on the black market. Petzoldt "had a whole damn bag full of German marks," and didn't want to take a chance on having it confiscated. He decided he might as well spend it. He made a few trips to southern Germany and France, and soon the cellar shelves were stocked with fine wines and cognac.

Since one of his duties was to entertain Russian officers, his liquor supply became very popular. Soon the Soviets indicated that they would like to have some of it. They also let him know that they had acquired substantial booty in German porcelain.

Petzoldt had learned a great deal about china from the Dean of Windsor, who was an expert collector. U.S. officers could ship anything home as long as they had receipts and swore the packages contained no military equipment or government property. He agreed to the trade, and in quick measure Russian chauffeurs appeared at his door with trunk loads of priceless ceramics to barter for brandy.

A German carpenter built a number of crates for him, and he shipped the porcelain to the United States. He sent them to the Holiday

Department Store, where he had worked while living in Laramie, Wyoming. They stored the boxes in an empty room upstairs.

"Crime doesn't pay!" Petzoldt laughed, remembering the events fifty years later. "When I was in Shanghai, I opened a letter from a friend in Laramie and here was this clipping from the newspaper: 'Whole block burned! The fire started in the Holiday Department Store. Nothing saved.' "

One day without any explanation, he received orders to go to London. Hoping he would have the chance to visit Dean Baillie, who had retired to the countryside, he took along a couple of cases of wine and bought some good Cuban cigars as a gift. The old gentleman was delighted to see him, and they spent two pleasant evenings sipping and puffing while they reminisced about past times.

In England the army offered Petzoldt an honorable discharge if he would go as a civilian to work for the Chinese National Relief Administration under K. Y. Chen, Nationalist China's chief of transportation in Shanghai. He would be employed by the Chinese government but paid by the United States.

America was contending with tons of excess military equipment that had been shipped to China in readiness for a possible invasion of Japan. After the atomic bomb was dropped on Hiroshima, the matériel was unnecessary. The United States did not want to go to the expense of reshipping the trucks, Jeeps, and other heavy wartime equipment and possibly disrupting the recovering economy at home. It seemed more practical to give the brand new vehicles to the Chinese.

But more than machinery, the Chinese needed food. There were some places in China where people were starving. Hundreds of water buffalo had been killed during the war, and farmers, weakened by hunger, had to drag their heavy plows by hand to work their meager rice paddies. Meanwhile, tons of unused American food sat on the docks along with the abandoned machinery. Petzoldt's mission was to find a way to get the foodstuffs to the people.

"The only contribution I made was to understand the graft that was involved," Petzoldt remembers. "This was one of the worst gangs that ever ruled a country. The Sungs and Kungs were more or less in charge, and it was awful. They milked the American government.

"You could take a one-dollar bill and go down to the black market

17. Paul on Mount Teewinot, 1940

18. Max Eberli, Paul and Elizabeth Knowlton on summit of La Reina, Santa Marta Expedition, Colombia, South America, 1941

19. *Wreckage of New Tribes Mission plane on Mount Moran, 1950*

20. (left) *NOLS Headquarters at the Sinks*

21. (below) *Paul on NOLS course on the tip of Isla San Pedro, Nolasco, Mexico*

22. (top inside right) *Ernest "Tap" Tapley relaxing during the first NOLS women's course, 1966*

23. (top outside right) *Paul and Eldon "Curly" on summit of the Grand Teton, 50th Anniversary Climb, 1974*

24. (below right) *Paul instructing rappeller on 39ers course, August 1971*

25. *60th Anniversary Climb of the Grand Teton, 1984*

26. *Nancy Carson, Paul, and Andy Carson on summit of the Grand Teton, 60th Anniversary Climb, 1984*

27. (right) *Paul with 60th Anniversary cake baked by Nancy Carson, 1984*

28. (below) *Paul and Ginny in view of Mount Everest, 1992*

29. *Paul Petzoldt still going strong at 90*

and buy 2,000 CNC (Chinese National Currency). Now if we were hiring Chinese to work at the airfields or anything, we had to pay them in Chinese money. But as a government, or the United Nations Relief and Reconstruction Administration (UNRRA), we couldn't buy this stuff on the black market. We had to buy it from the banks, and that was the Sungs and Kungs and Madame Chiang Kai-shek.

"The official rate was twenty to one. So in order to pay a coolie enough to live on, we had to pay him $200 a day—2,000 CNC. And it didn't go to the coolie. All he got was his bowl of rice. It all went into the banks.

"And little Madame Chiang Kai-shek coming over here and talking about the great Chinese democracy in front of Congress, and clenching her little fists and making all those guys get tears in their eyes! Wow! Over there they were killing and torturing people, cutting off their heads. Any opposition, bang! I saw the writing on the wall the moment I got there. We were fighting the Communists!"

So when he needed to transport food to the farmers, he played the game. He put a few goodies on top of every load that was shipped. Nylon stockings. Cigarettes. Peanuts. Canned sardines. Then he hoped that a few bags of rice would be left for the needy at the end of the run after everybody had taken off their cut.

It had been over a year since he had seen Bernice. She had stayed in Riverton with her mother while he was in Germany. Now that he was a civilian, he sent for her to join him. And bring along an American car. It would be convenient to have an automobile and, since vehicles made in the States were highly prized by the Chinese, he figured they could sell it for about $10,000 when they left.

They did. Petzoldt met a White Russian businessman who had escaped from the Communists and settled in Shanghai. He offered to trade a bag of pearls worth $10,000 for the car. He told Petzoldt that he had purchased the gems from American aviators who had brought them into the country on flights from Japan. Petzoldt made the deal.

But when he and Bernice arrived back in the United States, they were stopped by customs. They told the officers they had bought the gems in China, but the official identified them as cultured pearls from Japan and said there was no record that they had been recently sold in China. Therefore, they were considered Japanese property, and since the United States had defeated Japan, they belonged to the American government. The pearls were seized. The Petzoldts tried unsuccessfully to protest the confiscation.

They spent the winter of 1946 in Azusa, California. Friends from Dubois had told them about the town, and they thought they might settle there. They borrowed $10,000 on the GI bill to build a house. Professional contractors constructed a foundation and framed the thousand-square-foot bungalow, but Petzoldt and Bernice did most of the finish work themselves. They camped out until they completed the roof and walls and were able to sleep in the tiny home.

Petzoldt finished two bedrooms and plumbed a bathroom. He made regular trips to the junkyard to see what could be salvaged and found a pile of abandoned redwood planks which he bought for $50. He had the wood replaned and paneled the living room with it.

They moved in in the early spring. They were pleased with their good work, but something was missing. Each new day was like the last. There was no melting snow. No critters peeking out of their winter dens. No chartreuse sprouts on barren trees. No mountains to climb.

"Let's go back to Jackson," Petzoldt said one morning.

"I was ready a month ago," Bernice replied.

. . . .

CHAPTER 9

The Homestead

BUSINESS HAD BEEN SLOW FOR GLENN EXUM DURING THE WAR, WITH gas rationing and a virtual shutdown of the tourist industry. But the climbing concession remained intact for the duration, and there was never a threat of losing the business to competition because the government couldn't take it away from Petzoldt while he was in the service.

When he returned in the summer of 1947, he and Exum changed the name to the Petzoldt-Exum School of American Mountaineering and moved their headquarters out of the tepee and into a long clapboard barracks which had once been used by the Civilian Conservation Corps. The Petzoldts made a kitchen and sleeping rooms out of one section of the rundown building and filled the other half with mountaineering gear. These quarters were only temporary, however. Petzoldt still had some poker winnings left, and they were on the lookout for a better place to live.

Ever since the mid-1930s, when he used to drive up Teton Pass with Curly and Fred Brown to ski the untouched slopes on the southern flanks of the range, he had had his eye on the Crystal Springs Ranch in Moose. The 200-acre spread was not only blessed with a huge spring of pure water, it stood at the base of Rendezvous

Mountain, where the trio used to break trail for over four thousand vertical feet before plunging downhill into the pasture. Petzoldt always said the mountain, with its great bowls of snow and steep runs, would be an ideal spot for a major ski resort. When he learned that the property was for sale for $17,000, he tracked down the owner and pulled out his cash.

But he and Bernice scarcely had time to celebrate before the deal was canceled. The sale was not even out of escrow when the rancher came crying to Petzoldt with the news that his wife had changed her mind and threatened to divorce him if he sold her home. He offered to pay real estate and bank fees and throw in $3,000 for the inconvenience. Petzoldt took pity on the beleaguered husband and agreed to the cancellation. Eighteen years later, the Crystal Springs Ranch and Rendezvous Mountain became the $1.6 million Teton Village Ski Area.

That winter a friend from Riverton called to tell Petzoldt that the federal government was starting a reclamation project near there and conducting a drawing for irrigated homestead lots. Veterans were eligible to participate. Petzoldt figured his chances of winning were slim to nil but decided it wouldn't hurt to enter the lottery. If he did get lucky, it might be possible to get some stability into his life.

He could have returned to government service after the war and retained the same grade at the Department of Agriculture with all of the pensions and security to go with it. But the idea of pushing papers in the humid capital city for the rest of his life was repugnant to him. He belonged in the Rocky Mountain West where he could climb, ski, hunt, and fish.

On the other hand, if he won the drawing he would be a landowner—a farmer like his father. He could develop the homestead to get the deed and not have to depend on a three-month-long season of climbing to make a living. That January, his name was the third one drawn.

After carefully studying Bureau of Reclamation maps of the units, he selected 160 acres on a high plateau at the foot of Lost Well's Butte. His land stood above the sagebrush flats of the Riverton valley and within sight of the snow-topped Wind River mountains rising one hundred miles in the distance. He and Bernice moved in March.

Two 20-by-110-foot barracks from a Japanese detention camp were included in the lottery winnings. But the buildings were in Cody, almost two hundred miles away. Hiring someone to haul them or deliver them dismantled was expensive, and Petzoldt knew there were high costs for leveling and ditching property. On top of all that, they had to build a home and buy farm machinery and seed. Expenses would mount quickly. He told Bernice that collecting the barracks had to be a do-it-yourself project.

Petzoldt decided to saw the buildings into twelve-foot-wide loads and trail them behind their Jeep. They started with three sections, enough to throw up a makeshift dwelling until they could transport the rest of them to build a home. They jacked up the awkward segments and muscled them onto the trailer bed. Then they created a traffic jam when the tall load wedged itself under an arched steel bridge. While a string of cars waited, Petzoldt climbed up and sawed off the roof tops to release the load.

In April 1948, they assembled the three sections and placed them on a foundation made of redrock hauled forty miles from Wind River Canyon. They furnished their temporary home with army cots, homemade tables and benches, and an antiquated coal range. A used army stove heated the place.

When he finally hitched a small plow to the Jeep to clear brush and break up the soil, Petzoldt thought about his father laboring in the fields from before light until after dark. He rigged a rake onto the back of a rented tractor so that Bernice could help him. Together, they prepared the whole 160 acres and planted a crop of alfalfa seed and wheat before May.

There was still no water from the irrigation project. The reclamation office did not open the canals until June. When they did, a raging flood gushed onto the carefully cultivated fields and turned them to mud. Petzoldt's desperate shoveling failed to keep the flow in channels between the planted rows. They thought their hard work was wasted.

The next day they went to a Riverton hardware store to inquire about irrigation methods. They came home with hundreds of curved aluminum tubes. The shopkeeper told them to bridge the tubes between the irrigation ditch and the seed rows, then prime them to siphon out a controlled flow of water. The system worked, and they had a small harvest that fall.

In October they hauled the remaining barracks from Cody and commenced construction of a long ranch-style home and a bunkhouse.

Their second year the crops did well, and Petzoldt ran a couple of bands of sheep. He also leased more land and began raising alfalfa seed under government contract. Bernice started writing *On Top of the World*, a biography of her mountain-climbing husband.

The alfalfa seed was an experimental strain that had to be planted in soil that had never before been cultivated. Petzoldt's land, tilled out of sagebrush and greasewood, proved perfect for the plants. He became one of the area's biggest suppliers.

On the day before Thanksgiving 1950, Petzoldt was summoned back to the Tetons. Paul Judge, chief ranger of Grand Teton National Park, called to tell him a plane was down near the summit of Mount Moran in the middle of a blizzard. A rancher had spotted a light that could be a fire or possibly some flares. There might be survivors. They needed him to lead a rescue effort.

"Do you know whose plane it is?" Petzoldt asked. Judge told him that a DC-3 owned by the New Tribes Mission was four hours overdue on a flight from California to Montana. The missionaries had been on their way to South America. "My God," Petzoldt said. "I know those people. I showed them my K2 films in Chico before the war."

Driving over icy Togwotee Pass, Petzoldt remembered meeting the group. Paul Fleming, the impassioned evangelist leader, had characterized their overriding goal as, "Reaching new tribes until we've reached the last tribe."

But on their first mission, five of their members were massacred in the Amazon jungle. In a second attempt, fifteen missionaries were lost when their DC-3 crashed in the Venezuelan wilds. Now this.

Despite his concern for the planeload of women and children, he was not eager to climb the 12,594-foot peak. He had pioneered four routes up that mountain and knew it better than anybody. It had never been scaled in winter. There were places where sloping ledges were stacked like shingles and piled high with snow that was ready to avalanche. Danger was severe under normal conditions and would be greatly aggravated by the storm that now blanketed the peak in fog and snow.

When he arrived at Jackson, the weather had deteriorated to a whiteout. Mount Moran was completely socked in. There was still no verifiable proof that a plane was really up there. Someone claimed they had heard an engine. A rancher had seen a brief flash of light when the clouds parted for a few minutes. But the aircraft was far off its logged flight course, and it was impossible to send a search plane to look for the wreckage. Knowing nothing could be done until morning, Petzoldt went to the Cowboy Bar for a drink.

Nobody recognized him at first. People talked about the wreck and said newspapers and radio stations were calling from all over the country. Several rescue efforts that day had been thwarted. Air Force paratroopers, hoping to make an early morning jump to the accident scene, were foiled by snow and grounded in Idaho Falls. Park rangers Blake Vande Water and Merle Stitt then left on skis with mountaineers Richard Lange and Jim Huidekoper. They planned to carry first-aid materials to timberline and then make a technical climb to the wreckage. They were turned back on the glacier by the blizzard.

"The sheriff and the park have called Petzoldt," someone said. "Hell, they've got the right son-of-a-bitch now," said another. Any thoughts Petzoldt had of pulling out vanished.

On Thanksgiving morning he went to park headquarters to launch a rescue attempt. The chief ranger asked what he needed.

"I want Vande Water to go with me, a boat to get us across Jenny Lake, and about three of the army airmen as a support team," he said.

Before the party left he distributed copies of a diagram he had made of the mountain. The map was overlaid with a numbered grid so that the accident location could be pinpointed by the number on a square. If the plane was spotted from the air, the rangers could guide the rescuers by reporting the grid number on shortwave radio.

When everything was organized the party crossed the lake, attached climbing skins to their skis, and started up the mountain. The soldiers broke trail so that Petzoldt and Vande Water could save their energy for the difficult climbing ahead. They made timberline late in the day and established a base camp.

That afternoon, while the rescue party slogged through the snow, a private pilot circling the mountain located the wreckage. It lay far south of the direction the climbers were headed. The rangers tried to radio the information to Petzoldt, but the transmission apparently failed. In a desperate all-night push, Huidekoper, Lange, and Bill Ashley force-marched to the high camp and caught up with Petzoldt's group at 6:00 A.M. on November 24, in time to turn them toward the northeast ridge.

The five men roped up and gingerly made their way through deep, unstable snow and piles of rock to make a new camp. When they reached the area where the technical climbing would begin, Petzoldt and Vande Water left the others and continued upward alone.

"We took turns leading," Petzoldt remembers, "but we didn't get very far because we had to drive pitons, it was very steep, and we were trying to keep off the ledges. Sometimes we tried to avalanche a ledge. It was very dangerous."

Finally they reached a point about three hundred feet beneath an icy cliff which was studded with snowdrifts that looked as though they could plunge down on them any minute. Barely visible behind the shelf was a tangle of charred metal.

"When we looked up and saw that cliff—a smooth, ice-polished face broken with tenuously balanced drifts of snow—we just stared hopelessly at each other," Petzoldt said later. "We were worn out. We knew we couldn't make it in the remaining time and survive." With nightfall approaching they turned back to camp.

They tried again the next morning and reached the glassy cliff from which they had retreated the night before. The clouds were breaking up, and they heard cawing crows flying above them. They yelled. There was no answer.

There was nothing to do now but cross the ice ledge, where it was impossible to place pitons. They chopped steps as they made their way, listening for the warning "huuut" that signals an avalanche. An ice step crumbled under Petzoldt's foot, and he banged against the wall as Vande Water caught him with the rope. He regained his balance, and they continued while their movements tumbled little snowballs that threatened to trigger a major slide.

Eventually the gradient eased. The two exhausted climbers plodded through the powder to a small opening where pieces of wreckage were strewn over the snow. It appeared that the plane had crashed into a huge boulder and everything had compressed and burned.

"Nothing much was left," Petzoldt remembers. "The biggest piece [of a body] we found was a torso. The aluminum part of the back of the plane was there. One wing had gone off into the air, probably into the glacier because it's never been found. The fuselage, where people sat, there wasn't a seat, a piece of board, an electric wire, a lamp, there wasn't anything there except that aluminum. Everything else had gone right out and hit that big rock."

The sight dealt Vande Water an unexpected shock. "What impacted me really strongly was here were all these things, and the first thing that came to my mind was eyeballs. Terrible! I thought, impossible. Obviously, it couldn't have been that, but this was the first thought that came to me. On further examination I saw they were vitamin pills or some kind of capsule that had exploded and enlarged."

Petzoldt and Vande Water picked up some scattered papers, a briefcase holding books and flight logs, and a Bible. They placed the few remnants in their packs, took some pictures for the official report, and left the scene. It was ultimately decided that further rescue efforts would not be worth the risk to life.

It was almost dark when they reached timberline. Vande Water started striking and rolling up the tent to break camp. "What are you going to do?" Petzoldt said. "Let's just leave it here."

"Paul, this is my whole rescue cache," Vande Water said. "I need to have this for tomorrow or the next day." So they loaded the gear and hefted packs weighing over 100 pounds each.

"The snow was heavy," Vande Water remembers. "We thought when we got down a ways we could use our skis, but there was no base. We were sinking in and couldn't make turns.

"Then it got dark, and all those trees and no trails! We ended up lying on our stomachs on the skis and going until we'd hit a tree, then move over and go some more. Fifty feet at a time."

As they neared the bottom, they heard strange crashing noises. When they reached Moran Bay, they saw Ken Reemers in his lopsided boat. The boating concessionaire was making circles to break up ice in the freezing lake so that he could pick up the rescuers.

Several years after the Mount Moran rescue attempt, rumors started. People stopped Petzoldt and Vande Water on the street and asked, "Didn't you really get some money up there?" Gossip spread that the two rescuers had filled their packs with cash, watches, jewelry, and other valuables.

"That was so funny," Vande Water says. "Those people didn't have any money. They were poor missionaries."

"I knew the source," Petzoldt says. "The movie."

In 1956 *The Mountain*, a popular film starring Spencer Tracy and Robert Wagner, was shown all over the country. Tracy, a Swiss guide, took his brother, Wagner, up a great mountain and stumbled on a plane wreck. Only one beautiful young girl had survived.

"The no-good brother found a lot of money in the plane, took it and stashed it to smuggle out when they got back to the valley," Petzoldt says. "They had to bring the injured girl across deep crevasses. Tracy saved the girl but, as justice would have it, the wicked brother crashed through a snow bridge and fell into space with all the money."

The federal government had greater appreciation for the rescuers' risks than the Wyoming gossips. Petzoldt and Vande Water were each awarded the Department of Interior Conservation Award for their bravery. It was the highest honor bestowed by the department.

Petzoldt spent the rest of the winter tending his sheep and waiting for spring so that he could install irrigation on his new leases.

At the same time, he made a difficult decision. Finally, in 1955 he gave Exum the climbing concession. He did not feel that the school provided enough income to support two families and, with the demands of the farm, he would no longer be able to spend full time guiding.

"I had to do what I had to do," he says. "I had to make money. And if you've got debts, you have to pay them off. I had to make money any way I could."

His alfalfa seed business grew, and new problems arose. Wyoming did not have a facility to clean seed to meet government specifications, so after harvest Petzoldt had to truck his loads to the Platte Valley elevator in Sterling, Colorado. One day in the mid-1950s, after he had delivered about $150,000 worth of seed that was certified by the University of Wyoming, a friend called him from Sterling.

"You'd better get over here quick," he said. "There's a rumor that Platte's gone bankrupt. People are panicking. They might steal your seed."

Petzoldt jumped into the pickup and left at once. He sped through the black desert knowing everything he had was tied up in that seed. He remembered his experience with the onion field when he was a boy.

The warehouse lights were glowing like a lantern when he arrived about midnight. The building was an anthill of people and trucks weaving through high stacks of sacked grain. There was no sign of law enforcement. Farmers milled through the storehouse searching for their seed only to find that the government identification tags had been removed. Tension grew. People started grabbing anything they could get their hands on and tossing heavy bags into truck beds.

Petzoldt elbowed his way through the crowd looking for his seed. He found a large amount of it in a towering pile. He ran to his pickup and grabbed a double-bladed ax, then returned to station himself beside his property for the rest of the night. He was angry. He was big. And he had an ax. Nobody bothered him.

When the authorities arrived the next morning most of the grain was gone. Petzoldt stood wearily by his untouched store. It was obvious that he had the largest remaining supply.

A bank official approached him. He flashed the receipts that Petzoldt had given as collateral for a $20,000 loan. He said the bank had experienced grave losses. In order to recover, it must claim the seed it was entitled to. They had financed Petzoldt initially and given him the extra loan. They were sorry, but his seed belonged to them.

"I lost it all," Petzoldt remembers. "The elevator company was going broke so mortgaged itself, and everything that was in there, to a Chicago outfit which had a racket of taking over grain elevators that were in financial trouble. Then the crooks went in there and took the tags off all this government seed so it couldn't be identified.

"I never thought anything like that could happen. Most states had legislation to guarantee insurance protection for farmers who have crops stored in elevators. Colorado had a bill in the legislature the year before, but it didn't pass. I didn't know that at the time. I thought the certificates I had for seed were like money in the bank.

"Instead of being worth a quarter of a million dollars, I walked out of there owing $70,000. When all my creditors heard about it, they just closed in on me like a bunch of wolves. I owed for machinery, and one of the guys in Riverton started to collect on me and put a judgment against me. I owed the First National Bank $35,000, and they wouldn't loan me any more money so I had to liquidate at a very bad time."

Petzoldt filed a lawsuit and took it all the way to the federal court in Denver. He won, but only recouped enough money to pay his attorneys and cancel a portion of his debt to the bank.

When he and Bernice lost the farm, his brother-in-law, head of the agronomy department at the University of Wyoming, hired him to research another irrigation project near Cody. All winter Petzoldt interviewed GIs who had drawn 160-acre homesteads there, as he had done at Riverton.

He concluded that people could not make a living on small farms in that area any more. The high prices of machinery alone made the expenses prohibitive. He toured the county and tabulated figures about the farmers' overhead, what they raised, and how much they got for their crops. When the data had been collected, he helped produce a pamphlet about the findings. The publication showed that profits from production of wheat and alfalfa seed did not warrant excessive irrigation and equipment costs.

The study was a rallying point for the GIs who had put their life savings into the homesteads and were going broke. A number of them got together to hammer out a solution.

"They are opening up a new irrigation project around Yuma and Palm Springs," Petzoldt told the meeting. "We know we can make a living on 160 acres there if they would trade this poor land for property that can grow more valuable crops. The only thing for us to do is get together and send a representative group back to Washington, D.C., and talk to the head honchos there."

Petzoldt and three other men were elected to make an appeal to the Department of the Interior. After listening to their arguments, the secretary of the interior said, "It was a heck of an idea." Government soil samples in Wyoming proved the land was of poor quality. GIs couldn't survive there. On the other hand, the new systems in Arizona and California had plenty of water, cement canals, and crops adaptable to the soil. He thought they could work something out.

But when the project materialized and the Petzoldts moved to Arizona in the late 1950s, he was disappointed. The acreage he drew was hilly and covered with mesquite. It would cost a fortune to get it cleared and leveled.

Worse still, Bernice was acting peculiar. She suffered from sudden personality changes and had turned mean. She had always mimicked people and had a good eye for stinging detail. It used to be funny. But her sarcastic humor had turned ugly. She would be perfectly normal one day and then fall into a period of depression. Her episodes of erratic conduct were increasing. The ill-timed remark in India about *kundalini* had been the first real indication of the change in her behavior. Despite her remorse over that incident, the insults continued to occur. Especially after she had consumed a drink or two.

Was it because they couldn't have children? he wondered. Once they consulted a doctor in New York, but medical knowledge about sterility was not advanced at that time so the physician did not give them any definitive answers.

Perhaps it was the transient life they lived, or that they had not accumulated much money. He tried to talk to her about it, but she quickly changed the subject.

One evening when they were still in Jackson, Petzoldt confessed he was worried about her. Some city folks who were looking for property to buy invited them to dinner. Bernice was delightful throughout the meal. Then suddenly, with no provocation, she turned on one of the men. "You're a son-of-a-bitch," she snapped. Petzoldt made their excuses and they left.

"Why did you say that?" he asked when they got home. "Darling, I think we should get you some help."

"You're the crazy one," she shouted. The following morning she denied making any rude statement.

When they moved to Arizona, Bernice worsened. Petzoldt still loved her but realized he couldn't continue living with her unless she changed. He didn't think her problem was alcohol. She was not a habitual drinker. But a couple of cocktails set her off. He thought she might be schizophrenic, since her family had a history of that disorder. He begged her to go to a psychiatrist. She screamed back that he was the one who needed a shrink.

One night he awakened to see her standing over him with a large piece of wood poised to strike him on the head. He grabbed the weapon from her, and she ran for the door. He knew it was no longer safe for him to live with her.

"I think you had better go back to your mother's home in Riverton," he said when she calmed down. He knew as a Catholic she would not accept a divorce, but hoped her family could prevail on her to seek help.

"I loved her," Petzoldt remembers. "She was a wonderful person. I felt she was a normal person and then it got so bad with the changes that I didn't know how to handle it."

A few weeks later a man from Cheyenne offered to trade him the Ram's Horn Saloon in Dubois for the Arizona homestead. He jumped at the deal.

The Ram's Horn was a typical western hangout. Animal trophies hung over the bar and a leather band, depicting Wyoming's history in tooled pictures of Indians, trappers, covered wagons, cowboys, and ranches, stretched the length of the cafe wall. There was a little hotel upstairs, where Petzoldt lived in one of the rooms.

He tended bar for awhile but knew he would have to do something rash to raise enough money to repay the $70,000 he still owed on the Riverton homestead and to take care of Bernice. His sisters Lily and Gladys still lived in Long Beach, so he decided to go there and try the lucrative real estate business. He had always been a good salesman and the California market was hot. But after going to school and obtaining his sales license, he found it difficult to break into the field without contacts. So he switched to selling used cars.

"I was operating a little bit illegally," he admitted later, "but I was desperate and really making a lot of money."

He didn't have a used car lot of his own, but wholesaled vehicles to other dealers. He specialized in glamorous products like Cadillac convertibles with white leather interiors, long black Lincolns, and sexy sports cars.

"I used to buy ten cars at an auction with $100 in the bank and write checks for them," he said. "I had four or five bank accounts in California, Arizona, and Texas. Maybe I'd have to fix the transmission a little, shine them up, put a couple of hundred dollars work on them, but I could sell them for about $5,000 or $5,750.

"Well, it was a racket," he admits. "I played on the selfishness of people living in snorky subdivisions and trying to keep up with the Joneses. I'd give them a Cadillac with 10,000 miles on it, park it in their driveway, and take out an ad in the paper. This was 'Aunt Edna's car,' or something, you know, and she had to sell it. They would have to give me a deposit on the car so I could keep operating and catch up on my checks.

"A lot of people were afraid, and rightfully so, of buying cars from secondhand lots, but they would buy a Cadillac sitting out there in front of a $50,000 house. Hell, we'd sometimes make $2,000 on a car. I'd split it with the home owners.

"Soon as I got my bills paid, I came up to Pinedale and went off in the mountains with a pack on my back for a month by myself. Got a lot of beer out of my belly and cleared the air."

With his debts paid, Petzoldt bought Bernice a home in Laramie and returned to live in Dubois.

Dorothy Dewhurst Reed from Lander often drove to Dubois with a girlfriend to have dinner and attend dances at the Ram's Horn Saloon. Dottie managed the local radio station, which she co-owned with her brother-in-law, State Senator E. J. Breece. She and Petzoldt began dating regularly and their friendship finally developed into talk of marriage. The only thing that held them back was Bernice's religious opposition to divorce.

"Dottie had the type of stability and intelligence I liked," Petzoldt says. "She had had a very unhappy marriage with her first husband, so we just naturally gravitated together."

Petzoldt had done everything possible to provide for Bernice during their separation. But he no sooner bought her a $17,000 house in Laramie than she sold it and left for Arizona. Soon that money was gone. He moved her back to Laramie and bought her another home. This time he kept the deed.

Meanwhile, as his relationship with Dottie grew stronger, he sold the Ram's Horn and moved to Lander. He tried repeatedly to convince Bernice to grant him a divorce, but she held her ground.

One spring day in 1961, while hiking in the canyons above Lander, he ran into some local youngsters playing at rock climbing. They were all nerve and no skill, and it was obvious to him that someone was going to get seriously hurt. He wanted to help the kids and teach them a little mountaineering, but knew he would be liable in case of an accident.

He appeared before the town council and asked if it would be possible for him to instruct the young people under the aegis of the city. Jack Nicholas, an attorney and chairman of the Parks and Recreation Department, promised to look into the possibility. His investigation was positive, and Petzoldt received permission to conduct classes in a warming hut near the municipal ice skating rink. He started with just a few students, but his initial sessions with the youngsters were so successful that adults asked to participate. With official approval, he established the American School of Mountaineering and moved his courses into Sinks Canyon above town.

Overnight camp-outs became a family affair in Lander. One March a group of students, including Nicholas, even climbed the Grand Teton. Petzoldt's school was the first municipally sponsored climbing program in the country.

Adventure courses for youngsters were just developing in the United States. A year after Petzoldt started the Lander school, a branch of Outward Bound was introduced to America in neighboring Colorado. He read an article about it in *Reader's Digest*, and to his surprise he saw that the chief instructor was Tap Tapley, his fellow ski trooper.

Outward Bound originated in England following World War II. The school was born of concern about the numbers of young men lost in battle on the Atlantic Ocean. Rookie seamen escaping from torpedoed ships died unnecessarily. They proved less self-reliant than older, seasoned crew members who had a keen sense of weather and were sustained by an unselfish bond with their shipmates.

The first school was started by Kurt Hahn, a founding headmaster of the Gordonstoun School, where many English princes studied. The curriculum was grueling. For twenty-six days students were tested on endurance, strength of character, and the will to survive physical and mental challenges.

Besides general conditioning, they were taught map and compass reading, campcraft, backpacking, first aid, axemanship, knots and rope handling, rock climbing, fire fighting, mountain rescue, and development of group bonding and trust through tests on aerial rope courses and vertical walls.

But Outward Bound had an unstated goal that was equally as important as the demanding activities. Youngsters from all walks of life were removed from their familiar environments for an entire month and brought together with individuals from other ethnic, educational, and financial worlds to create a unique society of their own. As a result, the students began to scrutinize the real values, meaning, and purpose of their lives.

In March 1959, F. Charles Froelicher, headmaster of the Colorado Academy, a Denver boys' school, learned about Outward Bound. Although he realized the program was too vast to incorporate into his own institution, the concept fascinated him and he became enthusiastic about finding some way to start the courses in America.

A year later, Gilbert Burnett, a former operative for the Office of Strategic Services and the Central Intelligence Agency, also became fired up about Outward Bound when a reporter for the London *Times* told him about Hahn's enterprise and described Outward Bound's combination of severe challenges, raw adventure, and the idiom of compassion.

Burned out by almost twenty years of the dirty tricks and heartlessness of his intelligence work, Burnett was so deeply affected by Hahn's philosophy that he quit the agency and turned to education. He applied to John Kemper at Andover Academy in Massachusetts for the position of biology teacher.

On the day of his job interview, Burnett met Josh Miner, who taught at the school. When Burnett heard that Miner had been to Gordonstoun and had worked with Hahn for two years, his interest in Outward Bound rekindled. Later he learned of Froelicher's interest in starting an Outward Bound school in Colorado.

In January 1961, Burnett contacted Froelicher and they invited Kemper, Miner, Reagh Wetmore, and Ed Williams to gather for a brainstorming session. Two weeks later they voted to launch Colorado Outward Bound in the summer of 1962. They drafted Tap Tapley away from a job dynamiting avalanches and stringing fence for a mining company to get things rolling. He found an ideal location on an old mining claim above the ghost town of Marble. Courses began on June 16, 1962.

Late that summer Petzoldt contacted Tapley and said he would like to take a firsthand look at the new school. He was so impressed with what he saw that he accepted Tapley's invitation to return the next season as the mountaineering advisor.

When he returned home he decided to ask Bernice for a divorce once again. He told her that his life was taking a new direction. Besides, he and Dottie had waited long enough and wanted to get married. If she would sign the papers, he would give her the few thousand dollars in cash that he had saved.

She finally agreed. Hoping to finalize the divorce as quickly as possible, he went to Las Vegas, Nevada, to establish residency. He financed his stay in the gambling town by working as a dealer and shill at the Frontier Casino. When the waiting period ended, he took the legal documents to Laramie for Bernice's signature. He and Dottie were married on December 29, 1962.

The next summer Petzoldt became chief instructor for mountaineering at Outward Bound. Josh Miner and Joe Nold, who had taught at Gordonstoun for a year, took turns as director of the school that season.

Nold, a Canadian, frequently circled the globe, hopping from one teaching position to another and spending his vacations mountain climbing, skiing, and backpacking. He led groups of youngsters on treks in the Spanish Sierra Nevada, Morocco's Atlas Mountains, and the Himalayan foothills.

Miner had distinguished himself in teaching and motivating youngsters, but his outdoor experience was limited to hiking and camping in New England. He had never experienced a real mountain. So when he agreed to share the directorship, he arrived early in order to participate in Petzoldt's classes.

"I'd never seen a Rocky Mountain in my life," he says. "I could never have survived that summer if it hadn't been for Petzoldt. He was my mentor and coached me through it. I was in no shape to be a climber. At 9,000 feet, when I ran in the mornings to the run-and-dip, every tooth in my head ached and I was sick behind every bush."

One night shortly after he had taken charge, an instructor asked Miner if he could be relieved of his duty-officer responsibility. It was the eve of their first big alpine expedition, and he wanted to spend the last evening with his family in Glenwood Springs. "All you have to do is turn out the lights in the tent area at ten o'clock," he said. Miner asked him to show him the switch before he left.

At the appointed hour Miner flicked off the lights. The entire camp fell into total darkness. He had forgotten to bring a flashlight.

Cursing himself, he started to pick his way back through the blackness to headquarters. Then suddenly he fell into a hole dug that afternoon for a water line. A jolt of pain shot through his leg. It was broken.

Embarrassed as much as he was hurting, he yelled for help. Someone found him, carried him to the first-aid tent and got Petzoldt, who treated him with the unlikely combination of a morphine shot and whisky.

"We violated every canon of first aid," Miner remembers. "I lay on the floor with my leg on the cot, watching the ridge pole travel from right to left at 40 miles per hour. Petzoldt and I talked until I went to sleep.

"It probably saved my life because I don't think I could have survived Paul Petzoldt's alpine expedition leaving at four the next morning."

Following the incident Petzoldt suggested that Miner might be better off sticking to the business end of the school. "Look, you don't need to compete with us," he said. "You can just take care of the important things that have been neglected in this place—organization, planning, and general administration."

Miner agreed that the school had been overseen by mountaineers the first year and many administrative matters had been handled in a slipshod manner.

"So it was a perfect fit," says Miner. "My life was saved! I didn't have to take the expedition and I could take care of the things that had been neglected. Petzoldt was magnetic, able, forceful and colorful, and full of wonderful wisdom."

By the end of the season Petzoldt knew that the school had more than administrative problems. It lacked trained leaders. As he explains it:

> We had school teachers who were probably good leaders in
> their environment, but they didn't have leadership ability in
> Colorado—to plan and execute trips in wild country where an

accident would mean walking out ten miles for help. We had steep snow slopes, rock cliffs, loose boulders that dropped down from the mountains, big streams to ford, and severe thunderstorms to endure.

Some people knew how to do sports climbing and hang out all night on a mountain, but they didn't know how to plan and execute trips with ten or twelve kids. They weren't motivated to stand at the bottom teaching these kids; they wanted to do their stuff and have the kids watch them from down below.

A lot of them couldn't interpret maps. They might be able to read maps and see where the trails and roads went and how far they were, but they couldn't look at the various types of terrain, how rough it was, the elevation they must travel up and down.

They hadn't learned how to cook in a sanitary fashion. They would insist on taking things out into the field that could spoil, like sandwiches with mayonnaise, and they didn't know anything about calories.

So we had a showdown with Outward Bound. We said we've got to have these instructors here at least a week or ten days before they start school so we can teach them something. I practically told them their school was never going to amount to a goddam unless they had an instructor's training program.

When the summer of 1963 ended, Petzoldt knew that if Outward Bound, the Boy Scouts, church youth programs and others were going to succeed, they needed to have leaders who could not only motivate and teach youngsters to survive tough, Marine-like experiences but could also demonstrate safe and practical camping and mountaineering techniques.

As the outdoors filled with more and more recreationists who didn't know anything about practical conservation, implementing new laws and regulations would not be enough to protect the environment. Petzoldt was convinced that the only way the wilderness would ever be saved would be through education. And he was determined to train qualified instructors to make it happen.

CHAPTER 10

NOLS (National Outdoor Leadership School)

MID-DECADE—1964. AN ERA OF ENVIRONMENTAL AWARENESS. WITH more and more people trekking into the wild outdoors, it was obvious that the time-honored practices of legendary woodsmen and mountain guides were unacceptable. No longer could one break off pine boughs for beds, dig trenches around tents, build bonfires in a circle of rocks, pollute lakes and streams with cooking grease and soap, or litter campsites with glass, tin, and foil. Faced with sheer force of numbers, the concept that the world and its ecosystem could be thoughtlessly used to promote the immediate benefit of an individual became a thing of the past.

Heeding public outcry, Congress passed the Wilderness Act, which set aside certain unspoiled areas "where the earth and its community of life are untrammeled by man, where man himself is a visitor who does not remain."

Thousands of backpackers and campers headed for the hills to see this pristine paradise for themselves. Government agencies and educational institutions began to research methods of camping that would protect the newly designated wilderness areas.

Petzoldt thought the Wilderness Act was a great move in the right direction. He had even been in Washington to testify in favor of it.

But rules and regulations were not enough to get the job done. Few people knew how to properly use the wilderness they had fought for. Education was the answer. People had to be *taught* how to enjoy the wild outdoors safely and without harming it!

"The research that was being done was all on what people were doing out there," Petzoldt told journalist Molly Absolon. "I said I know what they're doing out there, they're lousing up the joint! There wasn't anything to *tell* us what to do."

When he returned to Outward Bound that summer, his insistence upon instructor training bore fruit. He became chief instructor (at a salary of $100 a month), and Tapley conducted the first leadership course by taking the teachers into the backcountry in an attempt to hone their outdoor skills before classes began. The instruction consisted of "Tapley taking off with the fellas for a hell of a trip," Petzoldt said. But that, like the Wilderness Act, still was not enough.

For a year Petzoldt thought about the problem. He envisioned a new branch of Outward Bound in Lander. It, however, would be different from the regular program,which was built primarily on physical and mental challenges and improvement of individual character. It would be the next step.

His school would give young people authentic adventure to replace the antisocial activities that teenagers often pursued in the name of adventure. It would provide leadership training along with opportunities to practice and master the outdoor skills they learned in the basic course. It would prepare leaders to take their friends, families, Boy Scout troops, or church youth clubs into the wilds safely and enjoyably and lay the groundwork for those wishing to become forest or park rangers or other professionals in the field. Most importantly, it would do away with the teacher who was inept at outdoorsmanship, the skilled outdoorsman who couldn't teach, the mountain climber who cared more about showing off than about motivating others.

Instead of basing students at a permanent camp, it would be a moveable campsite encompassing the whole Wind River Range of Wyoming. Provisions would be hauled to places that were reachable by Jeep or pickup, and the youngsters would hike between them.

"Of all of the mountain ranges I had visited in the whole United States, it was the best one to teach in," Petzoldt said. "The Colorado mountains were V-shaped mountains right down to the rivers. You had to climb over high passes to get from one place to another. In Wyoming there were all the teaching things right there. There were the rocks and the lakes, the forest and the flowers, the accessibility and the wild country. All the training environments that you needed right there."

Petzoldt was forthright with the hierarchy of Outward Bound about his dream. He promoted it openly in Lander, as well. As early as 1963, when Josh Miner had stopped there to discuss the idea of a pilot camp with town leaders, attorney Jack Nicholas had studied the Outward Bound incorporation papers and determined there would be no problem setting up a tax-free, nonprofit branch of the school, or a separate, unaffiliated institution, in Lander.

On July 30, 1963, Petzoldt had told the *Wyoming State Journal*: "We could start with half or a third of the regular program, to get experience at operating the program and not requiring nearly so much money to get started."

In 1964 Petzoldt wrote Miner a letter to elaborate on his vision. "My personal wishes, of course, would be to have an Outward Bound Leadership School here, drawing principally on the students who have finished a course in another Outward Bound school and who, then, are ready to profit by the training that we could give them here to make them real outdoor leaders for their communities, or, if you wished, for other Outward Bound schools in the future."

While he formulated plans for his own school, Petzoldt made certain that the existing Outward Bound program would run smoothly without him. He organized classes so that "the school can coast for awhile," and even tape recorded some of his sessions to help subsequent instructors know what had gone on before them. He resigned in August 1964, prior to the final session that season. Rob Hellyer left with him.

Hellyer had arrived at the camp in Marble unannounced in 1963. In his early twenties, he had lived abroad with his father, who was in the Foreign Service, and had completed three courses of Outward Bound in England. When he learned that the school was opening a branch in the United States, he headed for Colorado with the hope of getting a job.

"He arrived there at COBS in an old car that burnt out a rod in the middle of the Mojave desert," Petzoldt said. "He put it in himself. He wanted to get a job and we had no job for him. He stayed and in a week he was indispensable."

Hellyer created a job for himself in logistics and maintenance of equipment. He and Petzoldt hit it off immediately. "I wasn't there two days and Petzoldt wanted to go out and look at the country around there and he took me along," Hellyer remembers. "It was the biggest break of my life."

The two friends left Outward Bound to launch a two-month-long exploration of the Wind River Range and locate prime teaching areas for the various skills of the leadership course. They walked from Shoshone Lake above Lander over the peaks to Pinedale. In the mountainous terrain, much of which was unmapped, they found trout streams and lakes, granite cliffs and steep snowfields, virgin forests and alpine meadows—everything needed for an outdoor classroom.

"The classroom is the entire Wind River mountain range," Petzoldt said in a later promotional slide-narrative about the school. "The Wind Rivers are not only the least known of our great American mountain ranges but they are by far the most spectacular. Here we not only have the largest ice fields and glaciers in the Lower 48 but we have hundreds of beautiful mountains that have some of the finest rock for climbing in the world. Its glacial valleys rival Yosemite and perpendicular cliffs of two to three thousand feet are so common that there are literally hundreds of miles of them. Within this complex of high mountains, glaciers, and broad U-shaped glacial valleys with perpendicular sides, there are more than a thousand lakes stocked with trout."

Once Petzoldt and Hellyer completed the reconnaissance, the next step was to create an organization.

One evening, Petzoldt and Dottie, Jack and Alice Nicholas, and Dr. and Mrs. William Erickson attended a speech delivered by Governor Milward Simpson. After the program, they went to the Noble Hotel bar for a drink.

"We were sitting in a booth and Petzoldt was talking about the likelihood of getting Outward Bound being zero," Nicholas remembers. "Moreover, the way it was set up, we'd sort of lost interest in pursuing that."

Petzoldt, Nicholas, and Erickson had attended several directors meetings of Colorado Outward Bound and discovered it "had an organization like the British army."

"They wanted buildings," says Nicholas. "Needed about $300,000. No possibility! I think if we had chosen to underwrite all those requirements, we'd have gotten a charter that year. The idea was to underwrite it, and they take all the assets and control everything. None of us were impressed with the capabilities of the Outward Bound people."

A deciding factor was the apparent reticence of the Outward Bound officials to sanction a school in Wyoming at that time. They claimed it was premature, and too close to Colorado geographically.

As the three couples talked into the night, they became increasingly enthusiastic about forgetting Outward Bound and starting a school of their own. Finally, the others went home to bed and Petzoldt and Nicholas went to the attorney's office to draw up a checklist of things to do to start a corporation.

"So we went through and picked out a bunch of names for a potential board of directors, a scheme of capitalization, and chose the name," says Nicholas. "In the next day or two, I went ahead and sent in the charter."

Ed Breece, Dottie's brother-in-law and a state legislator, was invited to join Nicholas, Erickson, and Petzoldt on the board of directors. Petzoldt arranged to borrow some money from the First National Bank, and the other trustees signed the note. In order to provide an accurate description of the school's purpose and nationwide scope, they named it the National Outdoor Leadership School.

Now, all that was needed was students. They got a list of every college and school of higher education in the country, and Nicholas had his secretary write letters on her new automatic typewriter announcing the formation of the school. In Lander, Dottie broadcast public service announcements on KOVE to attract the locals.

Petzoldt also handwrote about forty letters a day six days a week to past clients in the Tetons and to students at Outward Bound. He contacted the youngsters directly, not through their parents. He wanted them to enroll because they wanted to, not because they were being farmed out for the summer.

And he contacted potential scholarship donors. One of his paramount purposes was to provide the means for less privileged youngsters to participate in the program. He took the "pay back when you're able" approach and was later gratified at the number of students who were able to do so.

"Everybody got a personal letter," Hellyer told NOLS historian Delmar W. Bachert. "The thing was pay back the scholarship when able. We wouldn't have had anybody, we wouldn't have gotten off the ground [without the scholarships.] In fact, if we were still in power today we would still be giving them away right and left."

In answer to later accusations that he purloined Outward Bound's membership card file without permission, Petzoldt claims that the addresses were given to him by his students. Hellyer concurs. "Petzoldt didn't take all the files," he said. "Petzoldt was like a course leader. As well as being an instructor he had his own patrol. These kids all gave him their name and address. That's what he had. He had no files pertaining to the school."

Josh Miner has "no idea" about the files. "I feel that NOLS is one of the great monuments to the success of Outward Bound," he says. "I never looked at NOLS as competition. It's a fantastic success story."

From the onset, Petzoldt considered NOLS a natural successor to the Outward Bound program. "The National Outdoor Leadership School is an advanced school, technically starting about where our program at Colorado Outward Bound School ended," he wrote Miner on January 19, 1965. "There is no competition between the National Outdoor Leadership School and Outward Bound."

By the spring of 1965, about $28,000, collected from $350 fees paid by prospective students, was in the bank. That was the only source of financing except for some money and legal services donated by Jack and Alice Nicholas.

"We did it from that," Petzoldt says. "I paid for the stamps. . . . We did the whole National Outdoor Leadership School without any donations.

"I was so stupid not to beat the bushes for money! I was taught not to do that. In Iowa, our neighbors would come to us to borrow a couple of pounds of sugar or something because it took all day to go to Creston for groceries. Of course, after they went to town, here came back the two pounds of sugar. Everybody did it. But the Petzoldts were not allowed to go asking. I was taught that was a sin. So I built NOLS without directly soliciting."

Meanwhile Tapley agreed to become co-director of the school, and they were in business.

Petzoldt's next move was to locate equipment. With the help of State Senator Alan Simpson, who sponsored a bill, NOLS was officially confirmed as a private school under the jurisdiction of the Wyoming Superintendent of Education and was therefore eligible to purchase government surplus. Petzoldt, an irrepressible bargain-hunter, went to Cheyenne with approximately $1,000 and returned with a truckload of bunny boots, sleeping bags, clothing, cookware, and anything else he thought the school could use.

Before the first course began, they had booked seventy-five students and started manufacturing nylon tents, parkas, and wind pants that were unavailable elsewhere and which were custom-made to meet their own specifications.

As city attorney, Nicholas got them a headquarters facility in Sinks Canyon above town. The Pacific Power and Light Company owned a dilapidated vacant building beside the sinkhole, where the Popo Agie River bubbles to the surface after running underground for a quarter of a mile. The power company was concerned about liability in case someone was injured breaking into the shack or falling into the sink. They wanted to donate the property to the city.

Nicholas worked a deal in which the city accepted the building as a gift from the power company and then NOLS leased it and assumed all responsibility. Petzoldt and a crew of volunteers restored the structure and furnished a modest office. The NOLS incorporators held their first meeting on St. Patrick's Day and named Petzoldt the official director at a salary of $650 a month.

On June 8, 1965, forty-three youngsters from twenty states arrived in Lander and were bused to Sinks Canyon, where they unpacked their bags and spread the contents on the ground for inspection. Petzoldt suggested they look at their gear more carefully.

"Everything you take will have to be carried on your own back," he warned. "Divide your baggage into three piles: items that are absolutely necessary, things you'd like to have, and stuff you don't need."

When the students complied, he and the instructors checked the stacks and added most of the like-to-have items to the don't-need pile. Then they fitted and issued backpacks, boots, sleeping bags, and tents.

The students selected their own rations from a storehouse of powdered and dehydrated foods, nuts, spices, and cheese. There were no canned or bottled goods, foil-wrapped prepackaged dinners, or fresh meat and produce that would spoil, be heavy, or pollute the environment. Petzoldt emphasized the need for a well-balanced variety of foods and ample calories to provide energy. The youngsters repackaged their provisions in plastic bags.

They divided into three patrols and took to the hills. For the next four weeks they learned how to take turns as leader, rappel down cliffs, ford raging rivers, glissade on glaciers, pull in rainbow trout, and develop camping and backpacking skills. Petzoldt and Tapley spent the entire summer in the field with the students, roving from one patrol to another and making certain that high teaching standards and innovative conservation methods were maintained.

They insisted that campsites be placed well away from bodies of water in order to preserve the scenic beauty. Students were taught to wash dishes a safe distance from lakeshores and streams to avoid contaminating them and to dig coverable sumpholes for waste water. Trash was burned or carried out, and trampled or charred ground was covered and smoothed to appear as natural as possible before leaving.

"The basic thing to remember is to camp and pass through an area and leave no trace of your being there," Petzoldt told them. His methods foreshadowed the "Leave No Trace" dictum now followed by environmentally concerned campers.

Petzoldt also devised a new concept which he termed Expedition Behavior. This involved an awareness of the relationships that connect individual to individual, the individual to the group, the group to the individual, a group to other groups and embraced the idea of multiple use in the region, recognizing the rights of others, including the administrative agencies and the local populace.

As he would later write in *The Wilderness Handbook*, "Human nature influences the success or failure, comfort or discomfort, safety or danger of an outdoor experience as much as equipment, logistics, trail techniques, rations, and other basic organizational concerns."

The vital subject of preplanning dominated all themes. Coining the phrases Climate Control Plan, Time Control Plan, and Energy Control Plan, he emphasized the importance of *avoiding* survival situations rather than solely concentrating on dealing with them once they happen.

Part disciplinarian, part father figure, Petzoldt reached the youth of a troubled time. Nightly camp meetings found him pacing before a gathering of students perched on boulders or sitting on the barren ground. His cottony eyebrows spiked out from under a battered felt hat, giving him a rather Mephistopholean appearance as he shot questions at the youngsters.

"What did you do today?" he would boom.

"We learned how to ford a river," a student might volunteer.

"Stand up when you address the group," Petzoldt would say.

The boy, a bit afraid, would get to his feet.

"How do you ford a river?"

With a hesitant mumble, the student would try to explain how to ford a river.

"Speak up! We can't hear you!" Petzoldt would interrupt.

The explanation would come louder.

"That was how you did it today!" Petzoldt would say when the student was finished. "But do you *really* know that's the best way? What if the circumstances were different? What must be taken into consideration? Judgment! A leader must use judgment!"

And the next morning, the student he had interrogated might be the one he spent an hour with fine-tuning his fly casting.

Every course concluded with a banquet catered by Dottie, Alice Nicholas, and Mrs. Erickson. A graduation ceremony followed. Then, a generation known for its rebellion against the establishment and used to disapprobation from its elders heard an unfamiliar message from their fifty-seven-year-old mentor.

"Never in the history of mankind has there been a generation of youth as great as you are," Petzoldt said. "You are physically stronger and healthier than any previous generation. You are better educated and better informed than the previous generation. You are more concerned with the problems of the world than our previous generation. You are more honest . . . more realistic . . . less hypocritical, fairer, more considerate . . . more independent of tradition and the old ways than any generation."

In 1965, at the end of the first season, Petzoldt reported to the board that, "Many or most of those who completed [the course] were now better qualified than most Outward Bound instructors." Only a handful were not entitled to a certificate of completion. He pronounced the initial year a success. "We expect to expand the course next year," he said. "We'll *even* try a course for girls!"

That winter he organized a party of NOLS graduates and instructors for a New Year's climb of the Grand Teton with the intention of developing a national rescue group in conjunction with the school.

Seventeen climbers, hailing from Pennsylvania, New York, Michigan, Illinois, California, Oklahoma, Colorado, and Wyoming, left Jenny Lake on December 29 in the middle of a blustery blizzard. They slogged through 50-mile-per-hour winds for two and a half days, their skis sinking into the deep powder with every step.

At timberline, they stashed their skis and proceeded up to the Lower Saddle on foot. There, in sub-zero temperatures, they built rock platforms for their tents on a 30-degree slope. Conditions were so fierce that they were forced to take shelter from the raging storm immediately.

"It was New Year's Eve, and we were all in our sleeping bags at six o'clock," Petzoldt said later. "The wind was blowing so hard we couldn't light our gas stoves. And the air was filled with snow so fine that it even sifted in through the air vents in our tents. By midnight most of the tents were covered, or almost completely so, with snow.

"At midnight, John Johnson got up so we heard this faint singing of Auld Lang Syne, and everybody else said, 'Oh shut up,' and went back to sleep."

The party failed to conquer the final 650 feet to the summit, but Petzoldt noted that the extremely difficult weather provided the best possible experience for the proposed rescue group.

The 1965 New Year's climb (which was to become an annual event) proved to have even greater benefits for NOLS. Both the United and Associated Press services carried extensive articles about the exploit, and the stories were picked up by newspapers, television, and radio stations throughout the country. Petzoldt also became the first

Lander resident to be named in *Who's Who in America*.

The locals were not so enthusiastic about the school, however. The conservative residents, wary in the wake of race riots and war protests, viewed the bearded, long-haired youths wearing "waffle stompers" and ragged cut-offs as hippies. To them, that meant drugs, shoplifting, vandalism. Many of them were furious with Petzoldt for introducing this element to their quiet town.

Given his own youthful experiences, Petzoldt related to the kids. He saw beyond appearances. He could empathize with their disillusionment and concern about the world. But considering the disposition of his neighbors, he agreed with Jack Nicholas, who later said, "The best thing to do was get them off the plane and get them to camp as quickly as we could."

The second year, when the then bizarre notion of enrolling girls in the five-week-long courses materialized, tongues wagged even more. "A lady just did not do things like that! . . . The weaker sex was not strong enough to shoulder heavy packs and do such strenuous hiking and climbing. . . . They would be way out in the wilds for five weeks where their mothers could not even check on them."

Petzoldt diplomatically put Tapley and his wife Lee in charge of the female patrol. Careful attention was paid to installing the girls in an area widely separated from the boys, limiting their loads to about 20 pounds, and excusing them from the three-day solo survival trek back to the trailhead that other prospective NOLS graduates endured.

The women's course inspired the first national magazine article about the school in the March 1968 issue of *Field and Stream*. That was also the year that Petzoldt almost ran for the office of U.S. senator from Wyoming.

As a county delegate, he attended the state Democratic convention in Casper. It was the year of the Tet offensive, student rioting at Columbia and other universities, and the King and Kennedy assassinations. Lyndon B. Johnson was stepping down from the presidency to leave the political battles to Hubert H. Humphrey and Richard M. Nixon. In Wyoming, Democrat Gale McGee was campaigning for another term as U.S. senator.

"A senator from Chicago made a speech first, saying how great McGee was, then McGee got up and made his speech," Petzoldt said, remembering the convention. "He raved about why we should back Nixon, why we should keep on with the Vietnam War, why we had to stop Communism, and all that sort of bullshit.

"When he finished, a few people clapped. I had a seizure. I had no intention of doing what I did, but I was angry. I got up and started making a speech."

He told the crowd that history doesn't necessarily repeat itself and that the days were over when a company of Marines could conquer a country.

"I went on and on. They said I talked half an hour. And I had their attention! The press said when I stopped, 40 percent of the people rose up and cheered for five minutes."

The following day, Petzoldt was on the front pages of the newspapers. Mike Swiler, owner of a popular local steakhouse and an influential Democrat, invited him to the university. He and his political cohorts urged Petzoldt to challenge McGee and run for the office of senator.

"I didn't say yes or no," Petzoldt says. "I told them I would think it over. People were trying to give me money. One guy tried to give me a check for $25,000. But after a few days, my answer was no. I got Mike to run in my place."

Instead of running for senate, Petzoldt went to college. He decided to compose a handbook about the mountaineering skills and conservation methods he had developed. At the age of sixty, he enrolled as an undergraduate at the University of Wyoming, where he would have access to the library for research. He took nine hours of creative writing, speech, and persuasion classes.

He lived in McIntyre Hall, the freshman dorm, where he attempted to study in the midst of blaring rock music and youthful confusion. This didn't seem to bother him unduly.

"I'm dealing with youth at my school," he said at the time. "I'm extremely interested in youth and in understanding them. . . . I'm convinced that youth today is just so far ahead of the youth of my day. There is no comparison."

It was a mutual bond. NOLS and Petzoldt were so popular with the younger generation that the school grew beyond his dreams. Then *Life* magazine ran Jane Howard's story, "Last Mountain Man? Not If

He Can Help It," in December 1969 and launched a spate of national coverage that moved NOLS into the big time.

"I was even slated to be on *Life*'s cover," Petzoldt laughs. "Then I was pre-empted by the murderer Charles Manson."

In 1970, the Aluminum Company of America featured NOLS on the Alcoa Hour with "30 Days of Survival," a television documentary directed by David Wildley.

A year later, the American Academy of Achievement named Petzoldt as a recipient of the prestigious Golden Plate Award, which was also presented to such notables as Lowell Thomas, James Michener, and future president Gerald Ford.

The school even earned local favor in 1971 when a few of the so-called hippies became heroes. On the morning of March 3, fire broke out at the Fremont Hotel across the street from NOLS headquarters. Staffers Skip Shoutis, John Cooper, and Steve Gipe, all in their early twenties, heard the alarm and rushed outside. They saw a frantic sixteen-year-old boy hanging out of a fourth-story window where he could not reach the fire escape.

Some men had run into the street to attempt to fight the blaze with a garden hose. Gipe grabbed the hose, and his buddies boosted him up to a cafe sign, from which he climbed eight more feet to reach the fire escape. He raced up the steps to the fourth floor and tossed the hose to the trapped boy.

"Tie it around your waist like a rope and hold onto the hose above your head," Gipe yelled. Then, belaying around his own body, he lowered the boy to the ground. "That's just what I'd expect from my boys," Petzoldt said later when told about the incident.

The publicity which resulted from all of the local and national media attention swamped the school with so many applications that he and Hellyer decided it was time to expand its horizons. With a proliferating cadre of NOLS-certified instructors, the school became more diversified. There were junior courses, college-credit classes for upperclassmen and graduate students, and 39'ers* expeditions for senior citizens.

---

*The name 39'ers was a reference to comedian Jack Benny's perennial claim of being thirty-nine years old.

But NOLS was outgrowing the Wind Rivers. In addition to increased usage by the school, growing hordes of the camping public crowded into the mountains. The environment was becoming severely threatened. Despite the school's innovative leave-no-trace practices, it was apparent that the numbers of students taken into the backcountry must be limited.

"For the first time in history, the citizens of this nation have become aware that wilderness areas are finite and that indiscriminate use will destroy them," Petzoldt told the *Wyoming State Journal*, on February 18, 1971.

In order to alleviate pressure on the eastern flanks of the Wind Rivers, NOLS started running courses out of Pinedale, where they could reach the less-used western side of the mountains.

Petzoldt and Hellyer made a good deal on a ranch to use as a base there. The asking price was $75,000, with a $30,000 down payment. The partners knew the ranch would appreciate in value and that it could be vital to the school's continued future in the area. They scraped the money together and obtained the deed.

NOLS started limiting classes to thirty-six participants, instigated a cap of nine hundred students per season, and sought other wilderness venues that could accommodate backpackers and provide more variety to the curriculum.

The school tested pilot branches in the mountains of New England and the spelunking caves of Tennessee. Hellyer and his wife Martha, along with Bill Scott, explored the possibility of sea kayaking and climbing on Mount McKinley in Alaska. A Washington branch in the North Cascades offered serious alpine mountaineering experiences. Tapley, who was still teaching at the Colorado Academy and had left NOLS, took a NOLS sailboat to Baja California and joined forces with Petzoldt again to teach sailing and snorkeling near Coyote Bay in the Sea of Cortez.

The diversity of courses dictated additional expenditures for specialized outfitting and increased manufacturing of NOLS-approved equipment. Little suitable outdoor gear was commercially available for wilderness backpacking in such variable environments. Much of it was designed for people having transportation and shelter close at hand, or using vehicles and horses to pack their provisions.

The equipment generally sold for expeditions beyond the trailhead was too expensive or, in some cases, superfluous. Often, it had not been tested in the field with large groups of people over long periods of time. Petzoldt felt NOLS was a perfect testing ground for new designs, but the school could not continue operating at the existing level if the manufacturing arm did not keep up with its growth.

"The board members at the time didn't wish to personally guarantee the finances necessary for the growth of the school nor were there any donations raised by the board for that purpose," Petzoldt said. "Therefore in order to equip and expand the school, Rob Hellyer and I borrowed money personally to secure equipment and real estate necessary for the continuation and growth of the school. As the school grew and expanded into regions other than Lander, more borrowing was done personally by Hellyer and me to equip and finance the operations."

Then NOLS lost the city lease at the Sinks. A new mayor, who shared the conservative views of many Lander residents and looked askance at the NOLS "long-hairs," was voted into office. She wanted to appoint her brother as caretaker of the Sinks and arranged for him to live in the house there. NOLS needed the building for an office and did not need a caretaker, so when an opportunity arose for them to purchase the Nicholas Office Building downtown for a headquarters, they made a deal. They also bought and remodeled a lumberyard at Fifth and Lincoln Streets for an outfitting station, made a bargain buy on a defunct Safeway store and turned it into a manufacturing center, and purchased the abandoned Noble Hotel for a student-housing facility. In addition, they acquired homes for the Lander staff, as well as headquarters buildings and housing in Alaska, Mexico, and Driggs, Idaho. Besides real estate, they purchased power boats, large sailboats, canoes, kayaks, horses, tack, winter grazing land, and trucks.

"All this investment, mostly on borrowed money, was done by Hellyer and me to service the school," Petzoldt said. "Through my personal efforts, we secured some donations for the school but all these went directly to the board of directors."

It finally became evident that the school and the manufacturing company should be operated as separate entities. Petzoldt realized that he and Hellyer were "single-handedly making a business and single-handedly borrowing money and were at the mercy of a board of trustees." Petzoldt owned 75 percent of the stock, and Hellyer held 25 percent.

Also when they asked the University of Wyoming and Kansas State Teacher's College to give credit for their courses, they were told it was "too hard to give college credit to private organizations." So in 1971 they switched the school to tax-free status in order to implement the affiliations. Petzoldt appointed John Walker, a physical education professor from the University of Wyoming, Dr. Robert Boles, a biologist from Kansas State, and Dr. Joseph Pease, athletic director at Fort Lewis College, to the NOLS board.

At the same time, so that the nonprofit status of NOLS was not jeopardized, they formed a new corporation under the name Outdoor Leadership Supply (later Paul Petzoldt Wilderness Equipment—PPWE). The firm manufactured gear for NOLS courses and sold it to other schools, camps, and the general public, as well as through mail orders. They also maintained a retail outlet to market brand name boots, climbing gear, wool garments, and skis. The nonprofit NOLS board managed the school offices, bookings, and other educational activities but had no voice in the dealings of PPWE.

Petzoldt experimented with a number of original designs and new materials. When the school first started, he scavenged thrift shops for worn-out, loosely knit woolen sweaters, then cut off usable tops and sewed them to salvageable bottoms to create knee-length garments that provided extra warmth.

Later, he designed a "NOLS shirt" of tightly woven wool with a Nehru-style collar and extra long shirttails. Unlike many wool shirts of the era, his were not lined with cotton. He had proven during his time with the ski troops that wool possesses insulating qualities to keep one warm even when wet.

He tested synthetic fabrics such as Fiberfill II for sleeping bags and designed a special tent to solve condensation problems when camping in Baja California. PPWE also manufactured extra large backpack sacks with oversized outside pockets.

The factory owned all the equipment, supplies, and real estate utilized by NOLS. The company had a contract with the school that it would receive a percentage of the tuition fees in exchange for this service.

Petzoldt fragmented his time between running the school, going into the field on various courses, lecturing, writing *The Wilderness Handbook*, and serving as a one-man public relations office. Despite his advancing age and being diagnosed with glaucoma, he remained healthy and energetic as he juggled and expanded his various projects. Success bred success—more and more equipment and real estate were needed to maintain the standards of the school, and Petzoldt's debts increased accordingly. Board members started to cluck that he was a great mountaineer but a poor businessman. They remained reticent about voting funds to fuel the school's expansion.

Dottie shared the board's worries as she watched Petzoldt's financial obligations climb. Her apprehensiveness grew when her daughter Jane Ryan, who had moved from the East to become Petzoldt's private secretary, talked of his latest acquisition or another bank loan. Her concerns were reinforced in discussions with her brother-in-law Ed Breece, who still served on the NOLS board. When Jane fell in love with trustee Joe Pease, Dottie gained another direct line to the school directors.

Petzoldt, Hellyer, and Hellyer's wife, Martha, continued to borrow money from the bank. Dottie refused to become involved and sign her name to the loans. Escalating liabilities resulting from PPWE providing equipment and services for the school's unshackled expansion caused her to worry that if she invested in the company she would become financially responsible if they went broke. Unlike Petzoldt, who was too fired up by his efforts to advance the school to worry about money, she felt the need for the security of cash in the bank and assured resources for the future.

She finally told him that she was opening a private bank account and would thereafter keep her finances separately. He took her actions to mean "that I paid all the bills and she kept all the money." Her unwillingness to give financial support to the school led to a rift and finally to the dissolution of the marriage.

"That was the beginning of the end because we were no longer really together," Petzoldt says. They were divorced in 1973.

Despite Petzoldt's personal troubles and an increasingly hostile board of directors, the school continued to grow. National media attention focused on the third successful completion of the famous annual New Year's climb of the Grand Teton. The following year, Petzoldt joined the Lander One-Shot Antelope Hunters and a number of astronauts on safari in Mozambique and later founded a NOLS branch in Kenya.

PPWE continued to expand with retail outlets in Iowa, Nevada, Tennessee, Montana, Colorado, Arizona, Alaska, Oregon, New Mexico, Idaho, Alabama, California, Wisconsin, Michigan, Missouri, Kansas, and Massachusetts.

But in June 1974, the main building of the four-unit warehouse complex, and approximately $500,000 worth of supplies and equipment, burned to the ground. Fortunately, there was no one on the premises, although at 6:00 A.M. the day before, scores of students had been in the building being outfitted for the field. Cause of the fire was unknown.

"It really hurt us," Hellyer said. "It took everything. A lot of it we had written off because it was valued at less than $100. We received $150,000 in about two months from the insurance company. All our winter stuff burned so we went out and spent all that and more to get ready for the winter. When we paid our income tax, we had to come up with $75,000 because this $150,000 was counted as income."

That July, at the age of sixty-six, Petzoldt decided to put aside his troubles and celebrate his long career. He invited seventeen friends to climb the Grand Teton in commemoration of the fiftieth anniversary of his first ascent.

The group was an unusual mixture of NOLS instructors and novices who had never climbed a mountain. Petzoldt's teenage nephew Jim Herrick was the youngest and his seventy-two-year-old brother Curly the eldest in a gaggle of grandparents, television photographers, writers, insurance brokers, ski area directors, and newsmen whose combined ages averaged forty-three years.

The party shouldered their packs and left the Lupine Meadows trailhead on July 11 with Petzoldt at the forefront setting a slow, easy pace. This was no high-powered mountaineering expedition. Rest stops were frequent, and the cameras clicked incessantly as Petzoldt identified wildflowers and mountain critters and related folkloric stories about the surrounding lakes and peaks.

For two days, the greenhorn businessmen and professionals doggedly zigzagged up the narrow mountain trails, clamored over car-sized boulders, scrambled over scree and talus, and kicked steps up the glacier to the Lower Saddle.

On July 13, close to the date that Petzoldt and Ralph Herron had set foot on top of the Grand in 1924, they reached the summit at one-thirty in the afternoon.

"Then we were all on top together, bolting peanuts and candy and snapping pictures, laughing as Petzoldt and June [Lehman] clowned with a sign some bizarre humorist had toted to the summit that cautioned: 'Climbing registration required for travel beyond this point,'" Leslie Gezon wrote. "Some of us were feeling so high I think we needed the warning."

Petzoldt and Curly hugged, patted, and joshed each other like a couple of kids. It was a sentimental moment for them. They had made the climb together many times and wondered if there would ever be another opportunity.

Everyone signed the register and took his or her own private moment to memorize the view and savor the experience. A few presented momentos of the occasion to Petzoldt. After such an arduous trek, the stay on top seemed exceptionally brief.

Euphoric with success and a goodly amount of sunshine, the party made its way down to the 150-foot rappel that was a shortcut back to camp. Petzoldt stationed himself at the edge of the cliff to oversee his novice friends descending on the rope.

"Remember to yell, 'All Clear!' when you are safely down, untied, and out of danger of falling rocks," he cautioned each rapeller. Without exception, the excited novices stepped backwards off of the ledge, lowered themselves to the ground, and, without untying and stepping aside, gave the clearance signal.

The carelessness worried and irritated Petzoldt. So when another climber reached the bottom and yelled he was clear, Petzoldt bellowed, "All clear? Like hell you're all clear!" He picked up a good-sized rock and hurled it over the precipice to shatter like glass at the feet of the people below. The remaining rapellers were careful to follow his instructions.

On April 23, 1975, NOLS received a letter from the Internal Revenue Service. District Director Robert M. McKiever notified the school that "the records of your organization revealed certain activities contrary to the purposes for which you were organized and determined to be exempt from Federal income tax under section 501(c) (3) of the Internal Revenue Code."

The notice went on to name the National Outdoor Leadership Supply Company (then PPWE) and Petzoldt personally on four violations.

The feds questioned the attempts in 1969 and 1970 to "convert the school into a private profit-making organization, and the organization of a foundation to support the private school."

They contested the contract with PPWE "to furnish all equipment, supplies, etc., [to NOLS] without the benefit of other competitive bids for such services and supplies."

They noted that on June 22, 1971, NOLS had executed a note for $87,779.84 to PPWE for the purchase of improved real property and other operating expenses. "The operation of the two organizations compared to that of a Brother-Sister Corporation wherein transactions were accomplished without formal action of the trustees."

Finally, the letter listed PPWE's purchase of the Noble Hotel and the Pinedale ranch and their subsequent resale to the school.

McKiever indicated that there would be no change in NOLS's exempt status since an IRS representative had met with the board of directors and had previously discussed the transactions with Petzoldt and board chairman John Walker on August 27, 1974. They had satisfactorily explained the dealings and subsequently corrected the school's operations. But he ordered that, "All transactions with the Paul Petzoldt Wilderness Equipment Company which were executed on June 22, 1971 [$87,779.84] are expected to be repaid as soon as possible."

The notice concluded with a warning. "The exempt status of the school will be adversely affected in later years if these transactions contrary to the exemption are allowed to reoccur. It is emphasized that the Board of Directors should exercise its authority in overseeing the operations of the school."

"The operations and equipment supply were managed in the field by Rob Hellyer for the tax-paying corporation owned by Hellyer and me," Petzoldt explained later. "At the same time I was serving as director of the nonprofit school and was able to use my expertise and leadership to build the outdoor education system into world-renown.

"Since Hellyer and I had personally secured loans to purchase equipment and real estate for the operation of the school and charged the school and others for their services, there was a suspicion that we were making a profit which some considered unethical. Hellyer and I feel the school had an obligation to use our facilities until our loans were paid."

"We ran our private corporation like it was a nonprofit corporation," Hellyer said in a later interview. "We just thought it was all the same. We never considered it anything but ours. Not ours, but this family thing. When I say family, I don't mean the Petzoldt family. I mean the students and staff."

Jack Nicholas (now a retired District Judge for the State of Wyoming) explained further. "You have to put this back in the light of thirty years ago," he said in 1996. "People did not have the sophistication about taxes that almost everybody does now. Neither Petzoldt nor Hellyer were sophisticated about taxes. In essence, what they did was receive a lot of money and spend a lot of money primarily on acquisition of more goods without creating a reserve to pay taxes. Without even realizing that the accountants called it profit.

"So they ended up with a tremendous tax liability for which there was no cash. The money had gone back into canvas, new boots, snowshoes, etc. And the source of the cash was tuition for the school, which came through the nonprofit corporation. The only way to return that was to buy goods from the leadership supply and have that show a profit which would generate cash to pay taxes. But to show more profit to pay taxes, you have to pay more taxes. Once you get behind on something like that, it's very hard to catch up."

On June 6, 1975, Walker wrote NOLS's attorneys at the Riverton office of Hettinger and Leedy that the IRS had informed him that "Paul Petzoldt is so closely related to PPWE that he cannot as President of NOLS enter into contract with PPWE and that the Board of Directors must be involved in this business."

201

At the July 11 board of directors meeting at the Royal Inn in Salt Lake City, Utah, the trustees moved "that Paul Petzoldt be removed as an officer of NOLS and that he no longer serve in any capacity with NOLS. The board discussed possible severance pay and agreed that he should receive $2,500.00." Walker and Breece were then appointed as an executive committee to act on the board's behalf, and Jan Hamren was named as director in Petzoldt's place.

Petzoldt knew nothing about the board meeting or the trustees' decision. But he had been suspicious for some time that a plot against him was afoot. He had heard vague rumors that the trustees were not going to renew his contract as director and wanted to get control of PPWE, as well. They probably thought that if they cancelled PPWE's contract, they could buy him and Hellyer out at any figure they wanted. Also, he suspected that Pease and Walker had their eyes on his and Hellyer's jobs.

That summer, the Quaker Oats Company asked him to appear in a television commercial showing that NOLS was using one of their new products on Mount McKinley in Alaska. They offered a $10,000 advance and told him he would also receive $250 in residuals every time the ad was aired. Petzoldt agreed to the deal but requested that the $10,000 go to NOLS as a tax-free gift instead of to him personally. He thought that would partially cover his debts to the school.

However, as soon as he returned from Alaska, he knew that there was something wrong. As he later recounted the story:

> I was no sooner back than I got a call from Bill Nightingale, president of the Central Bank and Trust Company.
>
> "Do you know what's going on?" he said.
>
> "No," I said.
>
> "Well, your trustees decided to take over the joint and put you out of business. Yeah. They came in yesterday and said they were going to fire you, they weren't going to renew your contract. They wanted to know if they could take over your Small Business Administration (SBA) loan. They said if they didn't renew your contract, you couldn't pay your loan, and wanted to know if they could take over the factory and hotel.
>
> "You know what I told them?" he said. "I told them they could go to hell."

"You did?" I said.

"Yeah. That was one of the greatest mistakes I ever made because they came back that afternoon and made the biggest single withdrawal I ever had in one day."

In accordance with the board's decision, all NOLS accounts for checking, payroll, scholarships, reserve funds, restricted donations, and general savings had been transferred to the First National Bank.

"They thought that if they went in and told the bank that they were going to get rid of me, the bank would somehow let them take over my Small Business Administration loan and they were going to own all the business and everything," Petzoldt says. "But the president of the First National Bank refused to lend them funds to acquire the SBA loan, despite the fact that they had made his bank's biggest single deposit that day. So that's when it hit the fan. It was the big steal."

"I think the problem with the board was more because of the problems between Petzoldt and Dottie," Jack Nicholas said later. "When there was a final falling out between Dottie and Petzoldt it had all sorts of ramifications. The end effect, Dottie got control of the school."

"Others were ambitious to take over the school and force Hellyer and [me] into an uneconomic sale with a threat of buying their own equipment and not using the tax-paying facilities," Petzoldt told the *Wyoming State Journal.*

But the board was in a bind. They didn't own any equipment, and they didn't have enough money to buy all of the gear and real estate. Without equipment, they couldn't book students for the next year. So they made overtures to Outward Bound about assuming ownership of the school.

"Josh Miner called me one night and said what's going on out there," Petzoldt remembers. "He said he had a call from the board of trustees and they wanted to know if Outward Bound would like to have NOLS. He told them they were not interested."

Petzoldt couldn't sleep that night. He wondered if he should start all over again and go on his own. "I didn't know if I could do it either," he said later. "I had the equipment but owed money and they had the list of all our students."

Then on July 12, Walker wrote him a letter inviting him "to give serious consideration to continuing to work with and advise NOLS and its staff in a consulting capacity for which you would be appropriately compensated."

"Boy, I had to make decisions, decisions, decisions," Petzoldt says. "You see I owed money to the bank for borrowing on the store, buying new equipment for Alaska, Africa, Baja California, and the Washington school. We had five schools going. We had a big deal. I'd imported $50,000 worth of climbing shoes from France. I was a wheeler-dealer, and I owed a lot of money. And now I was without income because they had canceled my contract. So what was I to do? Well, we could have let NOLS go under. Or I could have fought them and just said, 'I'm NOLS now, I'm starting a new outfit. I am Paul Petzoldt Outdoor Leadership School.'

"I didn't. See, I trusted people. So, what to do? We got with the lawyers and thought we made a compromise. They offered a deal that I was to be President Emeritus and an advisor and have a contract for $20,000 a year for ten years, which would be renewable. All I was to do was advise them, give lectures and be a figurehead, and they would pay my expenses. I thought that would keep my people in their jobs, and they would give me $200,000 over ten years for my equipment and my name.

"I had to make up my mind whether I wanted NOLS to go under. But I finally decided the important thing is to have NOLS go on. That was a hell of a lot more important than me because I'd never been interested in making money or thinking about my security, my old age. I was always interested in getting something done. In doing. So I made that decision, thinking that they were sincere."

Two days later he signed a contract to become Senior Advisor in Outdoor Education for the National Outdoor Leadership School. It was specified that he "shall act upon the instructions of the directors of NOLS, which instructions shall be in writing. . . . NOLS shall have the right to terminate the contract without payment of any sum thereafter to Mr. Petzoldt should he act contrary to the written instructions of the Director."

"We were going to be like one big happy family," Petzoldt says. He took the deal to mean that he would be meeting with the board, reviewing their plans, and continuing to outfit the school through

PPWE. The arrangement appeared to be satisfactory.

He found out differently when the owner of the Pinedale ranch contacted him and said he had an opportunity to buy another place and needed cash fast. He said he would sacrifice the ranch, give it to them for $30,000 and forgive the $15,000 balance.

So Petzoldt approached the NOLS trustees and asked if they would loan him the $30,000 with the deed as collateral. He and Hellyer would repay the debt over time with interest and the deed would be returned to them at that time. The board voted in favor of the transaction.

Then a buyer offered Petzoldt and Hellyer $150,000 for the property. The sale would enable them to cancel their debts to the school and clear matters further. Petzoldt contacted the trustees and asked them to give him the deed so he could finalize the deal.

"Here's the money and interest," he said. "We want the deed back."

"We have the deed," Petzoldt says they told him.

"You agreed to return it when I repaid the loan with interest," he replied. "It's in the minutes."

"They said they had talked about it, but it wasn't in the minutes," Petzoldt said later. "Then I knew that I was dealing with people who wanted our jobs, our SBA loan, our property, and were out to destroy me. The ranch would be worth about $200,000 today."

During this period of upheaval at NOLS, Petzoldt renewed a friendship with Joan Brodbeck from Milwaukee, whom he had met at the One-Shot safari in Mozambique in 1973. Their correspondence evolved into a long-distance courtship and in 1975 he proposed marriage.

That July she joined him in Washington, D.C., where he testified at confirmation hearings for former Wyoming Governor Stanley K. Hathaway, who was a candidate for secretary of the interior under President Gerald Ford. They were married before a justice of the peace in a local courthouse. His longtime friend Henry Nichol from Potomac, Maryland, witnessed the ceremony.

"It was quick work," Nichol says. "I thought Petzoldt needed a little bit more than that to get married, so I arranged a wedding dinner for them. My wife Betty was out of town, so I called up my friends, some had already met Petzoldt, and said we're going to have a potluck wedding dinner in the recreation room in our basement. We had a wonderful dinner and we were all dancing."

When the newlyweds returned to Lander, Joan, a former businesswoman, offered to manage PPWE while he traveled and lectured to promote the school. But Petzoldt's relationship with the NOLS board remained strained, and the supply outlet was in serious trouble.

That November, NOLS made an offer to purchase PPWE outright. A game of bidding Ping-Pong ensued until the board finally named a purchase price of $423,000 for the Noble Hotel, the lumberyard, and all outfitting equipment except the horses, tack, and three vehicles. They tacked on a noncompetitive clause forbidding Petzoldt and PPWE from competing with the school in the United States, Africa, and Mexico.

Petzoldt answered the offer with an unqualified "No." He claimed that PPWE owned all the government surplus property purchased for NOLS, and furthermore that the name National Outdoor Leadership School was actually owned by the tax-paying corporation and had been loaned to the educational arm solely for the purpose of preserving the name for use by both organizations.

The school threatened to sue and declared that "Paul Petzoldt is completely separated from all NOLS operations." Then all but a handful of NOLS instructors went on strike.

Petzoldt told the *Wyoming State Journal* that he saw three solutions to the dilemma:

> First, the resignation of most of the present NOLS board, especially those related to me through a former marriage, and putting NOLS instructors on the board, instructors who know the philosophy and education system we have built.
>
> Second, the instructors forming their own new board, in which case, Hellyer and I would arrange for them to use or purchase the equipment for operation.
>
> Or third, if all fails, we will continue the school and enlarge it as entirely a tax-paying company.

Then he concluded, "Whatever happens, I am not going to see my life-work in building the finest and most motivating educational system fail. Our school shall continue and I will be part of that school until I am sure it is in trustworthy hands—then I'd like to retire and go fishing."

In the meantime, the NOLS Instructors Association (NIA) and other employees banded together to demand that Walker, Pease, Boles, and newly named trustee Joe Kenney, Jr., be removed from the board. When that did not occur, they closed up shop. Only Janet Jahn, the business manager, stayed on duty.

Then everybody—NOLS, NIA, and PPWE—frantically began to mail press releases and newsletters to past and present instructors, alumni, and customers. In 50,000 PPWE mailings, Petzoldt announced that he had lost complete control of the name National Outdoor Leadership School.

"Therefore in order to carry on our teaching, our tradition, and our service to the outdoors and conservation, we are now all together again under a new name—College of Outdoor Leadership. In other words, the College of Outdoor Leadership became COOL. Which signifies our attitude about the change."

Meanwhile, Walker mobilized a handful of employees and announced courses would commence November 24, right on schedule.

Petzoldt submitted his resignation as senior advisor and affirmed that he would again be leading the annual climb of the Grand Teton on New Year's Day.

With the official opening of Lander's Christmas season, a truce materialized between the warring factions. The *Wyoming State Journal* reported an initial agreement between Petzoldt and NOLS for purchase of the hotel, lumberyard, and a large amount of outfitting equipment for approximately a half million dollars. Petzoldt resumed his post as senior advisor, and the instructors went back to work.

"We kept PPWE," says Hellyer, "but without the school it took the starch right out of us. There was a time there in 1975 that if I had wanted to be aggressive in that way, Paul would have let me take it over and do anything I wanted with it. Make a success out of it. I think I could have if I'd wanted to sit behind a desk, be an office manager and run a mailorder business. We could have gone overseas and had some stuff made."

As it turned out, Petzoldt gave Hellyer about sixty horses and a 50 percent interest in a ranch they owned on the Sweetwater River.

But for Petzoldt it was "the big steal."

"Once I signed the contract with them everything was hunky-dory until they got things set up. Then I was persona non grata. Peter Simer [the new director] started giving me instructions to do menial things. They even started rumors that the reason they had to get rid of me was that I was an alcoholic."

"But it was more than a job that Petzoldt lost," Molly Absolon wrote in 1995. "He says that NOLS was like a child that was stolen from him and his bitterness over that has—even now—mixed with his pride about where the school he started has gone."

On February 2, 1978, the NOLS Executive Committee produced a photocopied letter stating that Petzoldt had cashed a $1,700 royalty check payable to NOLS for a film entitled, *High in the Wind Rivers*. A legal opinion stated that the act was a breach of contract, and the committee voted to terminate the relationship with Petzoldt for good.

"I financed that movie myself!" Petzoldt says. "I loaned money to some graduate students from New York University who promised to pay me back. They had shown the picture and collected money on it. The check was rightfully mine."

One trustee submitted a written objection. "The system, the order, the vocabulary, the curricula, the personality of the National Outdoor Leadership School is directly derived from the magnificent mountaineer, whom we all, at one time, affectionately called 'Paul,'" Neil J. Short wrote. "I am unalterably opposed to modifying or terminating Petzoldt's contract . . . If he owes the school money, the debt should be deducted from his salary."

But his was a lone voice. The committee ruled that henceforth Petzoldt's contract as senior advisor was canceled, and his name and likeness would be removed from all NOLS publications. The break was complete.

·
·
·
·
·
·
·

CHAPTER 11

The Wilderness Education Association

WHEN HE REALIZED THAT HE WAS NOT GOING TO REMAIN AS A FUNC-
tioning part of NOLS, Petzoldt, now sixty-seven years old, changed
his focus to Driggs, Idaho. He wrote a small guidebook, *Petzoldt's Teton
Trails* (Wasatch Publishers, 1976; no longer in print) and independently took students to places rarely visited by hikers and climbers.
They scaled the back sides of the Grand and Middle Tetons and Mount
Moran, and ventured to primitive trails north of Driggs that the Civilian Conservation Corps and horse-packers had made years before.

Six years earlier, in 1971, he had refurbished a rustic lodge in Driggs
for use as headquarters for NOLS courses on the western side of the
Tetons. Long before World War II, he had recognized the recreational
potential of the Teton Valley. It was an ideal location for a ski area,
with mountainous terrain carved by natural runs, and powder snow
that fell in abundance and created one of the longest winter seasons in
the Rockies.

In the late 1960s, the local populace got the same idea. The
economy was hurting. Sales of agricultural products had declined, and
youngsters, sensing no future in farming and ranching, were leaving
for brighter pastures. Finally, the citizens of Teton County applied to
the U.S. government for an Area Redevelopment Loan to enable them

to construct a winter resort. They convinced one hundred investors to give $1,000 apiece in a bid to raise matching funds. Petzoldt was one of them.

The newly created company borrowed more money and started to build lifts and lodges and construct roads. The Grand Targhee Ski Area opened in 1969.

But as happened in many developing resorts in those days, the inexperienced entrepreneurs fell into financial straits. Transportation was a problem because the nearest airports were in Idaho Falls or across Teton Pass in Jackson Hole, and heavy snows often clogged the highways.

Equally troublesome was the fact that, even though the actual resort was in Wyoming, the Idaho border ran along the base of the mountain and the teetotaling citizens of Driggs and Tetonia were predominantly members of the Church of Jesus Christ of Latter-day Saints. Mormons frowned on alcohol and recreating on Sundays, but having bars, lounges, and apres-ski activities going strong seven days a week was integral to the success of a world-class ski resort. By 1973, Grand Targhee foundered.

As an original investor, Petzoldt learned that the company was $450,000 in debt, and he was approached to invest more money. He did not have any expendable cash, but he had a better idea.

He was a very close friend of William Robinson, an engineer and plastics magnate from Ohio who had sent his son to NOLS. Robinson had made a fortune by developing the method used for forming plastic into such things as coffee can covers, had sold one of his companies to Alcoa, and had given NOLS some very profitable stock in that corporation. In appreciation, Petzoldt had invited him to join the Mozambique safari. When Petzoldt later learned that Grand Targhee was in trouble, he thought the resort might be a good investment for Robinson.

Robinson flew to Driggs with a lawyer and an accountant to look over the facilities. Petzoldt assured him that all of the environmental work had been done and approved so that expansion would not be curtailed. Robinson bought the ski area.

Petzoldt, believing that land values would increase as Grand Targhee gained popularity and a demand for condominiums and second homes materialized, bought 600 acres at an average price of $500 an acre. Since the adjacent towns and Teton County lacked planning and zoning regulations, he placed covenants on his own property, dividing it into 10-acre lots that could never be re-subdivided.

Shortly after his purchase, he sold one parcel for $6,000. In subsequent years, he raised the price to $8,000, $10,000, $15,000, and on up to $30,000. In 1997, with five or six lots left, he set a minimum of $40,000 for a 10-acre piece.

IN THE LATE 1970S, A GROUP OF UNIVERSITY PROFESSORS, ENVIRON-mentalists, and public lands administrators invited him to a meeting. They shared his concern that America's outdoors was being impacted by increasing numbers of users. They contended that much of the growing impact was coming from the same people who had fought so hard to establish the Wilderness Act in 1964. The measures implemented with passage of the bill—building a stronger legislative fence, requiring permits to limit travel beyond established recreational sites and campgrounds, restricting hikers and campers to semipermanent camps and designated trails—were not working. Petzoldt had always held that these devices were merely stopgaps and would be ineffective without public education.

"It's like someone having a big party in a beautiful new home," Petzoldt says. "The hostess decides she can protect her house by inviting a limited number of guests and confining them to a particular part of the house. Then one of the invitees barges in, burns a hole in the sofa and spits on the carpet. People have to be *educated* about how to use the wild outdoors!"

Just as NOLS had been a step beyond Outward Bound, it was time to figure out a way to reach the community of outdoors professionals who administered public lands; the legislators who had the power to designate wilderness; the professors of environmental sciences, forestry, and wildlife management; and active laymen like scout leaders and members of the Sierra Club and other organizations concerned with conservation and limited use. The group agreed that the best avenue for disseminating information was through existing universities and colleges.

"There should be a formal certification system for users of all backcountry regions—the mountains, the forests, the waterways, and deserts that the American public is loving to death," Petzoldt suggested.

In order to be certified, a candidate would not only have to prove competency in basic camping skills—mastery of mountaineering, rafting or another specialized adventure activity, plus the know-how necessary for planning nutritious, low cost rations; selecting proper clothing for the location, activity and season; practicing environmentally sound health and hygiene procedures; navigating and developing travel techniques suited to the group's age and experience, as well as having knowledge of first aid and emergency procedures—he or she would also have to demonstrate judgment and leadership ability.

The candidate would have to understand and motivate interlocking relationships between his/her own group and horsemen, ranchers, hunters, and other parties using the area. Candidates would have to be aware of environmental ethics, promote minimum impact, be a communicator, and know the region's cultural and natural history. If all group leaders had these qualifications, Petzoldt vowed, outdoor education would filter more quickly into the public sector.

The committee agreed with his concept. But the question of how to make it happen remained unresolved. The recreation specialists could not reach consensus about how individuals could effectively prove their expertise and ability to lead others. Some recommended written lessons and testing. Others called for proof of actual experience. A few committee members thought potential leaders could learn on the job. It was finally agreed that only a combination of all these requirements would warrant official certification.

But which school, which agency or camp, was capable of formulating a certification system that would achieve national recognition and acceptance? An independent organization must develop such a program, they decided.

A few of the educators put their words into action and conducted field experiments to develop a workable curriculum for certification. Frank Lupton of Western Illinois University was the first to bring his students majoring in recreation to Petzoldt's lodge at Driggs for a two-week course in the Tetons. Charles Gregory of Pennsylvania State University and Jack Drury from New York's North Country

Community College followed. PPWE equipped the participants and Pete Peterson, a crusty local horse-packer, outfitted the courses.

The experiment was so successful that Petzoldt started to schedule his own classes. The vegetation of the west side of the Tetons was more lush than that on the east, with a wide variety of flowers due to heavier rain and snow, and the geology, primarily limestone with its uplifted beds visible, was more interesting than the granite to the east. Because hiking began at higher altitudes, it was easier and less elevation was gained than on the Jackson side.

"It was a perfect place," Petzoldt says. "It had cliffs, glaciers, big snowfields, and lakes full of fish."

A favorite trip was climbing Table Mountain from the north. It was there that the famous photographer William Jackson shot the first pictures of the Grand Teton in 1872. A large glacier leading to thousand-foot-high cliffs made a perfect classroom for Petzoldt to teach ice climbing, glissading, and how to burrow into packed drifts to make snow caves.

Other times, he taught courses on Maidenform Peak near Mount Moran. Climbing was excellent and from a camp at the divide there were views of the Sawtooth Range and the Tetons all the way to the Wind Rivers. There were many thickets of crooked, stunted trees called krummholz in the area, and in wintertime these were often studded with shining ice crystals.

By 1977, Petzoldt had proved that his courses and the concepts of other educators cooperating with him could work together to create a college-level curriculum. He chartered the nonprofit Wilderness Education Association to administer a comprehensive eighteen-point wilderness leadership program that would certify hundreds of educators, college upperclassmen aiming at careers in recreation, forestry, conservation, and other outdoor-related fields, and practicing professionals. WEA worked directly through universities and colleges willing to give credit for classes taken by future outdoor professionals.

But in the early 1980s, as WEA continued to grow, PPWE faltered. Without the NOLS connection and faced with increased competition from national firms with broad distribution and hefty advertising budgets, the factory failed. Petzoldt took advantage of an opportunity to sell the Safeway building for a good-sized profit and gave the sewing machines to the women who had operated them.

About the same time, he received a surprise letter from the Pakistani Tourist Bureau. The government was fed up with foreign trek operators coming into their country to lead expensive mountaineering expeditions. The companies and their tourists showed no respect for the local religion and customs, brought their own leaders and guides from abroad, and treated the residents like servants.

Deciding to emulate Nepal, Pakistan sought to get into the lucrative trekking business. The government invited Petzoldt and Joan to be their guests for a brief visit to assess tourism possibilities.

The trip was very different from his first expedition to K2 in 1938. Modern paved roads were everywhere, even along the Indus River all the way to Skardu and on to the Karakoram. What had been a primitive village in 1938 was now a bustling city with automobile repair shops adjacent to spice-scented bazaars.

Despite the fact that their visit was late in the season, their hosts insisted that they do a little trekking so Petzoldt could better evaluate the tourism potential. Teahouses closed for the season were reopened for lodging, but there was no heat. Cooks were rousted from their barley fields to prepare meals, but general levels of sanitation left much to be desired—even fifty years after the K2 expedition.

"Everybody got deathly ill," Petzoldt remembers. "Joan hated every minute of it. Every day somebody was incapacitated with bellyache, vomiting, and squirting out the rear end." He was the only one who escaped being sick.

"It was very interesting as a whole," he says of the trip, "but nothing ever came of it. We were hoping to take people over there on WEA courses, but it was so expensive and would have only been available to very rich kids."

In the summer of 1984, as Petzoldt approached his seventy-sixth birthday, he invited friends to celebrate the sixtieth anniversary of his first Teton ascent. Despite the deterioration of his vision from the glaucoma that had worsened over the past decade, he felt fit. The event aroused so much interest that reporters and photographers from television stations in Salt Lake City, Idaho Falls, and Casper, Wyoming, joined the group to film the expedition. Twenty other friends and former NOLS instructors completed the large party.

Many of the climbers had special bonds with Petzoldt and wanted to share what all thought would be his last attempt on the Grand.

Quincy Jensen, a sixty-two-year-old television cameraman from Idaho Falls, had been a fan of Petzoldt's ever since he met him when he was climbing with a friend some years before. The inexperienced pair had brought along a small lead rope and a 60-foot rope they had borrowed from the Utah Power & Light Company. When they reached a 150-foot rappel, they were stymied. Petzoldt came along just in time to lend them his rope and teach them how to get down the cliff and retrieve the borrowed rope.

Caine Alder from Salt Lake City had met Petzoldt in 1954 at the ranger station after making his second unsuccessful attempt on the summit. His companion had unroped after crossing the Crawl and left him stranded at the base of the ice-coated chockstone chimney. Alder, who was unskilled at the time, did not know what to do. Finally, unroped, he crawled back over the narrow shelf that hung above a chasm thousands of feet deep. When he accosted the leader back in the valley and asked why he had deserted him, the man replied, "Today I just wanted to stand on the summit by myself."

When Petzoldt heard the story, he felt sorry for Alder and offered to take him up the mountain.

"Paul changed my whole philosophy about climbing," says Alder, who is now an accomplished mountaineer. "I used to want to conquer the mountain, bring it down. Paul taught me that reaching the summit was not the important thing. I learned to savor the entire experience—the flowers, the rocks, the history, the geology—so that it is almost a religious experience."

On July 21, 1984, under pewter-colored clouds and a drizzling rain, the anniversary party made its slow way from Lupine Meadows into the forest. Hopes that the weather was just a temporary summer storm faded by the time they reached the first campsite in the meadow beneath the Middle Teton. The next day the Park Service radioed that a massive low-pressure system was racing north from the Gulf of Mexico. Petzoldt reluctantly told everyone to pack up and head for Jackson.

Two days later, the group, shrunken by half, started again. The weather held until they reached the boulder field thirty minutes away from the meadow. Then came a torrent. The climbers and everything

215

in their packs were soaked. When they reached the campsite, they hurriedly pitched the soggy tents and huddled inside, munching a dinner of cheese and raisins as lightning streaked and thunder boomed outside.

They awakened to fog swirling around the high granite peaks like veils of chiffon and savoured the clear air that sparkled in the wake of the storm. Encouraged, they broke camp and filed along the sawtooth trail over broken scree and up steep snowfields to the Lower Saddle. Then, just as they crawled into their tents, the pyrotechnics raged again.

It was pitch black and cold when they awakened in the clammy aftermath of storm at 3:00 A.M. the next morning. Petzoldt took the lead for the final attack. Wearing a jaunty tam-o'-shanter, knickers, and a red and black wool plaid shirt, he slowly traversed the steep talus slope.

The trail wound among miniature rock gardens studded with moss campion and then pitched toward the jagged Black Dike. They roped up to slither across a slab leading to the smooth "Needle," where they squeezed through the "Eye of the Needle," and followed a ledge to the "Bellyroll-Almost." Once around this obstruction, they found hand- and footholds up a natural ladder of jet-black rock leading to the crest of the ridge. Ominous clouds tumbled over one another, filling the void below them.

Racing against the storm, they scrambled over the ledges and traversed up the main couloir to the narrow Upper Saddle. They were only a few hundred feet from the summit, but the most difficult, technical portion of the climb was ahead.

"We'll wait half an hour," Petzoldt said, "and then decide whether to go on to the top or turn back." All eyes were on the clouds boiling up the canyons. Black, solid-looking legions of them with occasional spots of blue being obliterated almost as soon as they appeared.

Five former NOLS instructors and Rob Hellyer's fourteen-year-old son Jimmy decided to make a run for the summit. "Good luck," Petzoldt said.

He told the others they would wait a bit longer. In a few minutes, the mountain was completely socked in. "We're going down," Petzoldt told his companions. "I've got bad vibes."

On the descent, thunder crashed and echoed all around them. Lightning bolts crackled and pelting hail iced the gravelly trail with two inches of frozen slush. Instant rivers of muddy water gushed underfoot as the climbers tied into ropes and inched down the steep pitches and slick crags to the safety of camp.

Their cohorts fared worse. The six experts made it to the summit but, instants later, as they crouched beneath a boulder, a streak of lightning buzzed across their boots and singed one man's glove as he leaned against the rock. They returned to the Lower Saddle unharmed but ardent believers in the Tetons' fabled fury.

The proposed four-day expedition had lasted a week. Most of the party had run out of time and were forced to give up. Petzoldt was determined to try one more time.

On the morning of July 28 the heavily overcast skies began to clear. "Let's go!" Petzoldt said to the few remaining people. A television crew scrambled ahead to take photographs from the Black Dike. Petzoldt started out ahead of the others.

The lone figure of the man whose name had become synonymous with the Tetons, using his ice ax as a walking stick, in tam-o'-shanter and knickers, made its slow, even way up the trail. Fog drifted around the peaks only to dissolve in the distance, as if the Teton had spent its rage. Petzoldt, hiking doggedly up the slope, appeared to be stronger than when he started. Thunder rumbled and lightning flashed in the distance, but his instincts were "on."

Nancy and Andy Carson, former NOLS instructors and owners of the Jackson Hole Mountain Guides, which had outfitted the trip, soon caught up to lead him over the difficult pitches. This time they made it to the top. Signing the register, Petzoldt became the oldest person ever to summit the Grand Teton.

Not long after the sixtieth anniversary climb, the Petzoldts admitted their marriage was impossible and decided to divorce. It had been a rocky union fraught with arguments about money from the start. When Joan first arrived in Lander, Paul already realized that he had made a terrible mistake.

"She was disappointed to find that her husband was not as wealthy as his reputation and his new Cadillac connotated," Petzoldt says.

As WEA continued to expand, Petzoldt was in great demand to

lecture and attend meetings throughout the country. His book, *The Wilderness Handbook*, was so successful that *The New Wilderness Handbook* was published by W.W. Norton to expand upon his teachings. In 1985, he received an honorary doctorate from the University of Idaho.

Petzoldt often quipped that he was "a lemon in the garden of love," but he did not remain single for long. He had been friends with Virginia Stroud Pyle, of Maine, for almost twenty years. When it became evident that his marriage to Joan was a mistake, he and Ginny, then widowed, rekindled their friendship.

GINNY'S SON, WILTON, HAD ATTENDED NOLS IN 1966, THE SECOND season of the school. Petzoldt was so impressed with the young man that he offered him a job as instructor. He went on to graduate from Princeton University and then enlisted in the Marine Corps, where he was commissioned as an officer.

Wilton considered NOLS a seminal experience in his life. His sister Sherry and brother Dallas had both followed him to the school, and he wanted to assure his younger brother, Kenneth, of having the same opportunity. The last thing he did before shipping out for Vietnam was to leave Kenneth tuition money for a NOLS course the following season.

Wilton was killed in 1969 while rescuing one of his buddies only six weeks after arriving at the battlefield. Sensitive to her son's strong belief in NOLS, Ginny requested that in lieu of flowers friends give donations to the school. Petzoldt received a check for $8,000, the largest personal gift in the school's four-year history.

In 1970, when Petzoldt went to New York for the premiere of "30 Days of Survival," Alcoa's nationally televised documentary about NOLS, he decided to meet the woman who had made such a significant contribution to the school. They became good friends and over the next seventeen years they got together when he was traveling in the East.

Petzoldt and Ginny were very different. The wife of an Episcopalian minister, she was extremely devout and devoted much time to the women's guild and other church activities. Petzoldt, on the other hand, never cared much for what he termed "churchianity."

218

A lifelong easterner, her ancestors had come to America with William Penn and settled in Stroudsville, Pennsylvania. Later, her family moved to South Jersey where her father commuted to work in Philadelphia. They spent summers in her grandparents' log cottage at Lake Sebago, Maine. Petzoldt, conversely, was physically and emotionally tied to the West.

Ginny had hiked in the White Mountains with her family but had never backpacked into wild mountains and camped out until she participated in a NOLS '39ers course in the Wind Rivers about 1972. The wild outdoors was Petzoldt's life.

Petzoldt's ill-fated marriage to Joan had interrupted their relationship for several years, but after Ginny's husband died and Petzoldt was separated, they started seeing one another again. They married in 1987 in the presence of the Episcopal Bishop of Maine.

The decision about where to make their home evolved into a compromise. They divided their time between Ginny's family cottage on Lake Sebago and Petzoldt's "wickiup" in Victor, Idaho. She came to love the majestic Tetons and he related to the beauty of the wooded lake in Maine.

"Moving to Maine has been a big adjustment," he said. "Climatically, it's been wonderful. If I lived like most Mainers do in the dense woods where I couldn't see, I think I'd have a problem. But we live right on the east shore where the wind and waves blow in and there are mountains across the water. It's really beautiful."

Petzoldt did not feel entirely comfortable with the local Mainers for the first few years. They did not "talk his language," and he considered himself an outsider. He finally broke the ice by helping with fund-raisers for the church and presenting programs to scout troops. The town of Raymond later demonstrated its appreciation by naming him grand marshal of the bicentennial Founders' Day Parade.

In the fall of 1990, Petzoldt was invited to the twenty-fifth anniversary celebration of NOLS. The letter and phone call from Jim Ratz, executive director of the school, came unexpectedly. Petzoldt invited Ratz to the house and he told him about the upcoming event and asked if he would attend.

"Why?" Petzoldt asked. "Did your board make you do this?"

"No," Ratz said. "I haven't talked to the board at all."

"Why do you want me to come?" Petzoldt asked.

"Paul, you *are* NOLS," Ratz replied. "We can't even describe what the school is for without talking about Paul Petzoldt."

"Well, if I'm part of the thing, you'd better make me a part of it," Petzoldt said.

For years, everywhere he went in the United States people would tell him they had sent a son or daughter to "his school" and ask him questions about how it was doing. His estrangement from the school was awkward and seemed an unnecessary embarrassment, since the people connected with Dottie were no longer on the board.

"I'm still NOLS," he said in a later interview, "and I don't want to have to explain to people that a bunch of sons of bitches took it away from me."

He told Ratz that he would accept the invitation on one condition. That he be given the permanent title President Emeritus. Ratz agreed.

Hundreds of NOLS graduates attended the weekend celebration. Saturday night was the time for speeches and awards, but Friday was reserved for a gala birthday party with Petzoldt as the central character.

Everybody gathered on the grounds of the NOLS field station above Lander. Petzoldt stood on the grass in the middle of a huge circle, much as he had done so many times on the Wind River expeditions. Without notes or even much of an idea about what he would say, he began talking about the beginning of the school. He let them all know he was glad to be back.

"He held forth for about an hour until it got so dark we couldn't see," Ratz says. "He read the crowd. It was fabulous. I think most of the board members now would say that [bringing Petzoldt back into the fold] was the most significant thing I did in my term."

It was not in Petzoldt's nature to consider the tribute as closure, however. He told the board and staff that he would never volunteer advice without being asked, but he would be there any time they needed him.

In March 1991, the Petzoldts were invited to join seven other Mainers as delegates on an official exchange junket to Greater Portland's sister city Arkhangelsk (Archangel) in the extreme northwest corner of the Soviet Union. The visit was to take place during the city's twenty-fifth Winter Festival Jubilee celebrating winter sports and welcoming the sun back to the land 130 miles south of the Arctic Circle. The northern port had been an important shipping base during the time that Petzoldt worked on Russian Lend-Lease for the Department of Agriculture during World War II.

The Russians were very hospitable. The Petzoldts and other members of their group stayed in private homes and were even given spending money to use for shopping and seeing the sights.

Petzoldt met with some of the shippers who had been involved in his arrangement for Russian icebreakers to clear the way for American freighters sailing from Seattle during the Lend-Lease operations. He showed them copies of a *National Geographic* article, "America Feeds the World," in which he was pictured with local officials going over shipment charts. They presented him with a medal.

Some Arkhangelsk Alpinist Club members invited him to join them for an authentic *banya*—a village sauna where fellow sweatmates took turns swishing leafy birch branches over one another's backs as clouds of sizzling steam almost burned their tonsils. When Petzoldt thought he could take no more, the attendant opened a door and signaled for everyone to run outside. In the yard a flat concrete slab that looked something like a miniature runway was piled with snow. The men jumped onto the snow and rolled back and forth on the 100-foot snow-field. Then it was back to the steam room to start all over again.

On the third go-around, Petzoldt suspected that he was being tested. The hearty Russians were trying to see just how much the old mountain climber could take. So he jumped into the snow for the third time and rolled as fast as he could. Back and forth twice. His Russian friends started to laugh and patted him on the back.

The following summer, he realized another dream. Patricia McConnell (his friend Jack Nicholas' daughter, who had attended the first women's course and was a former NOLS instructor) and her husband, Robert, had participated in one of Scott Fischer's Mountain Madness ventures to Mount Everest. Disgusted at the environmental degradation that had resulted from the onslaught of trekkers, the McConnells organized a nonprofit foundation and solicited donations to send clean-up parties to major peaks throughout the world. They sought Petzoldt's participation to focus international attention on their cause.

In February, the Petzoldts flew to Hong Kong, where they stayed a few days before continuing on to Lhasa, Tibet. As they made the two-hour drive from the Lhasa airport to the city, they passed through a dry, dun-colored valley where the shallow Yarlung Tsanpo River cut between gray, boulder-strewn hills. Multicolored prayer flags fluttered over small clusters of cubical adobe houses that were enclosed by matching white walls. Now and then a brilliant likeness of the Buddha was painted on the cliffs alongside the road. There were a few barley fields and herds of cattle with an occasional long-haired yak.

The Holiday Inn was in the center of town off a busy street where gaudy bead necklaces and ornate prayer wheels were sold to vulnerable tourists. The hotel was modern, but an elaborate facade belied the drab, functional guest rooms that were typical of the rest of China. The Hard Yak Cafe coffee shop, with its yakburger specialty, added a bit of whimsy.

They remained in Lhasa for several days to acclimate to the 11,850-foot altitude and visit the imposing Potala Palace and temples once frequented by the exiled Dalai Lama. Then the caravan headed for Everest in new Jeeps imported from Shanghai and specially fitted with passenger handgrips on the sides and ceiling.

The modern roads, hacked out of the hills by thousands of Chinese laborers, soon ended. They rattled over a series of dusty switchbacks, climbing higher and higher and crossing lofty passes with views of turquoise lakes and distant glaciers.

"There were practically no bridges; we had to ford rivers," Ginny said later. "If the car doesn't work, you get out and push. The roads are paths and some were only about two feet from the cliff."

They traveled through ancient villages with mud houses decorated with orange, white, and black stripes to denote that members of a Buddhist sect lived there and cobbled walkways leading to massive stupas.

"Every hotel we stayed in was a riot," Ginny says. "They would be beautiful like an American hotel, but plumbing? The stuff was there but it didn't work."

They finally passed the Rongbuk monastery at the foot of Mount

Everest and began their project. Establishing tent camps as they moved along, they collected the bottles, cans, foil, and paper that littered the ground. They burned some of the trash and made piles of metal and glass that would be of use to locals so these materials could be taken back to the valley by yak.

The foundation donated a recycling machine to the monastery so that the monks could reprocess reusable paper.

In their five-day trek they reached about 19,000 feet, where snow fell during the night and melted in the morning sunshine.

"In going to Everest, I realized a life ambition," Petzoldt says, "Before World War II no American expedition could go to Tibet because it was restricted to the British. I only wished that I were younger so I could climb in the Himalayas again. That was a terrific adventure."

In the early 1990s, Petzoldt was inducted into the prestigious Explorers' Club. He was among six recipients of the Eddie Bauer Award for wilderness use and conservation. He received the Taft Award from Northern Illinois College for his contributions as an academic leader in outdoor interests. The Wyoming Parks and Recreation Association bestowed on him an award presented annually to an individual who has had a lasting influence on the parks, recreation, or conservation movements. Outward Bound paid tribute to his "life of commitment and to the impact it has had on the young people of our country" by presenting him with the Kurt Hahn Award. Even the U.S. Army Rangers issued him a certificate of appreciation after inviting him to Georgia to consult with them about training methods.

His membership in the American Alpine Club was also reactivated with all dues waived. For decades Petzoldt had been dogged by rumors that he had been kicked out of the Alpine Club. Some claimed that it was because of the 1939 incident in India. Others said the mountaineering community had snubbed him due to the "unconscionable" guiding fees he charged Betsy Cowles after the Santa Marta expedition. Petzoldt explained that he had purposely dropped his membership in 1947 because he was in the West and had little connection with the organization. "It cost money and I wasn't getting anything out of it," he says.

In a letter to the author on August 8, 1996, W. L. Putnam put the matter to rest. "There is no evidence that I have ever become aware of in the AAC (three years as its president and fifteen as its treasurer and a dozen more on its Board) that Petzoldt was ever subject to AAC criticism or suffered any revocation of his membership," he wrote.

With the personal honors, continued growth of WEA, reconciliation with NOLS, Ginny's companionship, and amazingly good health, old age was not so bad for Petzoldt. With one exception. The glaucoma had worsened. The reality of his blindness struck suddenly.

"It was gradually getting worse," Ginny says. "He could not adjust from light to dark. One day we were driving through a tunnel and his eyes didn't adjust. We almost went into the wall. There was a tanker behind us and luckily he was able to stop. I drove the rest of the way through. That's when I began to realize that he shouldn't be driving at all."

Petzoldt quit driving, but he didn't curtail many other activities.

"I'm writing now," he says. "I've quit the lecture circuit because I don't see well enough and my wife has to go with me.

"And I hate like hell to be falling off these platforms," he added with a chuckle.

His major project became the recording of "all the corny jokes and stories of Jackson Hole." With the editorial assistance of Kevin "Butch" Cassidy, he wrote *Petzoldt's Teton Tales, And Other Petzoldt Anecdotes*, which was published in 1995.

In 1994, at eighty-six, he astounded his friends by announcing that he would lead another expedition on the Grand Teton to commemorate the seventieth anniversary of his first ascent and raise the nation's awareness of his mission to promote wilderness preservation through education.

The event also served as a fund-raiser for WEA. People were invited to pledge anything from one-half cent upward for every vertical foot Petzoldt gained on the expedition.

Media coverage was nationwide. The University of Utah's television channel, KUED, produced a PBS documentary entitled "The Man and the Mountains," which was aired across the country. *The Boston Globe Magazine* covered the event, and Caine Alder published an article in *Climbing* magazine. The Associated Press and scores of local newspapers from Maine to Idaho carried stories.

Cocktail receptions and banquets preceded the climb. A mountain rescue dog introduced to the crowd was given the honorary name of Petzoldt. Friends and former climbing buddies bid hundreds of dollars for ragged stocking caps, gloves, and shirts which Petzoldt removed from his body in a lucrative WEA auction tabbed the Petzoldt Peel.

Petzoldt's ninety-six-year-old sister Violet from Twin Falls, Idaho, attended the kickoff celebration, as did Henry and Betty Nichol from Washington, D.C., and friends from far-off places, including Canada, Alaska, Hawaii, and even England. Glenn Exum delivered a tribute to his former partner, and then the two old-timers reminisced about the raucous times in Jackson Hole.

On the cloudless morning of July 17, fourteen hikers, accompanied a short distance by Ginny and a battery of reporters and photographers, left the trailhead to begin the historic climb. Steve Gipe, an emergency room doctor from Bozeman, Montana, and Skip Shoutis, a Forest Service ranger, both former NOLS instructors, stationed themselves before and behind Petzoldt as he slowly walked into the forest.

His near-blindness aggravated by the dim light, Petzoldt proceeded slowly, balancing himself with two rubber-tipped ski poles. He scuffed his boots along the path to seek out rocks and exposed tree roots, almost as if he had feelers in the soles of his feet.

The party crept out of the towering lodgepole pines onto a mountainside blossoming with bluebells, fleabane, Indian paintbrush, and Queen Anne's lace. The trail steepened and Petzoldt paused to rest more often as other hikers stopped him, asking him to sign autographs or taking pictures. Pretty soon, he started numbering his business cards, giving one to each photographer and exacting a promise to send him a print in exchange for one of his historic posters. By the time the four-day trip ended, he had distributed 222 cards.

It was late afternoon when they entered the giant boulder field below the meadow by the Middle Teton. Petzoldt maneuvered himself over the immense slabs of granite, using his tactile hands and feet as if they were eyes, while Gipe, Shoutis, and Geoff Heath, a structural engineer from Montana, carefully guided him across the obstacle, sometimes physically planting his boots on a steady rock.

"Clearly, they are celebrating the strength, courage, and heart of an outdoorsman who gave them the mountains," Maryalice Yakutchik of the *Boston Globe* wrote. "Many of them still have Petzoldt's handwritten 'PAY BACK WHEN ABLE SCHOLARSHIP' for the National Outdoor Leadership School, which he gave to just about any young man or woman who came to him looking for direction in their lives."

The next day another tedious climb took them past the Petzoldt Caves and on to the moraine of the Middle Teton glacier where, at approximately 11,000 feet, Petzoldt knew he could go no farther.

"I'm strong and feel great," he said. "But it would have taken too much time for me to go on with my eyesight. I would have to be roped practically all the time and although my body was willing, my judgment told me it was time to turn back. After all, I've been teaching judgment for sixty years. I was afraid if I tried the final pitch, I'd step on a rock that wasn't there."

The third morning, a number of the younger climbers symbolically carried Petzoldt's colors to the summit. When they returned to tell him of their adventure he vicariously shared their success.

"The mountain brought me a wonderful and exciting life," he said a bit wistfully. "But this is probably my last time on the mountain. It is kind of the closing of a chapter."

"That's what you said in 1984," his companions replied.

They headed down the mountain the next day. When they neared the Lupine Meadows trailhead, Steve Gipe asked Petzoldt to stop and rest for a minute. He took out a damp cloth and tenderly wiped the sweat from his old friend's face, adjusted the red kerchief around his neck, and tucked in his shirt. Then he gave the Grand Old Man of the Tetons a pat on the back and followed a respectful distance behind him as he made his final victory walk to the well-wishers waiting below.

Sources

Listed below are the sources for the quotations that appear in this book, keyed by page. Unless otherwise identified, quotations of Petzoldt's words are from interviews with the author. Throughout the text any unattributed quotations of the words of other individuals are paraphrases of conversations reported to the author by Petzoldt.

Chapter 2

Page 42. "I had to get . . . for the purpose." Paul Petzoldt (as told to Donald Hough), "Why I Climb Mountains," *Collier's*, June 18, 1949.

Chapter 3

Page 56. "When I was a very young curate . . . five minutes." Christopher Hibbert, *The Court of Windsor: An Intimate History of the Royal Inmates from William the Conqueror to Elizabeth II*, (New York: Harper and Row, 1964).

Chapter 4

Page 69. "Darling, you may . . . I love you." Patricia Petzoldt, *On Top of the World: My Adventures with My Mountain-climbing Husband* (New York: Thomas Y. Crowell, Co., 1953).

Page 70. "It had been . . . marry me after all." Ibid.

Page 74. "Many women have . . . lived to tell the tale." Ibid.

Page 76. "We climbed at an angle . . . ascent in the Tetons." Paul K. Petzoldt, "Winter Ascent of the Grand Teton," *Jackson Hole Courier*, December 26, 1935. Reprinted in *Nature Notes* (Grand Teton National Park), Vol. 2, No. 1, 1936, and in *Trail and Timberline*, May 1936.

Page 77. "Every night the men . . . with his bare hands." Patricia Petzoldt, *On Top of the World*.

Page 78. "Among our guests . . . had to be watched." Ibid.

Page 81. "Slowly and tremblingly . . . the narrow slope." Ibid.

Page 81. "Well, she's climbed . . . on her laurels." Ibid.

Page 84. "These mountains . . . by an avalanche." Ibid.

Chapter 5

Page 88. "We had put together . . . friendly person." Interview with Dr. Charles Houston.

Page 97. "If he dies . . . with the expedition." Ibid.

Page 97. "That was a . . . couldn't leave Paul." Interview with Robert Bates.

Page 98. "Before us the valley . . . swirling mist." Robert Bates, "K-2 At Last," in *Five Miles High* (New York: Dodd, Mead & Co., 1939).

Page 101. "When time lagged . . . 'iron ware.'" Robert Bates, "The Attack," in *Five Miles High*.

Page 104. "Our thoughts . . . seemed to do." Charles Houston, "Last Camps," in *Five Miles High*.

Page 107. "I think the weather . . . some sleep." Ibid.

Page 108. "My progress was . . . reached my limit." Ibid.

Page 109. "The whole world . . . but curiously content." Ibid.

Page 109. "I counted my . . . put them down." Ibid.

Page 111. "The high clouds . . . of the attack." Ibid.

Page 111. "Our mandate from . . . we were chicken." Interview with Dr. Charles Houston.

Page 111. "Ten days after . . . June and July." "Appendix. K-2: the Weather." *Five Miles High*.

Chapter 6

Page 117. "a tall, thin . . . almost fragile." Patricia Petzoldt, *On Top of the World*.

Page 118. "Now remember . . . a few days." Ibid.

Page 118–120. "Some of them . . . the master speak." and "Several of them . . . get hooked." In this section quotes from *On Top of the World* are combined with the memories of Paul Petzoldt.

Page 122–123. "You will know . . . will come closer." and "Do you remember . . . what we can do." Patricia Petzoldt, *On Top of the World*.

Page 123. "Mrs. [Johnson] said . . . add to it?" Ibid.

Page 125. "You are aware . . . as he fell." This part of the narrative is adapted from a report, "Memorandum Concerning Protection Case, Involving Paul Petzoldt and Wife," by C. E. Macy, American Consul, Karachi, India, dated April 3, 1939.

Page 126. "Nothing must be mentioned . . . hand over his face." Patricia Petzoldt, *On Top of the World*.

Page 126–127. "He said gently . . . precedes you." and "The master . . . left my shoes." Ibid.

Page 128. "They fabricated . . . of the accident." Letter from Paul Petzoldt to Charles Houston.

Page 128. "very upset, despondent and worried." "Memorandum Concerning . . ."

Page 129. "I'll pay you . . . can be done." Ibid.

Page 131. "The principles . . . immolation." and "How can we . . . be the consequences." Ibid.

Chapter 7

Page 137. The story of the Santa Marta expedition is taken from the Santa Marta Diary of Elizabeth Cowles (courtesy University of Wyoming American Heritage Center) and interviews with Paul Petzoldt.

Page 143. "Fiercely I watched . . . off balance." and "I was astounded . . . bulged in the middle!" Patricia Petzoldt, *On Top of the World*.

Page 144. The George Hopkins saga is taken from Mary Alice Gunderson, *Devils Tower, Stories in Stone* (High Plains Press, 1969), and Steve Gardiner and Dick Guilmette, *Devils Tower: A Climber's Guide* (Seattle: The Mountaineers, 1986) as well as interviews with Paul Petzoldt and Harold Rapp.

Page 148. "This was the . . . top of Devils Tower." Dale M. Titler, "Wings of Adventure." [magazine article, source unknown]

Chapter 8

Page 154. "Having never had . . . best of the unknown." From the video about the Tenth Mountain Division, *Fire On the Mountain*, produced by Beth and George Gage.

Page 155. "was a contemporary . . . pitcher blindfolded." Josh Miner and Joe Boldt, *Outward Bound USA* (New York, Morrow, 1981).

Page 155. "We camped . . . from him." Interview with Ernest Tapley.

Chapter 9

Page 168. "When we looked . . . and survive." Orrin and Lorraine Bonney, "High Country Challenge," [title of magazine unknown].

Page 169. "What impacted me . . . and enlarged." Interview with Blake Vande Water.

Page 169. "The snow . . . poor missionaries." Ibid.

Page 178. This anecdote was by Josh Miner in a telephone interview.

Chapter 10

Page 182. "The research . . . what to do." Molly Absolon, "Petzoldt Tells His Story," *The Leader: The Voice of the National Outdoor Leadership School* (Fall 1995).

Page 182. "Of all the mountain . . . needed right there." Delmar W. Bachert, *The NOLS Experience: Experiential Education in the Wilderness*, Ph.D dissertation, Appalachian State University, Boone, N. Carolina.

Page 183. "My personal wishes . . . in the future." Ibid.

Page 184. "He arrived there . . . was indispensable." Ibid.

Page 184. "I wasn't there . . . break of my life." Interview with Rob Hellyer.

Page 184. Jack Nicholas gave this account of the founding of NOLS in an interview with the author.

Page 186. "Everybody got . . . right and left." Bachert, *The NOLS Experience*.

Page 186. "Petzoldt didn't take . . . to the school." Interview with Rob Hellyer.

Page 186. "I feel that . . . success story." Interview with Josh Miner.

Page 186. "The National . . . Outward Bound." Bachert, *The NOLS Experience*.

Page 189. "Never in the history . . . than any generation." Adapted from Petzoldt's notes for a graduation speech.

Page 190. "We expect . . . for girls!" *Wyoming State Journal*, August 1965.

Page 190. "It was New Year's . . . back to sleep." *Wyoming State Journal*, January 9, 1966.

Page 191. "The best thing . . . as we could." Interview with Jack Nicholas.

Page 191. Raye C. Price [Ringholz],"Outdoor Finishing School," *Field and Stream*. Petzoldt later collaborated with this author to write *The Wilderness Handbook* and *The New Wilderness Handbook*, both published by W.W. Norton.

Page 195. "The board members . . . finance the operations." *Wyoming State Journal*. November 17, 1975.

Page 195. "All this investment . . . board of directors." Ibid.

Page 198. "It really hurt . . . as income." Interview with Rob Hellyer.

Page 199. "Then we were all . . . needed the warning." Leslie Gezon, "Fifty Years on the Grand Teton," *NOLS Alumnus* (Winter 1974).

Page 200. "The operations . . . loans were paid." "Petzoldt: I won't see my lifework fail," *Wyoming State Journal*, November 17, 1975.

Page 203. "I think the problem . . . of the school." Interview with Jack Nicholas.

Page 205. "It was quick . . . all dancing." Interview with Henry Nichol.

Page 207. "We kept PPWE . . . some stuff made." Interview with Rob Hellyer.

Page 208. "But it was . . . started has gone." Molly Absolon, "Petzoldt Tells His Story," *The Leader: The Voice of the National Outdoor Leadership School* (Fall 1995).

Chapter 11

Page 215. "Paul changed . . . religious experience." Interview with Caine Alder.

Page 219. "'Why?' Petzoldt asked . . . 'part of it,' Petzoldt said." This conversation is taken from separate interviews with Paul Petzoldt and Jim Ratz.

Page 220. "He held forth . . . in my term." Interview with Jim Ratz.

Page 222. "There were . . . from the cliff." and "Every hotel . . . didn't work." Interview with Ginny Petzoldt.

Page 224. "It was gradually . . . driving at all." Ibid.

Page 225. "Clearly, they are . . . in their lives." Maryalice Yakutchik, "Mountain Man," *The Boston Globe Magazine*, October 9, 1994.

acknowledgments

I have been taping interviews with Paul Petzoldt ever since I first met him in 1965, participated in the first NOLS course for women in 1966, and took part in a variety of classes during the writing of *The Wilderness Handbook*. These recordings comprise the major portion of my research, and I am grateful to Paul for his patience during these sometimes lengthy sessions. I also want to thank him for introducing me to camping and mountain adventure, which have provided wonderful experiences and memories.

The books, newspapers, and magazine articles mentioned in the "Sources" section at the end of the book have been most helpful to me, especially *On Top of the World: My Adventures with My Mountain-climbing Husband* by Patricia Petzoldt, *Five Miles High* by the members of the First American Expedition to K2, and *The NOLS Experience: Experiential Education in the Wilderness* by Delmar W. Bechert.

The insights and information gleaned from interviews with several other individuals have been extremely valuable to me. I am grateful to Ernest "Tap" Tapley and Josh Miner, who provided background about the early days of Outward Bound and the beginnings of NOLS, to Rob Hellyer, Judge Jack and Alice Nicholas, Henry and Betty Nichol, Skip Shoutis, Jim Ratz, and the NOLS staff members who made past board meeting minutes and other data available to me, and to Blake VandeWater, Harold Rapp, and Virginia Huidekoper for other historical information. My thanks to Ginny Petzoldt for her descriptions of Paul's recent years and travels and to Eldon "Curly" Petzoldt (now deceased) and Violet Petzoldt Herrick for stories about his youth.

I would also like to thank Dr. Charles Houston, William House, and Robert Bates for sharing their knowledge of the K2 expedition and William Putnam for information about the American Alpine Club.

The help I received from Walter Jones, Special Collections, Marriott Library, University of Utah; Rick Ewig and Jennifer King, American Heritage Center, University of Wyoming; and Ron Diemer, Teton County Historical Center, Jackson, Wyoming, is deeply appreciated. My special gratitude goes to a respected friend and mountaineer, Caine Alder, for his insightful reading of the manuscript.

It has been a pleasure to work with The Mountaineers Books, and I am indebted to Margaret Foster, Editor-in-Chief, for her enthusiastic support of this project.

Finally, a special tribute to my three daughters, Allyn, K. C., and Cam—all former NOLS students (K. C. has also served as an instructor)—and to my husband, Joe, for their constant support and love.

—Raye Ringholz
Salt Lake City, August 1997

photo credits

Figures 1, 2, 3, 4, 6, 8, and 9 (Cleve Petzoldt collection); Figures 5, 20, 22, 23, and 24 (Raye Ringholz collection); Figures 7, 10, 11, 12, 13, 28, and 29 (Paul Petzoldt collection; photographer, fig. 29, Linda Gagon); Figures 14, 15, and 16 (reproduced from *Five Miles High*, New York, 1939); Figures 17 and 18 (Elizabeth Cowles Partridge collection, neg. #26239 and 26203, American Heritage Center, University of Wyoming;); Figure 19 (Jackson Hole Historical Center); Figure 21 (National Outdoor Leadership School, Lander, Wyoming); Figures 25 and 26 (Andrew E. Carson collection); Figure 27 (Sandy Braun collection).

index

Index

Index

205, 206, 208, 211, 213, 218, 220, 224, 226; 39ers course 219; first women's course 191; 25th anniversary 219
National Ski Patrol 153
Nebel, Bernhard 136
Nevada, Las Vegas 178
New Tribes Mission 148, 166
Nez Perce Peak 47
Nichol, Betty 205, 225
Nichol, Henry 205, 225
Nicholas Office Building 195
Nicholas, Alice 184, 186, 189
Nicholas, Jack 176, 183, 184, 185, 186, 187, 191, 201, 203, 221
Nightingale, Bill 202
Noble Hotel 184, 195, 200, 207
Nold, Joe 178
NOLS Instructors Association 207
North Cascade Range 194

Ohio, Toledo 38, 39, 42
Olmstead, Ralph 149
On Top of the World 48, 166
Outdoor Leadership Supply—Paul Petzoldt Wilderness Equipment (PPWE) 195, 196, 197, 198, 200, 201, 202, 205, 206, 213
Outward Bound 176, 177, 180, 183, 203, 211
Outward Bound Kurt Hahn Award 223
Owen, Billy 25, 28–33, 35–36

Pakistan tour 214
Pasang Kikuli 93, 95, 98, 105
Pease, Dr. Joseph 196, 197, 207
Pempa 93
Petersen, F. L. 31–33
Peterson, Pete 213
Petzoldt Caves 34, 76, 226
Petzoldt, Herman "Dutch" 14, 15, 16, 17, 21
Petzoldt Ridge 142
Petzoldt, Bernice McGarrity (Patricia) 48, 49, 56, 60, 69, 70, 72–74, 76–85, 116–134, 136, 137, 142, 143, 148, 150, 151, 161, 162, 166 165, 172–175, 178
Petzoldt, Charles 5, 6, 13, 14, 15
Petzoldt, Dorothy Dewhurst Reed 175, 178, 184, 185, 189, 197, 203, 220
Petzoldt, Eldon "Curly" 14, 15, 16, 17, 21, 71, 75, 78, 79, 142, 163, 198, 199
Petzoldt, Emma Kiesow 5, 16, 17, 18, 20, 21

Petzoldt, Gladys 14, 21, 22, 65, 68, 174
Petzoldt, Joan Brodbeck 205, 206, 214, 217, 219
Petzoldt, Lily 14, 15, 16, 174
Petzoldt, Louie 13–17, 22
Petzoldt, Rosie 14, 21
Petzoldt, Violet 14, 16, 225
Petzoldt, Virginia Stroud Pyle 218, 219, 222, 224, 225
Petzoldt, Willie 13, 14, 15, 16, 21, 22
Petzoldt's Teton Tales, and Other Petzoldt Anecdotes 224
Petzoldt's Teton Trails 209
Petzoldt-Exum Climbing School 47
Petzoldt-Exum School of American Mountaineering 163
Pfeifer, Friedl 154
Phinsoo 93
Pico de Orizaba 83
Pinedale ranch 200, 205
Pir Panjal Range 93
Platte Valley Elevator 170
Plumley, Harold 71, 142
Plumley, William 71
Popocatépetl 83
Powell, Ike 34–36
Prince Rupert of Bavaria 57
Prine Cafe 23, 38, 39
Purdy, Charles 32, 33
Putnam, W. L. 223
Pyle, Dallas 218
Pyle, Kenneth 218
Pyle, Sherry 218
Pyle, Wilton 218

Quaker Oaks Company 202
Quinn, Joe 145

Radhi Soami sect 114, 118, 125, 130
Ram Bhagat 129, 130, 133, 134
Ram's Horn Ranch 72, 74, 75, 77, 79
Ram's Horn Saloon 174, 175
Rapp, Harold 144, 146, 147, 148
Ratz, Jim 219
Ravi River 131
Rawalpindi (Pakistan) 85, 89, 91, 112
Redman, Dorothy 43, 44
Reemers, Ken 169
Remsten, Harry 118, 123, 130, 131, 133, 134
Remsten, Mrs. Harry 118, 123, 130, 133
Rendezvous Mountain 75, 163, 164

Index

About the Author

Raye C. Ringholz is the author of eleven books, including *Paradise Paved: The Challenge of Growth in the New West*; *Little Town Blues: Voices from the Changing West*; *Uranium Frenzy: Boom and Bust on the Colorado Plateau*; and *Park City Trails*, a hiking and cross-country skiing guide. In addition to publishing numerous articles in newspapers and magazines, she has been a reporter and columnist for the *Salt Lake Telegram* and is a a past president of the Park City (Utah) Historical Society.

She met Paul Petzoldt over thirty years ago, when she took part in the first women's course at the National Outdoor Leadership School. Since that time, she has served on the board of the Wilderness Education Association and as Petzoldt's co-author on both editions of *The Wilderness Handbook*. She lives in Salt Lake City with her husband, Joseph F. Ringholz.

About the Mountaineers

Founded in 1906, The Mountaineers is a Seattle-based non-profit outdoor activity and conservation club with 15,000 members, whose mission is "to explore, study, preserve, and enjoy the natural beauty of the outdoors . . . . " The club sponsors many classes and year-round outdoor activities in the Pacific Northwest, and supports environmental causes by sponsoring legislation and presenting educational programs. The Mountaineers Books supports the club's mission by publishing travel and natural history guides, instructional texts, and works on conservation and history.

Send or call for our catalog of more than 300 outdoor titles:

 The Mountaineers Books
1001 SW Klickitat Way, Suite 201
Seattle, WA 98134
1-800-553-4453
e-mail: mbooks@mountaineers.org
website: www.mountaineers.org

Other titles you may enjoy from The Mountaineers:

THE DUKE OF ABRUZZI: An Explorer's Life,
Mirella Tenderini & Michael Shandrick
A vivid chronicle of the Duke of Abruzzi's exploration of K2, the pioneering of the Abruzzi Ridge, and the first ascent of Mount St. Elias. With historical photos and details of the Duke's personal life.

IN THE ZONE: Epic Survival Stories from the Mountaineering World, *Peter Potterfield*
True-life accounts of three climbers who faced the ultimate challenge in the passionate pursuit of their sport.

LOU WHITTAKER: Memoirs of a Mountain Guide,
Lou Whittaker & Andrea Gabbard
Highlights from the worldwide climbing career of renowned climber and Northwest native Lou Whittaker.

REINHOLD MESSNER, FREE SPIRIT: A Climber's Life,
Reinhold Messner
A chronicle of the remarkable career of one of the world's most innovative and disciplined climbers.

THE LAST HERO — BILL TILMAN: A Biography of the Explorer,
Tim Madge
The compelling story of the very private sailor, mountaineer and adventurer W.H. Tilman, who has been called "perhaps the greatest explorer of the twentieth century."

K2: CHALLENGING THE SKY, *Robert Mantovani & Kurt Diemburger*
A comprehensive photographic portfolio of the most dangerous and technically difficult mountain in the world to climb, including a history of the earliest explorations through the most recent ascents.

CLIMBING IN NORTH AMERICA, *Chris Jones*
The complete history of North American mountaineering, from the early nineteenth century through the 1970's. This classic brings alive the climbers and their routes, peaks, and adventures with a storytelling style and historic black and white photos.

OUTDOOR LEADERSHIP: Techniques, Common Sense and Self-Confidence, *John Graham*
The only handbook available on outdoor leadership with skills taught applicable to all endeavors and vocations. Practical advice, anecdotes and sidebars by noted outdoor leaders.